A Book of Answers

The Ultimate Oracle is You!
ILLUSTRATED EDITION

Mani Pureheart

FOTL Press

©1998 Mani Pureheart

ISBN#978-0-9745933-6-4

With all of the oracles and all of the oracular forms available in this entire universe, there is but one thing you **must** know. For your own answers, for your greatest development,

THE ULTIMATE ORACLE IS YOU!

FOREWORD

We are seekers. We are longing to know; to feel our connection with God, Creator, with Creation, the ATI, as Mani Pureheart speaks of; All That Is. The essence of our being knows it is connected to the One, yet many of us feel a deep sadness, separate and alone. We are asking big questions like, "What is my purpose here? What is my passion, what lights me up? Should I pursue my dreams? Why is there so much suffering? How can I help? What's life REALLY about? Where are The Directions?"

I invite you to use *A Book of Answers - The Ultimate Oracle is YOU* to help you find direction and focus. It is a profound tool for connecting with your inner guidance and a constant reminder to seek your guidance within. Many of our greatest philosophical and spiritual teachers have told us to look within. Eastern Religions stress the importance of quieting our minds and going, as Depok Chopra says, "Into the gap;" where we experience our connection with God, with the Divine Intelligence, with All That Is. Jesus also told us to seek within to find the Kingdom of God. If you're ready to look within and meet your Ultimate Oracle; to connect and stay open to our inner guidance, then this book and the accompanying cards have come to you today as a gift.

Mani gave me his first printed copy of A Book of Answers. I was honored and excited. This book had been a dream of his for many years and now it was real! His eyes were bright with the pride of a new father as I opened the book. I read the first few pages and then he asked me to use the book by opening it randomly. When I did, the word that appeared was "Confidence." As I read, I knew it was exactly what I needed to hear that day as I had been feeling stuck in an area of my work and was unable to move forward. The next day I began to take action toward my goal with confidence. That was the beginning of my journey with A Book of Answers. I've been using it daily since then and it has brought continuing clarity and peace into my life.

Each morning I turn to this book for centering and guidance. In our hurried and harried world, it is so easy to get hooked into the whirlwind of our over-booked schedules and the drama of our lives. When I wake in the morning my first thoughts too often are lists of what must be done that day. I'm already swept into the whirlwind and I haven't yet gotten out of bed! Staying in connection with our Ultimate Oracle; our Center, our Spirit, and our Higher Self is so important when we must make hundreds of decisions every day. I have found that having a morning practice is crucial to my ability to stay connected to my inner guidance. A Book of Answers has been a simple yet profound way to keep this connection.

I gift myself fifteen minutes to connect to the Source in the morning; to plug in and fill up for the day. Gratitude is always where I start; giving thanks for the many gifts in my life. I am so blessed! After about five minutes I'm filled with gratitude; a wonderful way to start the day. I then light a candle as a representation of the Light within me; my Ultimate Oracle. I repeat, "I am open to guidance" several times. After five minutes of allowing myself to see and feel "openness to guidance," I then turn to Mani's book.

I open it randomly (yeah, right!) and receive a focus for my day; a teaching. It is like having a wise elder come to me. Now, filled with gratitude and open to guidance; with a teaching to focus on, I'm ready for my day. Let the whirlwind begin! And it does! Throughout the day, situations come up where the teaching is so appropriate. It guides me to making my highest choices. Having a focus to center on throughout the day is what brings me out of the whirlwind and into my center where it is calm.

One morning, I received the word "Efficiency"—following the shortest path of greatest Light. It deals with cutting through the smoke screens and the illusions to find and grasp the heart of a situation. It implies that it is time to stop avoiding issues and face them directly. It's time to get to work!" Within relationships, it talked about how we don't communicate clearly and avoid addressing situations in a clear way, afraid of offending or angering the other. This only leads to frustration and distancing. Speaking truthfully always leads to greater understanding and harmony.

What I most needed to hear was that it was time to stop

avoiding issues and face them directly; to get to work. I recognize that I haven't taken action on my dreams! It's time to take action. I could see how my fears stop me over and over again. I'm grateful for the reminder to always choose my dreams, not my fears.

In my practice as a Mental Health Counselor and Expressive Art Therapist, I often use this book with my clients. They sometimes choose a word and it gives direction for the session. Choosing a word near the end of our time together provides clarity and guidance for that person to ponder and walk away with. The word may become a homework assignment to write about how it applies in their life today or having them practice being that word until our next session. My clients receive the perfect teaching every time they open this book.

My first client that day was a woman who just turned 40 and felt lost, had no direction, was depressed and very anxious. I listened to her talking about her life and then had her show me in the sand tray the warring aspects of herself. I was then reminded of the teaching this morning: stop avoiding responsibility for your life and face it directly; it's time to go to work. When I told her I saw her not wanting to take responsibility for her life, she readily agreed. She spoke about her fear of making a bad choice stopping her from making any choices.

I knew it was time to take action. We decided that we would probably make a good decision together. We talked about what she loves to do; what she is passionate about. In order to do what she would love to do, she knew it was time to go back to school. With the help of financial aid for school, her job search just opened up to take the jobs that are available. She now had a direction and possibilities and was committed to taking action. Just before she left I gave her the book to open randomly. She opened to Efficiency! She read it and left greatly relieved, hope-full and determined. I felt happiness for her and was grateful for the guidance. I used that teaching with every client that day and saw miraculous results with each. This book is such an incredible gift!

Just yesterday, when I opened *A Book of Answers*, the word was 'Contribution." The teaching I took with me for the day was: "Every personal relationship is two people who have consciously come together for the purpose of supporting and assisting one another in their growth; each making a Contribution to the other. Every interaction that we experience each day is a Contribution to our ongoing education and growth. Awareness of this marks the difference between being a victim or a student."

I thought a lot about this teaching on my morning walk. Looking at how my partner of twenty-eight years has encouraged and supported me in following my dreams; going back to school, finding my spiritual connection, starting a private practice and so many others, I felt such gratitude and love for him. I wondered if I was contributing as much to him in his growth. Last night, we talked about the contribution we make to each other as well as what we were doing that was slowing down our growth. We ended our day feeling close, connected, and loved; quite a gift from just a word!

A couple came to see me; struggling with their relationship; feeling angry, hurt, and disconnected. Remembering the teaching from this morning, Contribution, I asked them how they were contributing to each others' growth. The wife struggled with this concept, feeling that her partner only brought her anger and pain. As we talked more about the idea that they consciously came together to support each other and that neither was a victim, she began to identify the ways her partner had contributed to her dream of working out of their home so she could be there with their children. I had them going back and forth, telling the other how they had contributed to their growth. I could see them soften towards each other as they did this; the anger was gone as they felt appreciated, were able to thank each other for the support, and then ask for new ways that they could contribute to each other.

Near the end of our time together, I had them each open *A Book of Answers* randomly. She opened to Enrichment and read aloud, "Love does not take, it only gives, and in that giving lies the greatest reward. This is an opportunity and an invitation for you to do something wonderful for yourself by giving to your partner with and from Love." She cried as she admitted that she had stopped giving to her partner and had become focused on what she wasn't getting.

He opened the book to the word Deceit. His voice cracked as he read, "First you say you will and then you won't; then you say you do but then you don't. It is pretending to be a certain way or do a certain thing in such a way that others allow themselves to be placed in a position of trust and/or dependence, then suddenly and unexpectedly changing your position; doing that which serves you at the expense of the others involved." His homework was to take an honest look at this teaching and how he has been deceitful within this definition and come back next week ready to talk about this. I asked his wife not to contribute in this exercise but to stay focused on and practice her teaching of Enrichment. They left my office a little red-eyed but hand-in-hand and hopeful.

I use this book whenever I'm confused about a personal decision, or how to proceed with a client. Asking for guidance about that particular situation, I open the book to one or more words. I will often get clarity immediately as I am reading the teachings and other times the understanding comes later, always at the perfect moment.

Recently I've been trying to decide if I'm going to take my career in a new direction. I love what I do and I want to continue seeing clients and facilitating Expressive Art groups. I also want to teach what I am most passionate about, Art Therapy, and that would require going back for two more years of school. I turned to *A Book of Answers*, asking for guidance, and randomly chose three words. I opened to Perseverance, Synchronicity, and Visualization.

"Perseverance means going forward; completing even when you are tired or discouraged and want to quit... because it is the 'right' thing to do." This spoke to my fear that I won't be able to do the work required that it will be too hard and I will want to give up. I receive the word as a gift, affirming that I do have the Perseverance to accomplish this goal.

"Synchronicity means literally 'the condition of sameness of time'. Two things come together in space-time. It also carries with it the additional meaning of Divine intervention. Things that could not have 'just happened' happen anyway." I am a firm believer in Synchronicity, so I will move forward with the inquiry of finding a program, and if it 'comes together', then I will know that this is what I'm meant to do.

"Visualization—The first step involved in creating our physical reality is to create that reality in our minds and hearts. Drawing this word to you this day is an indication from Spirit that you have the power and the right to change your reality, and that Spirit is available and willing to help you to do so. The choice is yours and the time to choose is now." After reading this, I realized that I have been visualizing myself teaching for a long time. It has been my fears and doubts that have stopped me from pursuing my dream. I have the vision and the Perseverance, now I will allow Synchronicity to guide me. "The time to choose is now". I choose to follow my dreams. Thank you, Spirit; thank you Mani; thank you to My Ultimate Oracle for the clarity and the guidance to move forward, pursuing my dreams!

Along with inner guidance comes guidance from around us, from teachers who show up in our lives "when the student is ready." Mani Pureheart has been a teacher whose message of Love and whose healings have been beacons of Light as I and thousands of others have walked our paths, often in the darkness of our own blindness. When I first met Mani I was immediately drawn to him. There was Love emanating from him and a Light in his eyes that was extraordinary. After being with him for just a short time, there was no doubt in my mind and Spirit that Mani had the gifts of Seeing and Healing.

Mani tells of his amazing journey on his tapes The Story of a Healer and A Few Easy Lessons. He is often invited to speak at gatherings around the country and internationally, reminding us that "All of the teachings of all of the Teachers of Light have the same message: 'Be Love;' Be Love in every word, thought, deed, and prayer." I have experienced and watched many healings when Mani opens himself to "Be Love" and the healing energy pours through him. He is an open channel for Spirit and has committed his life to being of service.

We are seekers searching for our Spirit; our Ultimate Oracle. We are longing to connect with that part of us that Knows and to feel the peace that comes from having constant guidance. This book has come to you today as a gift from Spirit. Embrace it with gratitude. I invite you to commit to your awakening by using it every day for a month. Read it and use it yourself. Your Ultimate Oracle within will know Truth when it hears it.

I would like to thank Mani for the gift he and this book have been in my life. In my times of confusion and feeling lost, I know

I can count on the deep wisdom in A Book of Answers. In times of sadness it has brought comfort and often a chuckle. One of the things I love about Mani is his irreverence; check out his greeting cards! He laughs often and easily and has a huge heart filled with Love. Thank you, Mani, for being my friend and guide for all these years. And thank you for the gift of *A Book of Answers*! It has truly been a "God-send;" providing clarity, serenity and an ever increasing Knowing of my own Ultimate Oracle! You and this book are a gift to the world!

—Lila Deilke, MS., LMHC.

THIS BOOK IN A NUTSHELL:

A. We are all created of the Creator by the Creator. We are each and all a part of the body and the spirit of the Creator

Therefore:

B. We have no limitations except those we decide to accept for ourselves.

And:

C. There is no Journey, there is only an arrival. We are already Home because we have never left it.

As you can see, this book is totally superfluous unless, of course, you have chosen to stop doing things in the difficult manner to which you have become accustomed.

If that is the case, you may find this book to be invaluable.

This book is lovingly dedicated
to my father, my teacher, my friend;

Glen Ward

who art in heaven.

ACKNOWLEDGMENTS

(Written in Loving service to the Creator)

Thank you to all of the Angels in the multiverse whether you are conscious of your Angelic nature or in total rebellion against it. Each of us fills a niche in the heart of the Creator and plays a part in the growth of the whole.

To Michael Drake, for breaking the ice.

To my brother Dennis; for always being there—even when I wasn't.

For my children: Phil, Aaron, Summer, Christer; Thomas and Vroni, and all the rest of you.

To my mother Lillian for teaching me how to survive and be strong in my beliefs.

And to the countless others who have supported this work and me in so many different ways.

My special and loving thanks to my life partner;
chief supporter and earthly teacher;

Kim

You truly are the wind beneath my wings
and the anchor who keeps my feet on the ground.

I couldn't have done this without you,
...nor would I have wanted to.

A SHORT LIST OF DEFINITIONS

I have my own definitions for some of the words used in this book. Reading the following will make understanding the book much clearer and easier.

"LOVE."

Love, when spelled with a capital 'L' in a place where it would not be expected, refers to "Divine" Love as opposed to "human" love in any of its forms.

Spirit has defined **Divine Love** to me as: "The Love that you would feel for the concept of a beautiful field filled with newborn lambs frolicking or for the idea of a newborn baby. **Divine Love** is not Love for or of; it is simply Love, non-directed and without limitations."

Here is a statement included elsewhere in this book which was received from **Spirit** regarding **Divine Love:**

Beloved ones:

I have Loved you from the beginning of time.
I shall Love you when the worlds are dust.
There is nothing I would not do for your benefit.
There is no price, no cost to you
for this Love I give.

There is nothing you could do
to ever lessen this Love.
There is nothing you could ever do
that would make me withdraw from your side.

We are One in every way.
You are the heart of my heart.
You are the child of my loins,
and my fondest hopes.
You are the delight of my eye.

As you learn and grow,
Because we are One,
So learns and grows
the universe; and all in it.
Including Me.
For you and I
and All that Is

are One.

"SPIRIT."

Spirit has been my only major teacher. I have not read a lot of metaphysical or religious books nor have I followed any Guru. Spirit is defined by me as: "All of the Above". By that, I mean all of the Deities and helpful Spirits of all of the belief systems that ever will be, all wrapped into One. Because I believe that all beings are One and that One is the uncreated Creator; ultimately all beings and all actions are in service to All that Is.

Some of these beings and activities have taken the path of `darkness'; that is to say, they have chosen a path that is ego-filled and torturous (in every sense of the word). Very early on in my spiritual awakening process, I made a conscious choice not to allow anything of `darkness' into my life. I choose to work only with those beings and energies that directly and resolutely serve All that Is. That is the grouping of energies which I refer to as `Spirit'.

"PEELING THE ONION."

Refers to the practice of achieving growth and understanding one layer at a time. We overcome the immediate challenge only to find that it has been covering up another one hidden more deeply within our psyche. Spirit says: "When you peel the onion there will probably be tears with each layer, but as you remove each layer you will come closer to the core. When you finally peel away that final layer you will discover the nothingness which encompasses all!"

"ALL THAT IS."

Several years ago I noticed how very politicized the term "God" had become and how charged with gender-specific meaning. All of this really does not matter one iota to the Creator but it served as a block to reaching certain people with the message I was to bring. I asked Spirit what would be a good non-sectarian, non politicized, non gender-specific term to refer to the Creator. Spirit suggested the term "ATI". "ATI" I asked? "Yes" Spirit replied. "That is an acronym for `All that Is'. The Creator does not care what word we use to refer to Him, Her, It, Them, Us, All that Is, the Great Void. The Creator simply IS."

"THE SHORTEST PATH OF GREATEST LIGHT."

We have infinite choices available to us in each moment. Some paths are long; others are short. Some are entirely involved in the light, others follow a path through darkness. We can choose any combination of features as we walk our walk. We can choose the shortest path regardless of the consequences. This is the `quick and dirty' path. We can choose a long, involved path that is entirely in the light. While we eventually will achieve our goal, it is not a particularly efficient path. The ideal path would be the shortest path of greatest light.

"INTIMATE or PERSONAL RELATIONSHIP."

These are the relationships with wives, husbands, fathers, mothers, siblings, or any other extremely close relationship. It does not necessarily have to be a physical relationship to fall into this category.

"GENERAL or CASUAL RELATIONSHIP."

Any relationship which does not fall into the "intimate or personal relationship" category above. Our day-to-day' bumping elbows with' relationships are referred to with this label.

PREFACE

For as long as there have been humans there have been oracles. Some cultures have nourished and honored them while other groups have done their best to quash them. Those who have manifested these gifts of foreknowledge could not be stilled nor their gifts eradicated by mere decree. Many times; as in the case of the famed seer Nostradamus, the information had to be put into such a form as to hide its true significance.

Those of us who choose to manifest our gifts openly today are for the most part not directly denied the freedom to do so. Still, many times there is confusion on the part of the uninitiated or partially aware recipient of the information as to its true meaning and how it relates to their situation. This in turn creates fear and anger which instigates and supports repression and alienation feelings toward the psychic or reader.

When one receives a message from Spirit through a reader or psychic, there are certain words that are commonly used regardless of the method in which that message was originally received. Many times there is confusion or a lack of understanding regarding exactly what is meant by Spirit. These volumes support every word and tile oracle as well as readings from any other source. They explore and define over four hundred words that are commonly used in readings; discussing their possible meaning and influence in the context in which they are used.

In using this book the reader can simply make a list of the key words found in the message they have received and look them up in the index. While many of the meanings are broken down into various areas (i.e.: personal relationships, etc.) it is important to realize that Spirit doesn't do anything without a reason. You will probably find that it will add to your understanding of the situation in question and other aspects of your life if you will read the entire text that refers to the word you have selected. This volume also is a stand-alone oracle of great depth, and when combined with the Ultimate Oracle cards can provide even the beginner with accurate and in-depth self-knowledge and self-help tool of great value.

Many of us have been taught that we have to go to an outside source to find our answers to life's problems. We often pay a substantial fee for someone to tell us what we already know at some inner level.

There are many forms of Divination tools and oracles available at almost every metaphysical bookstore and some of us will go to the Bible or some other 'sacred' book for a spontaneous message. Whatever the apparent source of the information we receive,

THE ULTIMATE ORACLE FOR YOUR LIFE IS YOU!

The soul of each person is the best link between Creator and consciousness. Priests, books, readers, words, tiles, bones, inner voices -- these are all tools to help us focus on our own inner path.

The main purpose of this book is to throw open the doors of possibility so that each of us may use these wonderful tools to their full extent. I invite you to sit down and read the book cover to cover once before using it for your readings. Many of these words interact with and modify one another. I feel that it is important to at least become aware of those interactions. Several different methods for Divination will be offered as well as information regarding the meanings of the words in different circumstances. Spirit will supply additional information at the end of each word's subsection.

Comments and suggestions are welcomed.

Questions accompanied by a **responsible** donation and a **SASE** will receive a reply/reading.

Please visit our website at:
www.ManiPureheart.com

Or Email at:
Mani@ManiPureheart.com

If you have a word that you feel has been left out of these volumes and should be included, please send it to me at the above Email address. The first person to suggest each new word that is used in a later book will receive a gift from Mani and FOTL Press.

ABOUT THE COVER ART

When Spirit gave me the assignment of writing these books early in 1993, I was also instructed by Spirit to contact an artist whom I had recently met, in order to invite her to do the cover art for this work. When I contacted her and told her the story of what had happened and what the books were to be about, she graciously agreed to create the image of the angel of knowledge which you see in the center of the cover. Here is what Johanna (the artist) has to say about her image:

"Doug (Mani) called me one evening early this year (1993) and asked me if I'd paint him an angel for his new book. He said he'd like her to be the angel of Wisdom. The next morning she came to me brightly and clearly. When an image comes to me that quickly, clearly, and effortlessly I know that they are for real. I had the feeling of ancientness about her – not that she's old, but that she has been with us since the beginning of forever. She is known as the ancient Mother Sophia though she calls herself Arelite Sophia (Our-ray-lite – the light we all come from."

Arelite offers this message:

"Awaken now and acknowledge the Wisdom within you! You are ultimately wise – it comes with maturity; selectivity.
I am what you would call the Crone – the wise Grandmother.

Arelite – "our-ray-lite" – the light we came in on – our connection to the Divine – thus our inheritance of the Divine's Wisdom – a tiny strand of light that grows as we become still and at peace with ourselves – keeping outside of the business of our own thoughts, our "shoulds", "ought to's" and inner yammerings.

Ask me for assistance in this- I will be there to help you clear your channel so that you can access your own knowingness."

Johanna is the author of "Angels of the Rays", ISBN # 1880666677, published by Oughten House Publications. It is available in most bookstores or can be ordered easily.

CONTENTS

A SHORT LIST OF DEFINITIONS 15

PREFACE. 19

ABOUT THE COVER ART. 21

GROUNDING AND CENTERING MEDITATION. 31

BECOMING AWARE OF SPIRIT 36

USING THIS BOOK 40

SINGLE-WORD DRAW 45

THREE WORD SPREAD 46

THE TIME TRAVELER SPREAD 47

DETAILS SPREAD 47

STUMBLING BLOCK SPREAD 49

REVIEW SPREAD. 50

SEVEN WORD SPREAD 51

TEN WORD SPREAD 54

OVERVIEW SPREAD. 56

SPONTANEOUS MESSAGES 57

THE WORDS 59

THE WORDS

INDECISION	61	FLEXIBILITY	139
CELEBRATION	63	COMMITMENT	141
LEVITATION	65	PERSPECTIVE	143
PEACE	68	INVOLVEMENT	148
CHANGE	70	ACTUALIZATION	150
REST	73	YIELDING	152
WISDOM	75	VITALITY	154
DETERMINATION	78	ABANDONMENT	156
SELF-ESTEEM	80	DENIAL	158
SUCCESS	83	TOUCH	160
CLOSENESS	85	RESULTS	162
LEVITY	87	RESTITUTION	164
METAMORPHOSIS	89	WEALTH	167
STABILITY	91	PROGRESS	169
EXCELLENCE	93	CONFIDENCE	171
REBIRTH	95	CONSISTENCY	173
COMPASSION	98	FORTHRIGHTNESS	176
RESOLUTION	100	READINESS	178
CREATIVITY	103	WILLINGNESS	181
RELAXATION	105	HARVEST	183
NON-ATTACHMENT	107	GENTLENESS	186
HOPE	110	COURAGE	188
TRANSFORMATION	113	ASPIRATION	190
FOCUS	115	STEADFAST	192
RECOVERY	117	EASE	195
ALERTNESS	119	SEXUALITY	198
HUMILITY	122	DESIRE	201
EXUBERANCE	124	BLESSING	203
SPONTANEITY	126	PARTNERSHIP	205
SOLUTIONS	129	RELATIONSHIP	208
ACKNOWLEDGMENT	131	FORGIVENESS	211
ENJOYMENT	133	PLEASURE	213
GRATITUDE	135	PARTICIPATION	215
EAGERNESS	137	EMPOWERMENT	217

FUN	220	CONTINUITY	307
AWARENESS	222	UNION	310
ENTANGLEMENTS	224	SURRENDER	312
REASSURANCE	226	REVELATION	316
REJUVENATION	229	INSPIRATION	319
SIGNS	231	SYNCHRONICITY	321
VALIDATION	234	CEREMONY	323
VISUALIZATION	236	COMPLETION	326
RECOGNITION	239	FAMILY	328
UNIQUENESS	242	SERENITY	330
DISCOVERY	244	SHARING	332
CONTRIBUTION	246	BALANCE	335
LISTENING	248	MATURITY	338
PRACTICALITY	250	CONFUSION	340
GENEROSITY	252	IDENTITY	343
RESOURCEFULNESS	255	TRANSITION	346
OPEN-HEARTED	257	ADAPTABILITY	348
SENSIBLE	259	VULNERABILITY	350
CURIOUS	261	SOLITUDE	353
SIN	264	BREAKTHROUGH	355
AUTHORITY	267	INNOCENCE	357
REALIZATION	270	APPRECIATION	359
LAUGHTER	272	ASSURANCE	361
CALM	275	TOLERANCE	363
REJOICE	277	COOPERATION	367
JOY	279	EXCITEMENT	369
HUMOR	281	EMERGENCE	371
PROSPERITY	283	OPENNESS	375
TRIUMPH	286	ABUNDANCE	377
HEALING	288	CONSTANCY	379
DARING	290	GRACE	382
INVENTIVENESS	292	DECEIT	384
FRIENDSHIP	294	IMAGINATION	386
EXPERIENCE	297	WELL-BEING	388
FAITH	300	INTEGRATION	390
EMPATHY	302	WORTH	393
CLEARING	304	HAPPINESS	396

DEPENDABILITY	399	ENTHUSIASM	485
THOROUGHNESS	401	MOTIVATION	487
PERSEVERANCE	403	UNITY	491
UNKNOWN	405	DOUBT	493
ENRICHMENT	408	INFINITY	495
ASSERTIVE	410	SENSITIVITY	498
OBJECTIVE	413	VISION	501
ACCEPTANCE	416	NURTURING	503
ADVENTURE	418	FULFILLMENT	505
OPTIONS	420	VERSATILITY	507
CLUMSINESS	422	DEFIANCE	510
MAGNIFICENCE	424	REFLECTION	513
DARKNESS	426	OUTRAGEOUSNESS	516
INTUITION	429	PURIFICATION	518
SERVICE	431	OPTIMISM	520
OPEN-MINDED	434	CHARM	523
ENCOURAGEMENT	437	OBSERVATION	525
CHEERFULNESS	440	EFFICIENCY	527
PATIENCE	442	INTIMACY	529
EDUCATION	444	SELF-IMPORTANCE	531
WORRY	446	CHOICE	533
TREACHERY	448	WILL	536
SUSPICION	451	ORIGINALITY	539
DISCIPLINE	453	SPIRITUALITY	541
SIMPLICITY	455	COMFORT	543
SURPRISE	457	SENSUALITY	545
KINDNESS	459	BONDAGE	548
HARMONY	461	BEAUTY	550
ORDER	463	BIRTH	552
OBEDIENCE	465	BROTHERHOOD	554
PASSION	467	CLARITY	556
POWER	469	COMMUNICATION	558
OPPORTUNITY	471	DELIGHT	560
SATISFACTION	474	EXPECTATION	562
SECURITY	476	FREEDOM	564
RECEPTIVITY	479	BUILDING	567
DETACHMENT	482	INCOMPETENCE	570

ALPHABETICAL INDEX

ABANDONMENT	156	COMMITMENT	141
ABUNDANCE	377	COMMUNICATION	558
ACCEPTANCE	416	COMPASSION	98
ACKNOWLEDGMENT	131	COMPLETION	326
ACTUALIZATION	150	CONFIDENCE	171
ADAPTABILITY	348	CONFUSION	340
ADVENTURE	418	CONSISTENCY	173
ALERTNESS	119	CONSTANCY	379
APPRECIATION	359	CONTINUITY	307
ASPIRATION	190	CONTRIBUTION	246
ASSERTIVE	410	COOPERATION	367
ASSURANCE	361	COURAGE	188
AUTHORITY	267	CREATIVITY	103
AWARENESS	222	CURIOUS	261
BALANCE	335	DARING	290
BEAUTY	550	DARKNESS	426
BIRTH	552	DECEIT	384
BLESSING	203	DEFIANCE	510
BONDAGE	548	DELIGHT	560
BREAKTHROUGH	355	DENIAL	158
BROTHERHOOD	554	DEPENDABILITY	399
BUILDING	567	DESIRE	201
CALM	275	DETACHMENT	482
CELEBRATION	63	DETERMINATION	78
CEREMONY	323	DISCIPLINE	453
CHANGE	70	DISCOVERY	244
CHARM	523	DOUBT	493
CHEERFULNESS	440	EAGERNESS	137
CHOICE	533	EASE	195
CLARITY	556	EDUCATION	444
CLEARING	304	EFFICIENCY	527
CLOSENESS	85	EMERGENCE	371
CLUMSINESS	422	EMPATHY	302
COMFORT	543	EMPOWERMENT	217

ENCOURAGEMENT	437	INSPIRATION	319
ENJOYMENT	133	INTEGRATION	390
ENRICHMENT	408	INTIMACY	529
ENTANGLEMENTS	224	INTUITION	429
ENTHUSIASM	485	INVENTIVENESS	292
EXCELLENCE	93	INVOLVEMENT	148
EXCITEMENT	369	JOY	279
EXPECTATION	562	KINDNESS	459
EXPERIENCE	297	LAUGHTER	272
EXUBERANCE	124	LEVITATION	65
FAITH	300	LEVITY	87
FAMILY	328	LISTENING	248
FLEXIBILITY	139	MAGNIFICENCE	424
FOCUS	115	MATURITY	338
FORGIVENESS	211	METAMORPHOSIS	89
FORTHRIGHTNESS	176	MOTIVATION	487
FREEDOM	564	NON-ATTACHMENT	107
FRIENDSHIP	294	NURTURING	503
FULFILLMENT	505	OBEDIENCE	465
FUN	220	OBJECTIVE	413
GENEROSITY	252	OBSERVATION	525
GENTLENESS	186	OPEN-HEARTED	257
GRACE	382	OPEN-MINDED	434
GRATITUDE	135	OPENNESS	375
HAPPINESS	396	OPPORTUNITY	471
HARMONY	461	OPTIMISM	520
HARVEST	183	OPTIONS	420
HEALING	288	ORDER	463
HOPE	110	ORIGINALITY	539
HUMILITY	122	OUTRAGEOUSNESS	516
HUMOR	281	PARTICIPATION	215
IDENTITY	343	PARTNERSHIP	205
IMAGINATION	386	PASSION	467
INCOMPETENCE	570	PATIENCE	442
INDECISION	61	PEACE	68
INFINITY	495	PERSEVERANCE	403
INNOCENCE	357	PERSPECTIVE	143

PLEASURE	213	SIN	264
POWER	469	SOLITUDE	353
PRACTICALITY	250	SOLUTIONS	129
PROGRESS	169	SPIRITUALITY	541
PROSPERITY	283	SPONTANEITY	126
PURIFICATION	518	STABILITY	91
READINESS	178	STEADFAST	192
REALIZATION	270	SUCCESS	83
REASSURANCE	226	SURPRISE	457
REBIRTH	95	SURRENDER	312
RECEPTIVITY	479	SUSPICION	451
RECOGNITION	239	SYNCHRONICITY	321
RECOVERY	117	THOROUGHNESS	401
REFLECTION	513	TOLERANCE	363
REJOICE	277	TOUCH	160
REJUVENATION	229	TRANSFORMATION	113
RELATIONSHIP	208	TRANSITION	346
RELAXATION	105	TREACHERY	448
RESOLUTION	100	TRIUMPH	286
RESOURCEFULNESS	255	UNION	310
REST	73	UNIQUENESS	242
RESTITUTION	164	UNITY	491
RESULTS	162	UNKNOWN	405
REVELATION	316	VALIDATION	234
SATISFACTION	474	VERSATILITY	507
SECURITY	476	VISION	501
SELF-ESTEEM	80	VISUALIZATION	236
SELF-IMPORTANCE	531	VITALITY	154
SENSIBLE	259	VULNERABILITY	350
SENSITIVITY	498	WEALTH	167
SENSUALITY	545	WELL-BEING	388
SERENITY	330	WILL	536
SERVICE	431	WILLINGNESS	181
SEXUALITY	198	WISDOM	75
SHARING	332	WORRY	446
SIGNS	231	WORTH	393
SIMPLICITY	455	YIELDING	152

IN THE BEGINNING

There are several points that I would like to discuss before moving on to the main body of the book. These include grounding, centering, and protection. Much of the following information is taken from the book *A Few Easy Lessons, Vol. 1*. This book may be available at your local bookstore, or it can be ordered from FOTL Press at http://www.ManiPureheart.com.

Effective grounding and centering are the most important skills one can acquire and develop for enhancing meditation. I have met many meditators who have no concept of these skills and don't understand why their meditations seem to be ineffectual, or if they are effective, why that individual gets so "spacey" and disoriented. The following meditation is called "Grounding and Centering". An audio file of this and other meditations by Mani Pureheart as well as other inspirational and meditative tapes are also available. Contact Mani at the website above for a list of these and other available items.

GROUNDING AND CENTERING MEDITATION

You will probably have a much easier time with this if you enlist a trusted friend with good reading skills to read the meditation or order a tape of this with three other meditations from the website.

Make yourself completely comfortable. Loosen your clothing if necessary; take care of any personal needs and dim the lights.

Be seated now. Close your eyes. Relax and place your hands and arms in a comfortable position on your legs. Take a slow, deep breath and release it slowly and completely. Repeat the breath process a couple more times.

I would like for you now to become aware of your root chakra, or; if you are not familiar with your chakras, I ask you to focus your attention on the tip of your tailbone.

With an act of your own will, create a line of force -- of your own life energy -- extending down through the seat, the floor, and into the earth below.

Watch this cord with your inner vision as it travels down, down, down through the layers of the earth below your feet.

As the cord continues down through the earth, shift your attention to the center of the earth where you will find yourself standing in an enormous cavern. You look up to the roof of the cavern and see the connecting cord that you have created dropping down through the empty space toward a spot near your feet.

As this cord nears you, you observe a transformation in it. It becomes a massive, powerful, beautiful, healthy Oak tree trunk. As the cord; now the Oak's trunk strikes the center of the earth near your feet, your vision shifts once more and you watch as the Oak sends down tremendous huge roots. The roots travel miles and miles into the Earth's heart and as they do, they put out more roots. Those roots put forth still more and more until you are so completely and absolutely rooted to the loving heart of Mother Earth that the only force in the entire Universe that would be able to disconnect you would be an act of your own will.

This is called 'being grounded'.

Being grounded has several useful features. In addition to the material-world benefit of stability in your day-to-day activities and responses, you will find this grounding cord extremely useful for ridding yourself of all forms of negative energy, including physical pain.

I would like for you now to bring into your thoughts a recent event that created anger, distress, or anxiety.

Take a moment now and dwell on this event.

Let the emotions become as strong as the original moment.

Now allow that emotion; the concept of the emotion or the circumstances that have created the emotion to flow down the grounding cord toward the loving heart of Mother Earth, much like relieving yourself.

Shift your vision once more. Watch the bundle of emotions as it spirals down the outer surface of the cord toward the cavern.

As the bundle continues to travel down toward the center of the Earth, watch as it is absorbed into the body of the cord.

When these emotions enter the tree portion of the cord they fall freely down through the trunk, shattering into billions of pieces as the bundle strikes the level of the cavern floor.

The pieces are then absorbed into the large roots and follow the root system miles and miles into the loving heart of Mother Earth.

They pass through the roots and into the heart of the Earth where they are transmuted by Her great love into Divine Love, understanding, acceptance, and peace. Finally, this Loving energy is reabsorbed into the roots and travels back up, from the smallest roots to the largest. It then flows back into the tree.

From the tree trunk, it re-enters the grounding cord and travels back up the cord through your root chakra.

From there, the energy spreads throughout your being; replacing all of the previous negativity with a feeling of Love, understanding, and peace.

This same process works amazingly well with physical pain such as headaches or arthritis.

Take a moment now and just experience the feeling of peace and well-being.

Being completely grounded; now is the time to turn your attention to centering yourself.
Imagine for a moment that your physical body does not exist. See yourself as a tiny, beautiful, dancing flame of soft violet light. If you were to gaze into this flame you would see the cosmos as a tiny speck in its heart. This is the true essence of self; the self as All that Is...and as nothing.

Create now, with an effort of your own will, the illusion of your own physical head formed around this flame so that the flame floats midway between crown to throat; midway from ear to ear.

This is what is referred to as being centered.

Imagine and create now a tiny round mirror at the juncture of the eyebrows, facing inward. Shift your consciousness to the flame and gaze from the flame into the mirror -- and see the universe.

The universe is yours, Dear Children and the universe is YOU!

This is the basic "position" for meditation. All worthwhile meditation occurs most readily and effectively when one is completely grounded, totally centered, and totally within that place of One-ness with ALL THAT IS.

Take a few moments now and savor your connection.

It is now time to return your consciousness to the physical here and now being-ness.

Slowly and gently, as you can and as you wish, return your consciousness to the body. You may begin to move your fingers, then your wrists. You may begin now to wiggle your toes and move your ankles.

Now stretch. Bring yourself fully into the body and as you do, open your eyes and be here now.

That is the end of the grounding and centering meditation. It is not unusual for some individuals to take several minutes to return to the body. Do not be alarmed if this is the case. If, after a minute or so, they have made no physical motions indicating return, keep repeating in a quiet gentle voice the person's name and the phrases: **"It's time to come back now. It's time to return to the body. As you can and as you will, return to the here and now."**

BECOMING AWARE OF THE ENERGY OF SPIRIT

The "feeling" of the energy of Spirit is quite subtle and yet once it has been felt it is impossible to mistake or forget.

Now that you have become grounded and centered it is an appropriate time to focus your attention on the tingling sensation on the palms of your hands.

If you will briskly rub your hands together for a few seconds you will sensitize them further.

I would like for you now to extend your arms as far as possible to the sides at shoulder level. Now turn your hands so that the palms face one another while still maintaining the full spread of your arms. Focus your attention on the sensation in your palms and begin slowly bringing your hands closer together. It may help you to concentrate if you close your eyes. Usually about one-third of the way inward, (although it can vary widely), you will 'feel' a subtle but distinct resistance or barrier. When you find this, 'back up' and go through it several more times in order to better familiarize yourself with the sensation of the energy and what your perceptions of it are as you pass your physical body through your energy field.

This first area of resistance represents the thickness of that portion of the aura that most 'seers' can detect; only doubled. This is because the two fields (one extending from each hand) each apply a small degree of pressure on the other as they make contact. That pressure is transmitted to the energy centers or 'chakras' in the palms of the hands.

If you then continue through this first layer and bring the palms ever closer to one another, some of you may sense a second, stronger field of resistance. Those who are choosing to allow less sensitivity will only feel this inner field and not the outer. There is no blame or fault associated with this; it simply is a reflection of your current level of self-limitation. This innermost level is a representation of your 'prana' or life force doubled and overlapping itself.

Do not be disturbed if you do not feel anything. This does not mean you are dead. It simply means that at this time you are allowing the societal programming overlay to block your own native abilities. We as a people have allowed the priesthood of almost every religion to take our 'power' -- our inner connection to and strength of ALL THAT IS while convincing us we have no power and no right to that power in any active format. I suggest going back to the grounding and centering meditation a few more times over the next few days or weeks in order to learn how to overcome this imposed and false 'reality'.

Regarding 'protection': there IS a very simple and effective way to determine the alignment of any energy or entity which comes to you. Early in my own awakening I was quite concerned about being seduced by negative forces and asked Spirit how best to identify or avoid them and how best to protect myself.

Spirit provided a method it considered rather crude since the method uses physical reactions rather than 'knowingness'. However, Spirit's method is useful; and with practice leads to developing a 'knowingness' in these matters.

Spirit suggests that you take part in meditation, prayer, or whatever Light-filled activity you do to go to your highest spiritual level. At that point, take stock of the physical sensations within and around your body. Most people will experience a wonderful feeling of lightness, a tingling sensation, an expansive sense of well-being, and a slight to pronounced lightheadedness.

If you were to experience energy other than that of the Light, you would probably feel yourself withdraw or fold in on yourself. Stomach muscles will tighten and an entirely different sensation or 'chill' -- a definite icy coldness -- may be felt. This is easily 'cleared' by simply inviting the Light of Divine Love to surround and protect you. You'll be able to feel an instant and powerful change for the better. If for some reason you are unable to get a 'clear' reading on any entity's alignment, there are a couple of 'backup' measures that may be used. Spirit has given me an extraordinarily effective means to remove any negative influence.

Ground and center yourself to the best of your ability. Create the following scenario in your own words and your own way.

"Father*, I request your help.

I request an appropriate number of nurturing guardians be dispatched to me and those close to me. I further request that these guardians surround me and those close to me, separating from us any entities who are not of the highest light.

I further request that even more guardians, in an appropriate number, be dispatched to us in order to surround each of those darker entities in a cage of living Love. (Due to the tremendous difference in the energy levels and vibration rates involved, it is extremely uncomfortable for the lower-level entities to come into contact with the higher energy patterns of the guardians.) *I now ask that those guardians ascend and as they do, I ask that they increase their vibration rate still further. This forces the now surrounded entity to increase its vibration rate a like amount, thus becoming a being of Light. If it chooses to be stubborn it simply ceases to exist as a discrete entity and returns to the Source. In either instance, these entities are completely and permanently converted by the one effective tool against them, which is Love. They will never again have the opportunity or desire to affect anyone negatively.*

I ask that guardians in an appropriate number remain around me and those close to me for an appropriate time frame to ensure our continued healing and strengthening.

Thank you, Spirit.
Amen.

---

* I occasionally use the term "Father" because that is how I think. I recognize that the Creator is genderless and can correctly be referred to as Him, Her, It, Them, Us, The Great Mystery, All That Is, The Void, etc. Because of the current gender politics regarding this issue, Spirit has suggested another term that is completely apolitical, non gender specific and absolutely accurate. That term is "ATI" (pronounced Ah'tee), that is an acronym for "All That Is".

It is not at all unusual for the person making this request and those nearby to truly feel the presence and ascension of the guardians as well as the conversion or dissolution of the entities involved.

You will notice the continued use of the term 'appropriate'. This leaves the numbers and process in the 'hands' of the highest Spirit, whom we can only assume knows these things at a more intimate level than does our consciousness.

Some people may also wish to request the Christ Force, specific Angels, or some other specific energies be present in the room, sometimes even in specific positions in the room. The simple matter of a heartfelt request easily accomplishes this. As an individual becomes more sensitive the change in energy in the room can be easily detected.

USING THIS BOOK, THE CARDS, AND THE WORDS

1)   Let the book fall open wherever it will offer an "instant message" regarding your day to come or any particular question or event you wish information concerning.

2)   Using the word list and a pendulum, intuition, or any other random or guided selection process, select the word or words that seem to call to you for the day's message.

3)   Building on another reading from any other source is a simple matter. Simply write down the essence of that reading and select the words of greatest importance. Look up the words of the greatest importance for an even deeper understanding of the reading.

THE CARDS

The cards that this volume supports are probably totally different than any you have seen or used before. If you cannot find them locally, contact FOTL Press at www.ManiPureheart.com for information on obtaining your set. The first and most noticeable difference is the sheer number of words available to you. This in itself assures one of receiving an in-depth and detailed reading.

While it is very possible to use these cards as you would any other deck, simply drawing a word for a particular purpose or position in a spread and reading what the book has to say about it, Spirit designed the cards to be round for a very specific reason.

As you can see by the diagram on the next page, each card can be infinitely variable in its meaning. It varies in intensity from top to bottom and in gender alignment from side to side. A word falling squarely in the center, i.e.: as these words are aligned in the book, would represent plain vanilla — simply information for your perusal.

The details to be extracted from the position of the word as it looks up at you from the face of the card are the major difference in this system of readings compared to any other card-based system. The sheer number of words available to you represents another great difference. Combined, these two features enable the reader to arrive at a complex and detailed analysis of a particular situation. This system allows you to see in great depth all of the aspects of each word and the deeper and often hidden interactions and interrelationships as the different aspects of the words are revealed. When taken in combination and analyzed carefully this results in a tremendous amount of useful information and understanding for the recipient.

Example 1:

If a person were to draw the word shown below, oriented in the way demonstrated, this would be the message:

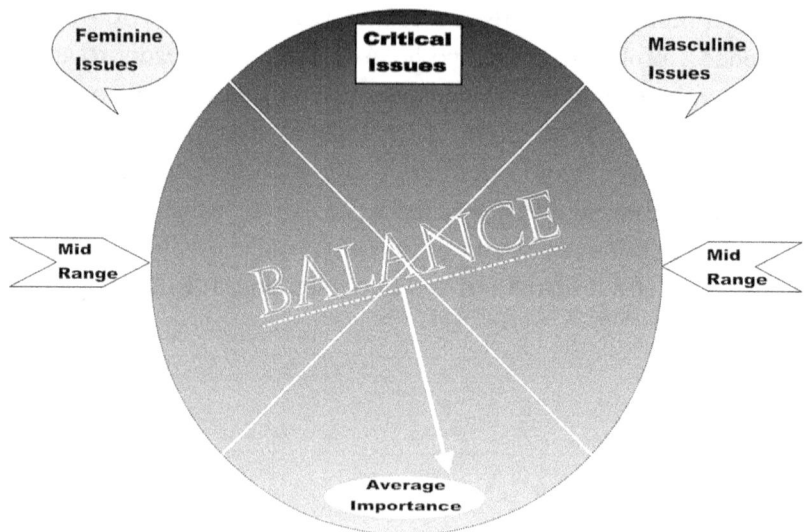

As you can see, the word "Balance" is almost but not quite aligned toward the vertical meridian, or "average". This means that while the word is important in the reading (or it would not have been included), it is not tremendously vital within the overall scope of the reading.

Because the word is tilted somewhat to the right, it indicates that whatever challenges are occurring within the realm of "Balance" are occurring with a male 'twist'. That is to say, there may be a tendency to be somewhat aggressive or controlling within the situation. The fact that the tilt is slight and well within the "average" quadrant indicates that the challenge is minor, but that "Balance" is still one of the aspects to be watched and improved upon if possible.

Example 2:

In this example, the word is aligned in such a way as to be more closely associated with the horizontal meridian, or "troublesome". It is oriented toward the male direction again, indicating that the problem has to do with those tendencies most commonly associated with male-ness. This would indicate that the person involved is experiencing challenges realizing "balance" because of a strong tendency toward being of a controlling and aggressive nature. The position also suggests strongly that this is an area where many and/or strong lessons are to be experienced if a change is not initiated from within immediately.

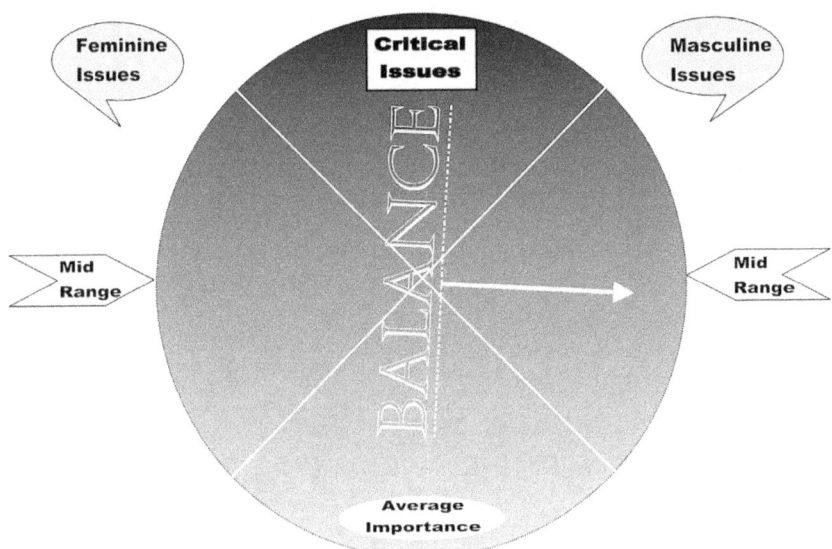

Example 3:

Here we see an example of a serious warning/admonition from Spirit regarding a situation.

The word is almost completely upside down; oriented toward the left or feminine side of the chart. This would indicate that there is a severe lack of balance in the situation and that the individual is being entirely too passive. Spirit suggests that when a word is upside down like this, it is time to put away the words, shut the book and get to work on solving the situation **NOW!**

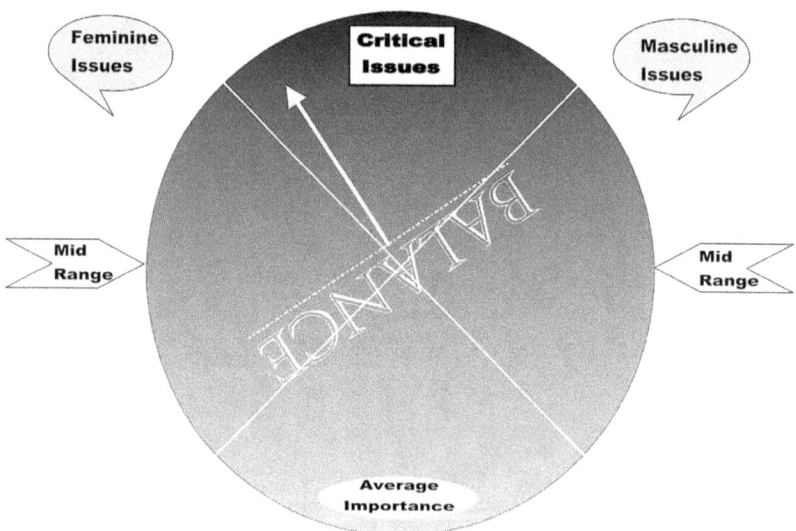

SINGLE-WORD DRAW

This first method is ideal for the beginning student of metaphysics or for receiving a quick and accurate guide to a specific question or situation. It will also encourage the beginner to have more faith in the information provided by Spirit and by the Angelic forces. My own experiences indicate that when we begin to trust the information we are presented with, more information as well as more detailed information is offered to us.

It is always a good idea to take a moment for silent meditation and thank you to whatever or whomever you consider your source or sources to be. Many people will then either close or avert their eyes from the words that are normally placed in a loose pile or a large bowl and gently stirred before drawing from them. Others will carefully study the words to see which one leaps out at them or which one is hanging over the edge of the bowl or is separated from the pack. Still others will simply pick a page at random or let the book fall open on its own. There is no wrong way to pick your word and there is no way that is more correct than another. Whichever method works best for you in the moment is the 'right' method to use at that moment.

Formulate your question and draw a single word. If you do not understand how the word you have drawn relates to the question you have asked refer to the text of this book under the heading of that word for further evaluation and different perspectives.
Another tool I have found useful is to replace the card in the pile, stir the words gently and ask Spirit for further data. If you draw the same word it means that Spirit is unwilling to give you more details at the present time and that it is important for you to figure out for yourself what the message contained in the single word refers to. At this time it might also be advantageous to perform a larger spread of words on the same subject.

Many times people will simply leave the words out in a convenient but unobtrusive location. As they go through their daily activities they may pass that spot a dozen times. Suddenly as they are passing by they will have the urge to reach out and grab a word. This spontaneous act is perhaps the method by which we interfere the least with the information Spirit intends for us to receive. When we use this method, the word drawn tells us:

1. The energy that Spirit has placed around us for that time period;

2. The lessons involved in the experiences we are about to encounter;

3. The lessons we are about to assist someone else in receiving

OR:

4. A combination of the above.

Many times the lessons we assist others in receiving are a modified version of the same lessons we are trying to give ourselves. Helping another only gives us a chance to see it from the outside instead of the inside.

THREE WORD SPREAD

At times we would like a more detailed answer than can be easily derived from a single word. At these times there are several options. One of these is the three-word spread which can be used in several ways.

The following pages outline possible methods or layouts. It's very important to remember that whatever you decide that you want the words to mean as you are going into the reading is exactly what will be reflected as the words are drawn. These readings have NO LIMITATIONS other than those we wish to impose on them.

PERCEPTION CREATES REALITY! WHAT'S YOURS?

THE TIME TRAVELER SPREAD

When we have a question regarding a relationship or another developing situation and we would like to know in what direction we are being led, this is a very good spread to use.

Focus upon the situation or on your specific question and draw the first word. Do not look at this word yet, but place it face down on the left or write it on the left side of your notepad. This word represents the past of this particular situation and what aspect of that past has led you to your current position. Draw a second word and place it in the middle position. This word reflects the situation as it is now. Repeat the process a third time. This word, placed on the right of the three, represents either the stumbling block you must overcome, the nature of the lessons you are offering yourself, the energy of the change that is occurring, or a combination of the above.

Meditate for a moment on the questions you have had regarding the past aspects of the situation then turn the word on the left to receive further information and understanding of that situation from Spirit. Repeat this process for the center word to more fully understand the situation as it exists at the present. At this time it may be appropriate to offer a prayer for understanding and the ability to perceive and follow the shortest path of greatest Light as your situation moves into maturity. Turn over the last word now and receive the message that Spirit would share with you in answer to your question.

DETAILS SPREAD

In the case of a single-word draw that did not seem to provide enough information or in any other situation in which more information or a deeper understanding would be helpful, this three-word draw will be quite useful.

Drawing the words as outlined for the Time Traveler, the first word to the left after the draw describes the area of out-of-balance attitudes or perceptions which resulted in creating the situation as it now exists.

The middle word represents the area of focus that Spirit is leading you toward, encouraging you to look at how to change your attitudes or behavior patterns to progress toward your immediate goal of growth and learning. Spirit uses a combination of persistence and escalation when offering us the lessons we have requested from our soul level. First, Spirit taps us on the shoulder (figuratively speaking) to gain our attention and generate changes in the direction of our growth into the Light. If we ignore these subtle hints (small things 'going wrong' or out-of-balance in our lives), Spirit 'escalates', making its demand for our attention more obvious. If this still fails to have the desired effect, things can begin to become downright uncomfortable in our lives. Spirit is not out to hurt us or cause us pain but only seeks to access our consciousness in an effort to help us learn the lessons we have requested from the higher levels. At times we can become quite deaf to Spirit's call. Like many children, we also can 'choose not to hear'. When a friend tells us an incredible tale of woe, listing all of the horrible things which are going wrong in their life, it is almost certain they have turned a deaf ear to Spirit's message for quite some time. This can result in some rather pointed attempts by Spirit to obtain their attention. We control the severity of our experience by determining how soon we decide to "get the message".

The third word deals with the direction and focus of the move you should consider in order to follow the shortest path of greatest Light. In other words; how we might behave to get from "here" to "there" in the shortest time and with the least hassle.

STUMBLING BLOCK SPREAD

"Where did I go wrong?"
            "How did I get into this mess?"
"What happened?"
            "Why can't I transcend this?"

These are the sorts of questions we often ask ourselves when life hands us a rude surprise and we have absolutely no idea what the whole thing is about. If you have run the "Details" spread without sufficient understanding of what Spirit's communication is about, this one may help you to understand more clearly. It can also be used to understand exactly what it is that is impeding your progress. You will have probably noticed by now that the only real difference in these three word draws is the intent we have when we draw the words. This is one of the Great Truths -- our will is the author of our own life experience and our intention is the pen with which we write that experience.

Feeling physically, emotionally, or spiritually blocked can be extremely trying and frustrating. As we have discussed before, events in your life only get to this level if you have ignored the more subtle hints. Let's go to the words and see what they can tell us.

Draw the three words as before.

The first word, placed to the left, indicates what stopped you in the first place. Take a moment and meditate on the deeper meanings of the word on the word. Don't limit yourself to what the dictionary or this book has to say about that word. Truly go within; spending several minutes if necessary to really come to a place of understanding regarding what your stumbling block was in the first place.

Once you feel comfortable with your answer, you are ready to go on to the middle word. This word tells you where Spirit thinks you need to focus in order to understand 'why' and at what point you stepped off of the shortest path into lesson land. Meditate on this word as it relates to the first word. Refer to your memories of actual happenings in the light of that first word drawn and in reference to the second. This should bring you to a greater understanding of exactly what your stumbling block has been in this matter and where you stand regarding this issue.

Once again the last word indicates the area you might choose to focus upon in order to rise above the situation and move forward.

REVIEW SPREAD

When we have finally gotten through a particularly rough growth phase we sometimes feel like it's time to lean back, take a deep breath, and relax for a moment. This is a particularly good time to reflect on what we've just been through and what we've accomplished. This spread will assist that process.

Meditate for a few moments on the events involved in this growth step and what you feel you have gained.

Think for a moment about where you think you have grown the most as a result of this step. Draw your first word. Leave it face down and place it in front of you if you are using the cards or simply place a piece of paper with the number '1' written on it as a bookmark.

The second word is a reading of the slant Spirit would put on what your first word indicates. As an example; if you had just experienced some growth in the area of learning to Love someone you don't particularly like to be around, you would probably feel that your area of growth was Love. Your first word may well have been compassion, as it is necessary to have understanding and true compassion for another's situation before one can really Love another. The second word could have been abundance. This would indicate that you have made an admirable beginning but Spirit would like for you to learn to Love much more.

The third word represents the reward you will receive from yourself and Spirit as a result of this growth. An example might be education. Now that you have learned how to overcome your dislike of a person or situation, Spirit is going to see to it that you are given the opportunity to exercise that new ability to help you to lock it in, and not lose this new skill. Of course, now that you know the secret it will be a simple matter to utilize it in these lessons.

SEVEN WORD SPREAD

For an organized and truly in-depth look at an overall situation, this is one of the spread formats that Spirit has suggested. Using the sacred number 'seven', I am told, helps to cut through the mysteries to the root of the problem.

Here are a couple of spreads you may wish to try.

Remember:

What you decide that the words will represent will create the reality of the spread.

First Method

Ground and center yourself as outlined in the meditation. Focus on the question at hand. Draw the first word. This is the core issue. This is the root from which the rest of the spread will grow. Place this word in front of you or write it on a piece of paper in a central position.

The next word should be drawn and inserted slightly to the right of the first one. This word speaks to us of the area of our masculine energy patterns involved in the resolution of this situation.

The third word is now drawn and laid to the left of the first word. This message relates to the area of our feminine nature that is concerned with this issue.

These three words together should provide a definitive look at the situation from several different perspectives. Understanding the situation is an important key to moving through it gracefully.

The next two words will discuss the path involved in this movement.

Draw your fourth word at this time and align it above and between the middle and right-hand words, forming a pyramid shape on the right side. This fourth word indicates the path your male energies will need to follow to find the shortest path of greatest Light toward your goal.

Draw another word and put it above the middle and left-hand words of the first row. This word relates to the feminine energy's shortest route to that same goal.

At this time you can pull out one more word and set it at the top, completing the six-word pyramid. This sixth word represents the goal to be attained through the successful fulfillment of this series of lessons. Spend some time with this word and you will find that the entire picture will come into a fairly sharp focus

Now reach into the deck one last time. Position this word at the bottom of the pyramid. This is the word I refer to as the 'bottom line'. The message of this word relates to the focus of this series of adventures; defining the greater lesson which lies at the bottom of this experience.

Please be aware with every word you draw that you could be on the receiving end as easily as the giving. As you read about the meaning of the words remember that these doors always swing both ways.

Second Method

To have a completely accurate reading, it is suggested that you make a diagram on a piece of paper and return each card to the deck, and reshuffle before re-drawing for the next information. As you draw a word for each position you can write that word on your diagram in its proper location. Don't forget to indicate the direction and orientation of the word, i.e.: left, right, slight, moderate, red flag, etc. If you are using the cards, you can return the word to the pile or bowl and gently stir the words once more. In this way, all possibilities are available for each position of the diagram. In a spread of this detail, that is quite important.

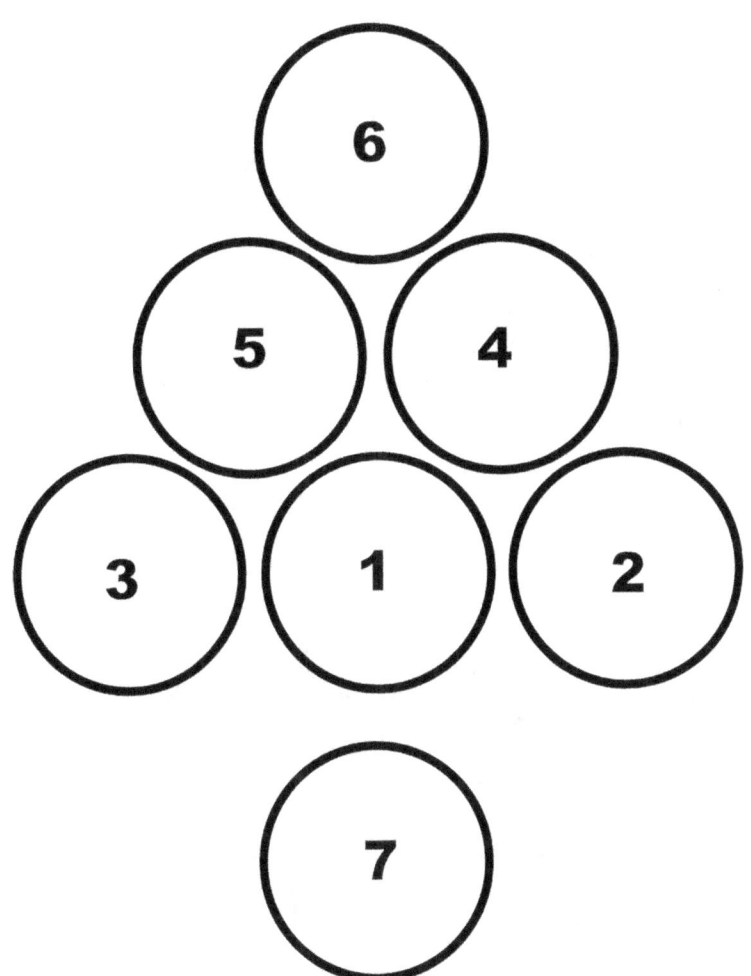

TEN WORD SPREAD

This is a particularly good spread for those seeking clarity regarding a relationship.

We are speaking of a complex issue dealing with far more than emotional or intimate issues. Relationship occurs whenever we interact with another in any way. Your child's teacher, your lover, your ex-lover, your next-door neighbor, your deceased parent, your best friend, Spirit, and your worst antagonist all have relationships with you. This spread may be used to investigate any of those associations more deeply, understand why they are as they are, where they are leading each of the participants and why.

Ground and center yourself and focus for a moment upon the relationship in question. Draw the first word and place it directly in front of you or write it in the center of your paper and return the word to the deck for possible use in another position of this spread. Be sure to note the orientation and degree of urgency for each word.

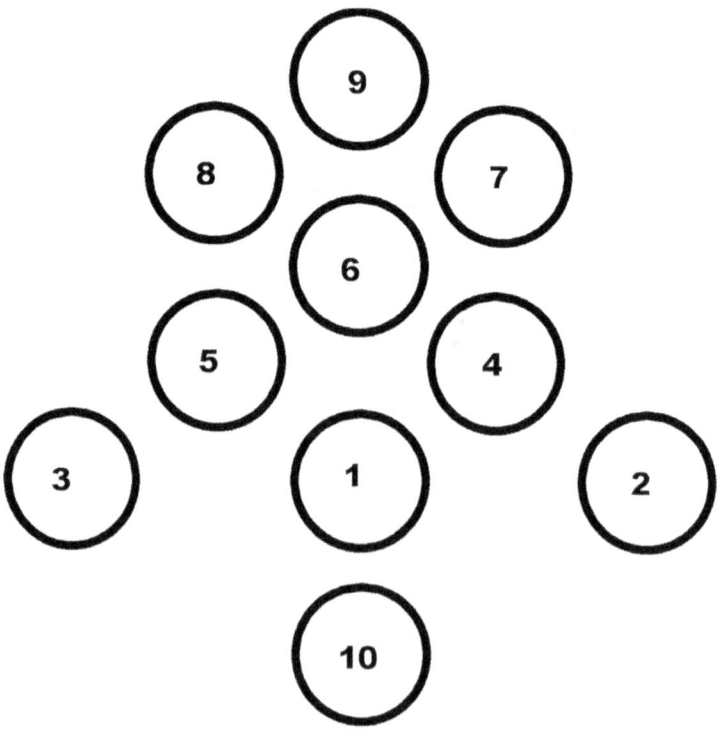

This word represents the starting point -- where the interaction is at this point in time.

The next word drawn is placed on the right side of the first and indicates the area to be focused on for the masculine side of the equation

The third word drawn is placed on the left of the first and reflects the feminine side of the problem or situation.

The fourth word is drawn and situated to the right of and slightly higher than the first, between, and above the first and second words. This word indicates the path of experiences or improved awareness your aspect could select in order to move to the next level within the relationship

The fifth word that you pull out will reflect the direction suggested for the other party in this transaction (you don't need to tell them -- Spirit will guide their steps). Insert this word in a similar position to the left of and above the center word.

Once either or both of you have processed through your segment of this level, you will come to the next tier. Select another word (6) at this time to indicate this mutual intermediate goal. Locate this word between and above the last two words so that the words you have taken so far form a pyramid shape. This intermediate goal is the stable place from which you each launch yourselves into the next growth experience.

Repeat this process to place the next three words (7, 8, and 9). Word 9 will indicate the immediate goal of the entire growth experience described by the eight words below it.

Select the final word and put it directly in front of you. This is your 'bottom line'; showing the underlying lesson for this entire series. It also represents the first step of your next growth opportunity.

Note:

Depending on how you draw your words, it is possible in any of the spreads suggested to wind up with a word in place but upside down. When this happens, you may consider this to be a strong message from Spirit that the word represents an area requiring immediate, focused, and unrelenting attention. The reversed position can be considered a 'red flag' of warning or an indicator of a serious lack of the energy referred to by the card. Spirit says: "Close the book, put away the words, and get to work on solving this RIGHT NOW!"

OVERVIEW SPREAD

Overview is the 'spread' that I, personally, use most often. It requires the use of the Ultimate Oracle deck of cards. This method allows Spirit to directly determine what it is that I need to be aware of. I find that this method is a very effective way of doing just that.

First, you may wish to focus either on a certain field within your life experience or consciously give Spirit free rein to inform you of whatever it is Spirit finds necessary or desirable to bring to your attention at this time.

Run your fingers through the cards, stirring them gently for a moment or two. Take a group of at least ten to fifteen cards all at once by pinching them between thumb and finger. You may take any amount up to the entire deck if you feel that it is appropriate. The important thing is to realize that whatever number you pick is exactly the correct amount.

Hold the group of words vertically about a foot above a cleared flat surface. Slowly and gently release your grip letting them cascade down onto the flat surface a few at a time. Some will fall face up, others face down. Separate the face-up words and read them all to get an idea of the energy of the message. When you feel that you have a pretty good idea, take just one of the 'face down' cards as your 'bottom line' for this spread.

While it would be impossible to give the meaning of each word for every possible circumstance, I will attempt to give some fairly complete guidelines. Don't forget that when drawing multiple words, every word you draw influences every other word you draw.

A somewhat advanced technique based on this mutual influence that can be used with almost any multi-word layout is to take the face-up words and intuitively 'cluster' them into groups in order to achieve even more understanding. This is not something that can be taught, but rather comes from within. It is a result of your comfort in dealing with Spirit and your confidence in your own ability to do so.

You never know how well this method will work if you don't try, so feel free to work with this continually. You'll be pleasantly surprised at how quickly you'll 'catch on'.

SPONTANEOUS MESSAGES

Many times as I am going through my day-to-day business and walk past my dish of cards I am moved to choose a word. I find that almost always the message is both accurate and timely.

Another method that seems to work well involves gently stirring or mixing the words, then drawing the word or words which have fallen outside of the pile or seem to be begging your attention in some other way. Remember—there is no wrong way to do this.

ENJOY!

THE WORDS

The section of this book that follows gives information for each of the words in the deck. The information for each word will be offered in reference to several different possible areas of application.

We will speak first about the basic meanings or applications for the energy referred to by each word.

We will then explore the possible meaning of the word in relation to a personal or intimate relationship. A personal relationship within the purposes of this book can be any close connection with any person. The connection can be biological, emotional, marital, physical, or a combination of all of these. We never seem to tire of trying to figure out what is happening to and within our relationships. This area specifically addresses how the energy of the word will affect that area of our lives.

We will then take a look at how the word relates to our mundane life in the world. How will the energy of the word be of use in our day-to-day interactions? This section offers some insights.

Ultimately, the only work we do is on ourselves. You will find that if you were to read all aspects of each of the words you draw, they all could be placed into the area of how it applies to self. I've tried to boil it down to a more direct and understandable form.

Harsh aspects appear to be present for most concepts – but are they REALLY harsh? This section addresses that perspective and suggests ways to avoid discomfort.

And finally, I offer COMMENTS FROM SPIRIT. Spirit has a wonderfully clear and concise way of stating its position. Spirit assigned me the wonderful task of creating these books and I have invited Spirit to add a closing remark for each one of the words. Sometimes the comments surprise even me!

The Words

INDECISION

Indecision is a positive event. It means that you are no longer satisfied with life as you have been experiencing it and you are ready to assimilate your lessons and experiences in order to move off in a new direction. The major difficulty lies in generating enough faith in ourselves and our process to be able to step away from the sometimes shaky security of what we think we know and into the unknown.

Should I stay or should I go? Will he come back; and if he does, should I take him back? Does she really love me? Our lives are often filled with this kind of question. We spend so much time playing "what if" that we sometimes forget that there is life beyond personal relationship. Live in the now -- and let the 'what ifs' sort themselves out in their own way and in their own time.

Usually, in general relationships, our Indecision revolves around something that we would like to do versus what we feel we should do or what we feel is expected of us. Living a spiritual life requires us to always do that which we know to be 'right' and to avoid those actions that we suspect are ego-directed. Remember: evil is simply the misuse of ego.

While Indecision is a positive experience preceding growth, when carried to extremes it becomes paralysis. Continual movement is a requisite for living. Stagnation means that a part of you has died.

COMMENTS FROM SPIRIT:

Coming from the heart of hearts; from the knowingness of Spirit, assures that there will be no Indecision in your life experience. The path is brightly lit if you will but open your eye to it. Any step away from the light is unthinkable in these circumstances; thus there can be no Indecision.

Blessings.

CELEBRATION

Celebration is Light, Joy, and Delight all rolled up in one with a few other aspects thrown in for good measure. Celebration is sometimes performed in a somber manner but this is not the true essence of Celebration. The true essence is the bubbling overflowing of Love and joy into the world when the body and soul can no longer contain them.

When this word is drawn into your life Spirit is inviting you to focus on and Celebrate the 'good' aspects of your relationship. It is also suggesting that you reflect on the lessons and purpose for those aspects that trouble you as these are the greatest blessings of all. The troubling aspects contain the teachings and lessons that your soul has requested. Do you choose to be a victim -- or a student?

Spirit invites you to Celebrate all your friendships, all your conflicts, and all your other mundane experiences. Everything that occurs in your life is a gift of Love whether you are able or willing to perceive it in that manner or not.
Celebrate!

Our entire life becomes a Celebration of our greater self when we grow into that spiritual place where we can see the beauty and Love in every aspect of every day. In the meantime, look to the light that is in your life in even the apparently darkest moments.
Celebrate!

There are no harsh aspects to joyful Celebration, except perhaps excess. Your Celebration need not offend or interfere with the process of others.

COMMENTS FROM SPIRIT:

One of the true purposes of your experience called 'life' is to learn to Celebrate the spirit that you are in each and every moment.

LEVITATION

    This interesting word has several meanings. Even the more common and mundane of these meanings is an unusual concept to many. That is the art of physically lifting material objects with the power of your thoughts. This is a reality and is being done by adepts around the world. It is also an almost totally useless toy and can indeed be a trap to those who become enamored of its glitter to the point where they lose track of the gem of far greater worth that lies at the end of their journey of inner discovery. This will not be the meaning to which this word refers in this text.
The Christian Bible has a phrase -- 'Lift up thine eyes unto the hills.' In the time of Christ the attitude of prayer -- of communication and communion with Spirit -- was with the head uplifted and eyes open.

This word is a reminder to you that Spirit is your best friend; that the Creator awaits only your sincere communication to place into action the changes and effects you request or require (the two are not always the same).

A third meaning is to uplift your attitude; to improve the perception that you place on the events, real and imagined, that you observe in your life. Remember that all things are in Divine order at all times -- whether we like them or not, and whether we understand them or not. Trust in the Creator to provide you with precisely what you need in each moment. If it seems unpleasant, lift up your eyes and your heart by communicating openly with Spirit.

Drawing this word in response to a question regarding a personal relationship means that it is time to place that relationship on a higher level. Whether there has been a problem of communication, divided attention or anger, misunderstanding, or any of the other problems that relationships are susceptible to, it is time to raise the energy and the level of communication and integrity. This word in this context asks that you and the other(s) involved act in a Creator-centered and impeccable way.

Impeccability is called for here. It is time to walk your talk even when the other party or parties refuse to. No one can ever cheat you in the long run. They can only cheat themselves.

It is so easy and so common to lie to ourselves about our true motives in various actions and situations. The fascinating part is the ease with which we ignore that which we know to be true – that which we know to be the 'right' action- as we continue blissfully down the primrose path of self-delusion. Once more, Levitation calls for the highest ideals and the highest action. To do anything less for any reason lessens you and empowers the forces which work counter to your growth.

As we strive to ever elevate our consciousness there is the danger of losing our footing and our grounding. The object of our growth is to expand our perception of self, not just to move it 'upward'. There is a phrase shared with me by a fundamentalist Christian friend. She says that some people are so heaven-bound that they are no earthly good. That is the condition to which I refer here. In the process of growing ever closer to Spirit, don't forget to keep your feet firmly anchored in this material reality which you have chosen at this point.

COMMENTS FROM SPIRIT:

Lift up your heart, your soul, your consciousness, and your aspirations to the mighty pinnacle of All that Is. You are this above all else. The sadness we feel at your reluctance to fully allow and manifest your own Divinity within the great Divinity of the Creator!

Children! Listen to us, please. You are the chosen. You are the elect. You are the heart; the Loving breath of the Greatest of all. How can you refuse for so long to see; to manifest this in your every breath and heartbeat? Lift up your eyes, beloved ones, and see who you are.

Blessings.

PEACE

     Literally speaking, Peace means an absence of disruptive influence. That is a passive Peace. When dealing with Spirit, however, there is a greater Peace; a Peace which is active in our daily lives and which reflects in our words our demeanor, and our attitude. When you meet someone who fully manifests this Divine Peace you will never forget it or them.

     Drawing Peace in reference to a question of personal relationship indicates that the time of conflict is coming to an end and that a resolution is at hand. Reflect for a moment on the situation that you find irritating, then attempt to reflect on the concept of Divine Peace. Do you feel your body relax as you attune to the energy of Divine Peace?

The feeling of Peacefulness in our daily excursions into the world is to be desired and is a very good thing when it happens. The small annoyances of everyday interactions can build up to an intolerable level quite quickly if allowed to. Inviting this energy into your living pattern dissipates those negative responses before they get a chance to fully form. This makes the day much more pleasant for all concerned. Once we learn to be at Peace at all times we find that life becomes much more simple and more enjoyable.

Inner Peace is 'a pearl of great value.' It is one of the finest gifts we can give ourselves. Imagine never losing your temper -- even a little bit. Think of how nice it would be to exist in total tranquility at all times and in all circumstances. This is the goal toward which the energy of Peace will lead you. It is up to you to follow.

COMMENTS FROM SPIRIT:

Peace is a word that describes the state of being at rest in the heart of Love; floating forever in total inner and outer harmony. One-ness with all that is and knowing that all there is, is Love beyond your greatest measure. Peace be yours, now and forevermore. Blessings.

CHANGE

"Nothing Changes but the Changes."
Change is one of the greatest blessings that we can receive. It is also one of the most disconcerting and potentially one of the most disruptive. Change is the essence and purpose of the physical realm. Nothing is without Change. At times, Change can even be perceived as degeneration or death. From the viewpoint of Spirit, these are only the loops in our paths that allow us to review areas that have been neglected. When the lessons are learned further loops in that area become unnecessary as Change has occurred which now enables us to move on to our next level.

Personal relationships are loaded with Change. Change is

their primary purpose and function. Any partnership is a tool that all concerned may use to help them to move forward on their path. Every interaction with an intimate partner reaches far deeper into the heart of "who you are" than with any other individual at any other time. It is because we have allowed our defenses to be lowered with our partner that this is so. "Intimate", in this usage, does not necessarily mean nor is it limited to physically intimate partners.

We are forever buffeted by the Changes that each person and each group of people experience in their mundane relationships with the world around us. As their reality modifies itself to fit their pattern of lessons the part of our reality that is touched by theirs is also altered. This is part of the flow of growth that we as a group are experiencing. The interactive aspect of this growth assures us of a never-ending variety of experiences. It is important to recall that all of these experiences are gifts of Love that we have given ourselves as an opportunity to learn and grow. We always have the choice to experience these events either as a student or as a victim.

Our entire reason for experiencing this material realm in the manner called 'life' is to enable ourselves to have the opportunity to Change in the direction of our own Divinity and to move ever closer to Spirit. Change is a great blessing. Enjoy it. Lack of motion equals

stagnation and death. You will accept that which falls within your pattern of truths at this point in your development. As you grow; as I grow, our patterns of truths change while the Great Truths remain forever constant. It is only our stage of development and our level of receptivity that cause the appearance of changing realities regarding the state and nature of ourselves, Man, the etheric, and God.

Each of us creates our own reality as we travel this path. This reality is both gift and trap for it is something that is intended to be transitory and changing as we grow. Many of us come to a wide, comfortable spot in our road, lie down, and wrap ourselves in the dream, halting all forward motion. Do not fear change; rather look for it, study it, accept that which seems "right," and seek to understand that which we find 'uncomfortable' for that part serves us as well. This is the growth we all seek.

COMMENTS FROM SPIRIT:

Change is the heart's blood of existence. Were it not for this thing you refer to as change, there would be no purpose to existence. Change is the road to the godhead of self, and the doorway opening to the future.

Blessings.

REST

    For every step in any journey, fatigue accrues; energy is expended and must be replaced. This word indicates that you have reached a place in your path where it is appropriate to honor the fact of your weariness. Stop awhile in this beautiful wayside Resting place and lean back against the giant tree. Listen to the birds, the water, and the song of the breeze around you. Take the time to take the time. It's important.
    Personal relationships -- even the best of them are a lot of work to maintain and nurture. One might think of this effort as the beating of the heart of the relationship. If the heart stops, the relationship withers and dies. Even the human heart Rests between beats. Take a 'time out' for yourself. Treat yourself (and your partner)

to a little quiet, alone or special time. You deserve it and it can help tremendously!

In our day to day dealings with the 'outer' world it is easy to become callous to the needs and emotional state of those around us. This word invites you to mentally 'take five' and come back to the world more refreshed and sensitive in order to better reflect the Divine Love within to those around you

How often in the daily rush of life and living do we forget to honor the needs of our body and psyche? Rest is every bit as important to our well-being and growth as food and warmth. Meditation is an excellent form of Rest, surpassing even sleep in some instances.

The Incas of South America only had three rules to live by: Don't lie, Don't steal, and don't be lazy. Inappropriate use of Rest in order to avoid responsibilities is laziness and was listed among the Christian's seven deadly sins as sloth.

COMMENTS FROM SPIRIT:

Come, my children, and Rest your hearts in the Love of the Creator. This is your home, your sanctuary, and your place of total peacefulness. When you be One with All that Is, the peace of the Creator is the hallmark of your existence. Rest of the highest order is and always has been the birthright of all.

WISDOM

Wisdom is an elusive prize. It has nothing at all to do with intelligence and everything to do with knowingness -- the ability to perceive and connect with the flow of the river of life all around and through you and the others around you.

Wisdom, as it regards a personal relationship, involves instinctively tuning yourself to the pulse of the relationship and the inner and outer needs of both yourself and your partner, flowing in the path of least resistance and greatest light. This can only be accomplished by constantly attuned sensitivity and caring. Remember: Love does not take, it only gives. Love does not possess, it only shares.

The important thing in any relationship of any kind is to attempt to remain balanced and attuned as much as possible. If you are becoming angry or irritated with a situation or person it is only because you are not allowing yourself the Wisdom of seeing the situation through the eyes of Spirit. Everything that we (at the Soul level) allow ourselves to experience is a gift of Love and an opportunity to learn. We have two choices in this circumstance. We can either be students or victims. A student learns and grows (Wisdom) from the experience and does not have to repeat it. A victim has not 'gotten the message' and is condemned to repeat the lesson -- usually in increasing intensity -- until they do.

An example of this can be found in an early arithmetic class. The teacher tells the class that "two plus two equals four." Everyone understands it except you. "TWO PLUS TWO EQUALS FOUR," the teacher repeats. If you still 'don't get it', she may have you come up to the blackboard and write it ten times. If that doesn't work she may demonstrate the concept with blackboard erasers. If you still don't get it she may give you the homework assignment of writing the equation one hundred times. If you still don't understand you may have to stay after school in a study hall to help you. If that does not get through to you, you may have to attend summer school. If that doesn't work you may have to repeat the class.

Spirit tells me that "Infinite Love has infinite patience." We can keep coming back as often as we want—or need—to get a particular lesson. Every time it is offered to us and we 'don't get it', it travels around the wheel of our life once more and approaches us from a slightly different angle—and with greater intensity. This process continues until we finally 'get the message (becoming a student) or until the message is coming to us so loudly and with such force that all of the other aspects of our life must take a back seat until that particular lesson is learned. This is the reason that it sometimes seems that our entire life has gone to heck. It is only Spirit Loving us enough to offer us an important lesson in a way that we cannot ignore. As soon as we get the message, Spirit (the teacher) offers us another one built upon the last but offered in the gentlest of fashions.

"Two plus three is five."

Wisdom in use on the personal level is a blessing of the highest order. When you allow your connectedness to All that Is to be the ruler (in both uses of the word) of your life, you will find that your life flows much more smoothly. There just doesn't seem to be anything that upsets you. You understand that all things are in order and that the entire universe supports you and your growth.

There are no harsh aspects to true Wisdom. Allow yourself to hear the Creator and you cannot make an error.

COMMENTS FROM SPIRIT:

The greatest Wisdom is to simply BE Love in every word, in every thought, in every deed, in every prayer. Manifest the order of all in the most mundane and the glory of the highest in the act most humble. That is all.

DETERMINATION

As with so many other things, Determination can be a mixed blessing. The direction from which one comes in this Determination is the critical factor. If one comes from a place of self-serving or ego the Determination reflects that. If one comes from the higher aspect of self and that Determination is to serve the creator, it is quite a different matter. This word invites you to examine the motives behind your Determination in whatever areas are activated at this time

To be Determined in a personal relationship can also be either a blessing or a curse; again depending on the underlying reasons. If one is Determined to see through what seems to be an untenable position or situation, this is most likely a position that will provide growth and understanding as long as the experience occurs from a mental state of the student rather than as a result of a feeling or perception of victimhood. If on the other hand, one is Determined to 'bail out' of a seemingly 'bad' situation, this offers a completely different set of lessons. I recommend you also read 'relationship'.

Determination in a general relationship is almost always an aspect of Ego and should be recognized as such. It comes into being when the participants have conflicting ideas of how something should occur and invest themselves in that idea, regardless of its merit or the merit of any other ideas propounded.

Determination on the personal level speaks once again of intent. Drawing this word is an invitation by Spirit to inspect your inner workings and positions and to look at your motives and attachment behind your recent or proposed activities. Listen to Spirit -- It knows what It's doing!

Determination can become an obsession when carried to an extreme. Anything that serves to tie us to the material form called reality by most is not a direct path to our spiritual nature. It may provide many wonderful lessons in the long run, but it will be exactly that -- the long run.

Obsession is not the shortest path of greatest light.

COMMENTS FROM SPIRIT:

Determine to live within the Creator and to allow the Creator to live within you. Determine to BE LOVE in every moment and every aspect of your living. This is the only form of Determination that is not of, from, and for Ego. Be at peace, BE LOVE, and be Loved.

Blessings.

SELF-ESTEEM

Self Esteem can be defined as a sense of self as a worthwhile and worthy being. Each of us is created of the Creator by the Creator. Each of us is a part of the whole and connected to that wholeness whether we are aware of it or not. The way in which we choose to perceive ourselves determines how many of the blessings of our heritage we will allow ourselves in each moment.

Self Esteem in a personal relationship situation is revealed by the dynamics of the day-to-day relating of the partners involved. Do you feel so insecure as to need to dominate your partnership? Or does it take the other path of allowing yourself to be dominated? Either way dishonors not only you and your partner but also the reason for the relationship to exist in the first place. This is not to say that this is not in Divine order. It simply is not the shortest path of greatest Light for most people in most cases. Drawing this word invites you to look at whether or not you are recognizing that the Creator moves, lives, and speaks through you and your partner. How could the Creator not be worthy? How could the Creator not be loved and honored? Love and honor yourself enough that those things that you KNOW to be the shortest path of greatest Light are followed in each moment and in every way. Be still within and know that Thou (and your partner) art the Creator!

The message on the personal level is to esteem yourself in accordance with your birthright. Humility and great strength go hand in hand and complement one another. You will naturally manifest both of these things, as well as compassion when you are in balance. At that point, you will have an accurate picture of whom and what you truly are instead of the facade you have allowed yourself and the world to place on your shoulders that would paint you as less than that. When you find yourself in this state of balance you will find yourself truly Loved by many about you. Most importantly of all, you will truly Love and be content with yourself.

Sometimes we create within ourselves the illusion of superiority in an effort to find true Self-Esteem. This is nothing of course but a manifestation of ego and as such is probably not in line with our shortest path of greatest Light. Assess yourself carefully as you enter new levels of Self Esteem. Make sure there is not more steam than self.

COMMENTS FROM SPIRIT:

Esteem of the self is a form of acknowledgment of our Divine origin and connection. There is no difference among you. There is no difference between yourself and the Creator save the self-imposed limitations created by yourself in order that you might learn of your own limitless nature.

Blessings.*

*Spirit has often reminded me that we are created of the Creator by the Creator; and as such may be considered part of the body and the spirit of the Creator much as a freckle is a tiny part of our corporeal body. We think of that freckle as a discrete and minute part of ourselves yet it is intimately connected with and a part of the entirety of our 'self'. In that same way, though we may be as a molecule of water in the Earth's seas if we will but expand our consciousness and connectedness to encompass that greater wholeness we inherit the majesty and grandeur of that greater being-ness. Carried to its extreme this process leads one back to the One-ness that existed before Creation. One does in fact become the Creator.

SUCCESS

    A simple definition might suggest that Success is the opposite of failure. Since there is (on the level of Spirit) no such thing as failure it then becomes necessary to redefine Success. Success in the general sense has to do with completing a task or phase in such a way as to have grown in the process. Even what may appear to the world as a dismal failure may be deemed a Success if only you have learned and grown -- even a tiny amount -- in the experience.

    A good personal relationship is marked by a constant flow of small Successes. The major purpose of personal relationship is to provide a fertile ground in which to grow (see Balance). Whether or not we choose to use it as a growing and learning experience or whether we choose to experience it as a victim marks the boundary between a Successful and unSuccessful relationship.

Many of us will often choose to mark our Success in a general relationship in terms of material gain or the appearance of power over another. Unfortunately, this is indeed the way the world seems to keep score but this is not the type of Success of which we speak. Success in the arena of general relationship is measured by how often and to what extent you overcome the urges to keep score according to the world's rules. Points in day-to-day life are earned by subordinating your desires in favor of what is 'right'. Helping another without thought of benefit for self is the only rule. Spirit has noted your efforts to move your consciousness in that direction and is about to throw Its weight behind your inclination. Enjoy!

The most satisfying of all forms of Success is personal Success. Because the only adversary that we have is our own ego-centered desires and our own created limitations all Successes are ultimately personal Successes. Any time that we are able to step beyond those desires and limitations we have achieved a Success. Congratulations!

There is a saying about not letting Success get to your head. At times, a small Success can bring forth a tremendous bloom of ego. Don't let this happen to you. Remember -- only you can prevent flaming ego!

COMMENTS FROM SPIRIT:

Success is another one of those Human-created concepts. When one achieves in consciousness the total One-ness with which one was brought into being, the knowledge of that one's total perfection in each moment becomes a beacon to the completeness that knows not Success or failure. It simply exists.

Blessings.

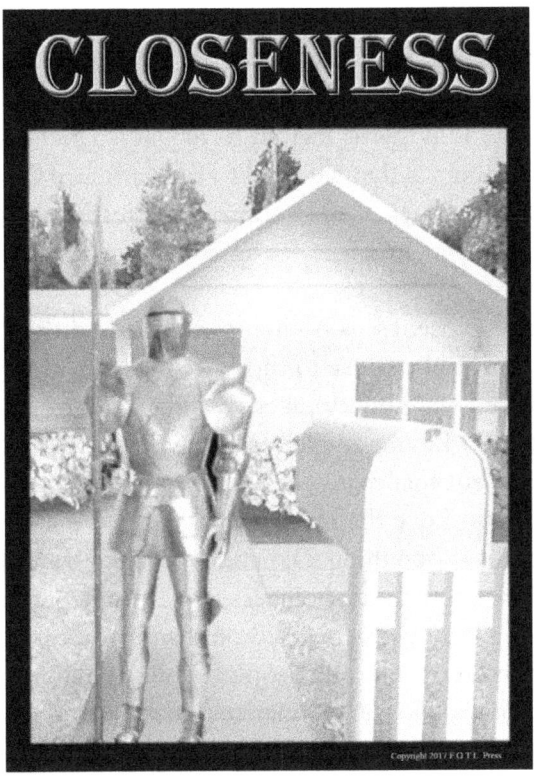

CLOSENESS

This word can have several meanings. In the context of a spiritual reading, it generally refers to one's Closeness to the Creator. It can also refer to one's nearness or proximity to a new level of awareness or existence. The third major possibility deals with an association with another in a relationship.

Closeness received in response to a question regarding personal relationship often speaks of a need to increase the emotional Closeness (especially after a series of harsh lessons) in order to assist one another to heal and grow. It can also refer to a need to be aware of how your quest for Closeness is affecting the other party. In many cases, it can actually create a strong desire for more separation if your partner feels pushed or pressured. It is critical that you always come from Love, not need.

In many cases when dealing with the world at large Closeness is a factor that creates fear. Fear is nothing more than the absence of Love; most often self-Love. This word invites you to recognize that we are all One and invites us further to recognize that which irritates us most about others is that we need to look at more Closely in ourselves. Rather than anger, a more appropriate response might well be gratitude to the others involved for agreeing on the Spirit level to be your teachers.

Personal Closeness is both important and difficult. We tend to choose to want to be Close to those we like and admire. Most of us do not feel that way about ourselves and go out of our way to avoid knowing and Loving ourselves at that level. It is from this lack of self-nourishment that many dis-eases arise. This word invites you to get to know and Love the inner you.

Closeness is one thing. Dependence is quite another. Come together from strength and wholeness, not from dependence and need. Crutches are meant to be used only until you can stand on your own two feet and most rational people are very anxious to be done with them as soon as possible. Practice this in your search for and use of Closeness. If Closeness serves to buoy you up when you need it; fine. If you are seeking it in order to avoid inner work it will be detrimental to your growth and will probably bring lessons to that effect.

COMMENTS FROM SPIRIT:

There is truly but one Closeness; the Closeness to the Creator that springs from the awareness that you reside in the heart of that Creator who is the source of all Love for all Eternity. When you allow this Closeness there is none other necessary in your life. God's Love transcends all.

Blessings.

LEVITY

Levity, in its strictest sense, means "the act or process of lightening". Bringing forth this word at this time suggests that you learn to 'lighten up' and pull yourself out of your current focus on the apparently negative and weighty issues of your life.

There are moments of heaviness, anger, and sadness in the best of relationships. Receiving this word indicates that it is time to become aware of them and to take an even closer look at them to see how you can lighten the situation. Another possible meaning is to expect joyousness to enter your life in the moment. In either case, find the joy!

Our dealings with the outer world are often marked with a somber and often antagonistic appearance. What you send is what you receive. This word invites you to send Love and joy in order to prepare yourself to receive it. (You may wish to be a little roundabout in this. The world doesn't know how to handle unadulterated Love and joy. You sort of have to break it in gently.)

Lighten up on yourself is the message here. Remember that we are generally much more judgmental of ourselves (if we listen to what we think and say) than we are of anyone else. Don't take yourself (or your self-perceived faults) quite so seriously. Give yourself a day off from self-criticism. You might just find it to be a pleasant happening and decide to experience it more often!

Lighten up!

Laugh *with*—not *at*.

Remember to BE Love!

COMMENTS FROM SPIRIT:

Lightening of the Spirit is exactly what this concept called 'Spiritual Growth' is all about. You are held on the physical plane by your sense of heaviness in body, mind, and Spirit. These concepts are self-imposed prison walls and are totally imaginary. Release yourself from these concepts and you set yourself free in the ultimate sense. Come home, children -- We Love you.

Blessings.

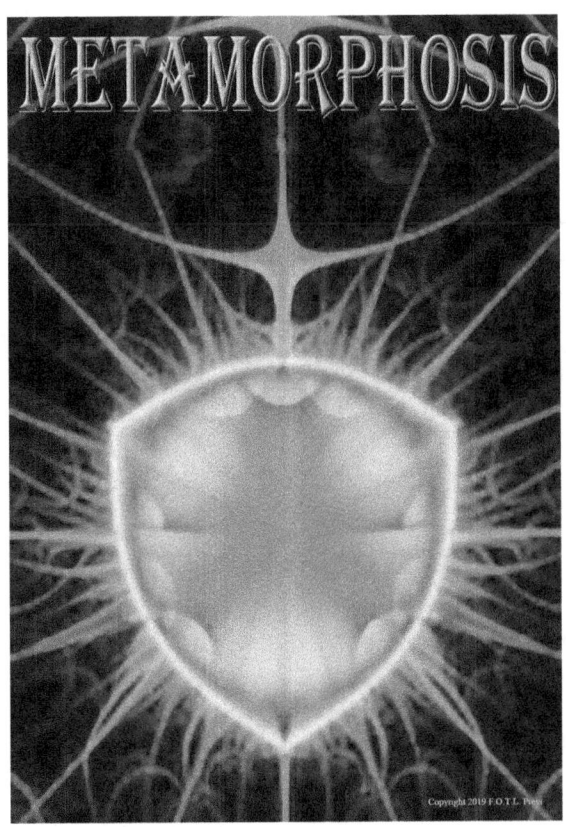

METAMORPHOSIS

This is one of the words that may be considered to be a great treasure. Metamorphosis refers to something becoming that which it was not, to begin with. It is positive change incarnate, applied personally.
Another view of Metamorphosis is Chaos: sudden, radical, and apparently random Change in and around you. It means that the lessons you have been working on are moving to a new level and most likely a new series of lessons. Consider the butterfly. Remember: change is good. To not change is the death of the spirit.
Remember -- what you were is not who you are.

Personal relationships provide the most intense opportunities for change in any aspect of the human experience. This word at this time indicates that it is time for a new lesson!

Remember -- what you were is not who you are.

The world around us is in a constant state of flux and transformation. As we are a part of that reality we are caught up and swept along in the flow of that change. Enjoy the unexpected for this is Spirit at work.

Remember—**what you were is not who you are.**

The greatest challenge of life is to change from within. To see that we are not yet perfect in our every thought and action, and to determine and resolve to allow ourselves to approach that perfection more closely is the goal.

Remember—**what you were is not who you are.**

COMMENTS FROM SPIRIT:

As the caterpillar learns to forsake the reality and supposed security of the earth and ascends into the heaven above while retaining the same persona, we invite you to forsake the perceived security of the world and yourself as you think you know them and ascend into the heavenly state of consciousness and being that is your birthright. Dear Children, learn that the only limitations you have are those which you impose upon yourselves. You are indeed the children of the Most High and are Loved and Blessed with the greatest gifts your Parent can give. You need only decry the heaviness of the rules that this world; this society would have you blindly accept, and you can accomplish miracles of the highest order within and without.

Blessings to you.

STABILITY

    While the ability to accept and absorb change is integral to the human growth experience, there comes a time when it is appropriate to be still within and without and simply be. There are times when the world and its motion seem to be going awry and you feel as though it falls upon your shoulders to "be the rock" for those around you who seem to have lost their footing and balance in the whirl of events. Drawing Stability at this time indicates that that time of strength and solidness is upon you. Take the time and have the intent to be -- and to remain -- well centered and well balanced. This is not only for the benefit of others but for your own growth as well. The sea heaves and swells; ebbs and flows; has storms and calm but the sea is always the sea. That is Stability in the midst of change.

Personal relationships thrive on change. It is both troubling and a blessing. There is a quote from the Orient that states "That which does not kill me strengthens me". The same is true for a relationship. Strong and constant change is the life's blood of a growing, healthy relationship; but as in the human body, the heart must rest between beats. This is a time to relax and evaluate where your relationship is in this moment to identify those aspects worth emphasizing and nurturing them into further growth. Search out and identify the areas that form the solid base of your partnership and honor the Stability of those while appreciating and honoring the changes which occur.

Much the same could be said for general relationships. There are certain aspects that provide a Stabile solid ground upon which your everyday relationships grow. Find, honor, and nurture those aspects that promote steady and lasting growth opportunities and grow your Stability day by day and moment by moment.

It is important to maintain inner Stability within a dynamic whole. To remain perfectly static invites petrifaction and stagnation. To thrash wildly and without limits to your movement invites destructive chaos. Freedom of movement within the parameters of your highest goals provides both Stability and growth. Bringing this word into your consciousness at this time invites you to do just that.

Stability is a balance between fossilizing and flying off into the nether regions of existence. The middle path -- moderation in all things -- is strongly recommended. Stability should be a living breathing and moving form; not a monument to immobility.

COMMENTS FROM SPIRIT:

There is but one form of Stability that we would discuss. Be strong and certain in your awareness of the Creator within and allow that to manifest in your every moment. That is all. We are done.

Blessings.

EXCELLENCE

To Excel means to surpass the average. This word in your life at this moment urges you to become much more than ordinary in your material and spiritual manifestation.

Excellence in a personal relationship requires a conscious and honorable focus on maintaining, nurturing, and improving that relationship. Don't settle for an average relationship and don't settle for being an average partner. You are invited by this word to Excell! One can always strive for perfection. The higher you go the better is your view of the remaining potential for improvement. This is a win-win situation!

Being in integrity with what you believe and within the framework of what you believe to be appropriate in the moment is of the essence when seeking Excellence. Excellence is often a demanding and always a rewarding partner.

It is so important to be totally honest with and within yourself at all times and in every way. Be in total integrity with your highest beliefs in each moment, and you live in Excellence.

There is a Christian saying: "You are so Heaven-bound that you are no earthly good". Remember that even though you are not of this world you have chosen to be in this world. The only responsibility we have is to be the tallest, brightest, clearest, and purest reflector of the Creator's presence that we can be. That is what Excellence is all about! It is not up to us to force another to emulate our efforts or path. If that other chooses to look up and see the light that we reflect and to say to themselves: "I, too, am that", that is a wonderful thing. If that same other chooses to look only downward into fear and control then that is also a wonderful thing and is exactly appropriate for them at this time. We are fulfilling our responsibility to Excellence and to Spirit. They are growing toward their goals at their own pace and in their own way.

COMMENTS FROM SPIRIT:

Excellence is another of those strictly human terms. It compares 'less than Oneness' with 'approaching Oneness.' When you choose to allow yourself to exist in Oneness, Excellence is a 'given.'

Blessings.

REBIRTH

That which has been no longer is and yet you still exist. You are becoming new or have evolved a different set of awarenesses and reactions. That is what Rebirth is all about.

We seem to feel on a Spiritual level that it is very important to balance all of the outstanding Karma that we can because we are at the end of a planetary and spiritual cycle. This is why so many of us have chosen such intense life experiences.

In this time of the world's history, the 'normal' process of life and death has changed. In 'normal times' when we complete the 'contract' under which we returned to a material body, we no longer require the body and lay it down in the process known as death. When we come to the end of a contract period under the current conditions we will often choose to experience a life-threatening occurrence. At times the process can also occur without that trigger. Many of us have 'near death' experiences where we will 'check in' with the Spirit realm for further instruction and 'resetting' of our parameters then return to our old body. The reason for this is that it can be very advantageous in the interest of balancing Karma to have a fully formed adult body and because time is limited on the physical plane we are better off keeping our old one rather than growing a new one. One of the signals of this Rebirth process is a falling away of the tools that were necessary for the old lessons to be received. If your whole world has crumbled around you; if your partner and children seem to have been taken from you; if your hobbies and habits have suddenly and radically changed; if your employment or field of employment is pulled out from under you and it seems like the end of the world, it is! It is the end of the world that you created in order to complete the old contract. Over the next several months, you will begin to gather around you the tools you need to grow and learn (and be of service) at your new level. You are being reborn - giving birth to yourself. There is no birth without pain and you will have to learn to walk and talk your new reality. What a blessing -- what a gift you are giving yourself!

Personal relationships go through the same process. When you arrive at a juncture where the relationship must die; giving birth to an entirely new body (a new partner -- or no partner) or being reborn with the same partner in a new level of understanding with a whole new set of challenges, lessons, and blessings. That time is now!

General relationships are much the same though usually not as intense as a personal relationship. The choice is yours. Do you allow this relationship to die or do you make the conscious choice to pass through the difficulty and re-birth the relationship at a new level of understanding and co-operation?

Rebirth within oneself is, of course, the most important of all. This form of Rebirth involves a petit mort -- a small dying. It is not always as intense or overwhelming as the Rebirth discussed earlier but is every bit as important and transformational. It generally involves but one aspect of your life pattern at a time.

As long as your direction is forward -- toward Love -- Rebirth is favorable. It is only when one chooses to retreat into Fear and avoidance that the process may be perceived as unfavorable.

COMMENTS FROM SPIRIT:

Rebirth involves returning consciously to the Love, Light, and Wholeness that was yours from the start. Come home, Children -- you know the way.

Blessings.

COMPASSION

Compassion is the helpful side of Brotherhood. It occurs when you see the pain or predicament of another, and because of your Love for all beings attempt in some way to ease the situation.

Even in the closest personal partnership, there are areas of our lives that are many times unpleasant. Our natural tendency is to hide these areas from our partner. This is an act of Compassion; performed to spare our partner concern because of our pain. Remember: love is the heart of every personal relationship and communication is the life's blood. When the blood ceases flowing the heart will always wither and die. This word invites us to open up these areas of discomfort in order to experience the healing Compassion of our loved one(s). We are also encouraged by the presence of this word today to become more aware of our partner's discomforts so that we may assist them in healing.

Compassion in our daily activities is critical to spiritual growth. The Bible urges us to "Love our neighbor as ourselves." Take the time for unexpected expressions of Divine Love toward strangers. Don't be amazed if you receive a pleasant surprise when you've selected Compassion as your word for the day.

Because we know ourselves so intimately we cannot deny the truths of our thoughts and actions. Most of us who desire spiritual growth can tend to judge ourselves quite harshly. Add to this the emotional wounds and lessened self-image many carry from their childhood. The programming and self-chastisement can be very effective in holding back our growth. When the energy of Compassion enters our lives in response to a query about ourselves it is an invitation to ease up on ourselves and accept that like it or not, understand it or not all things (including our thoughts and actions) are in Divine order at all times. As long as we do everything we do with and from Love, we are following the shortest path of greatest Light.

There are of course no harsh aspects to Compassion practiced in harmony with the comfort of others.

COMMENTS FROM SPIRIT:

All that Is; is Love. Manifesting this Divine Light through words, thoughts, and deeds brings us closer to Oneness. Love your brothers and sisters, and all living things, for we are all related -- we are all One. Give freely of yourself and your energy without thought of return, and you shall gain the Universe. None can cheat you -- they can only cheat themselves.

RESOLUTION

    Resolution in this format can have two main meanings. We will mention the second and focus on the first. The first meaning is the completion of a process as in resolving a chord or a conflict. If this meaning fits the question asked it is time to wrap up a project or phase that you have been dealing with whether it is a relationship, your employment, self-doubt, or any of a myriad of other unfinished subjects.

    The second meaning deals with the strong desire, commitment, and ability to see through a project in your life. Usually, this form is a prerequisite for the first form.

    In our personal relationships, there is always 'work in progress'. Encountering this word at this time indicates that it is time to bring closure to some aspect of that work in progress. Fear or reluctance might accompany some applications of this message. Once you know what it is that you must do it is very important to do it and to do it with and from only Love.

Quite often we hold resentments and grudges about an interaction that did not seem to be favorable to us. Try to remember that every experience that we have has been 'pre-approved' by our own soul and by Spirit. How we react to it is up to us. Every experience bears a lesson. We can either become a student; see the lesson and move on to the next one, or we can choose not to 'get the message', perceive ourselves as a victim, and guarantee that the lesson will be offered with greater intensity another time. Even if we have chosen to be the 'victim' in a specific circumstance we can resolve it by stepping away from our personal involvement, identifying the root lesson or lessons then bringing that awareness back into the personal. In so doing we have chosen to become the student and the lesson in that area is ended for now.

The majority of unresolved issues within one's own psyche have to do with self-worth or the lack of it. These are issues regarding the ability to accomplish a given task or whether or not one is 'lovable', cute, smart, desirable, intelligent, etc., etc. ad nauseam. Every single one of these feelings stems from a lack of self-worth or self-assurance. Those in turn are directly caused by 'fear' which is really nothing more than a deficit of Self-Love. The remedy is to go within and see yourself as the tiny spark of the Creator that you truly are in the depths of your being. Once you recognize that innate Oneness; ask yourself the following questions.

Given: **I am created of the Creator by the Creator, and, thus, I am a part of the body of the Creator.**

How could the Creator be unworthy?
How could the Creator be unLoved?

COMMENTS FROM SPIRIT:

Children, we invite you to the ultimate Resolution. We are here, awaiting your return. We hold out our arms to you in Divine Love and welcome you into them. Come home, Dear Children. Find us in your hearts and know that we are you, and you, Divine.

Be Love and you will be Home.

CREATIVITY

    Creativity is the outer expression of the inner self. Expression can take almost limitless forms, from whistling under your breath to the creation of a new YOU-niverse
    What areas of your personal relationship are dull and lackluster? Creativity invites you to look into new, interesting, and exciting ways to express and improve your relationship.
    Drawing this word invites you to find new ways to express yourself in the world or indicates a further exploration of the skills you already use.
    Creativity in response to a personal issue opens a limitless realm of possibilities to you. Sit down with your 'problem'. Turn it round and round in your mind and see how different it looks now

and how many new and different solutions present themselves. You are hereby invited to expand your concept and perception of self.

If indulged from and with Love, there is no harsh aspect to Creativity.

COMMENTS FROM SPIRIT:

Creativity is the human reflection of the use of the Creator's Love in the fabrication of this universe and is on-the-job training for all who would consciously co-create in this material realm. You are invited to do your part.

RELAXATION

Relaxation is the opposite -- the release -- of tension or coercion. It literally means 'to return to a state of lax-ness. Lax means freedom to move without restraint or stress which is almost always generated from fear (the absence of Love). Relaxation in this interpretation therefore literally means 'returning to the (natural) condition of liberty'.

Relaxation regarding a personal relationship refers to being less concerned about the path and apparent outcome of that relationship. It refers to not being so concerned with the emotional and physical spaces that it seems destined or directed to be passing through in the future. It suggests that the shortest path to greatest Light would be to reside in the moment; doing those things that seem to be 'right' in the spiritual sense and which reflect Love without concern for the future. It is only in this way that Relaxation can be truly achieved and appreciated. When this occurs often enough it becomes a habit and your life flows much more gently as long as the habit is maintained. It all boils down to trust in yourself and trust in Spirit.

In a general relationship, Relaxation simply means to have or achieve a certain level of comfort with the process as it is occurring. Trust is an important element of that process. Trusting those of the material realm; trusting that what they are doing will not 'hurt' you is one way of achieving this. Trust in Spirit is much more important in the process, however. By having trust in Spirit (also known as 'faith') and knowing with absolute certainty that all things are in Divine order at all times and in all ways whether we like it or not and whether we understand it or not we can indeed be totally Relaxed in even the most trying of circumstances.

Relax your grip on yourself occasionally for it can become a chokehold that will cause the cut-off portions to wither and die just as a tourniquet would. Every part of us is there for a reason. We must learn to accept that and to deal with the unpleasant aspects from a place of Love and understanding. You cannot fight hateful things with hate. That only serves to strengthen them and weaken you. The only effective tool for overcoming hate or anger is Love. Following a lesser path only serves to align you with the lesser energies.

COMMENTS FROM SPIRIT:

Relax, Beloveds. Take a break from your constant efforts to grow, to learn, to expand, and to excel. When you become quiet within you will find that you are already all of those things that you pursue and that the only goal that is needed is to Relax and allow yourself to manifest the Divinity that you are in each and every moment; in each and every circumstance. To BE Love is the ultimate manifestation of your ultimate form. BE Love, Dearest Ones and Relaxation shall be your constant condition and state.

Blessings to you, each and all.

NON-ATTACHMENT

Many teachers and schools of thought urge us to be 'unattached' to a person or situation as a method of maintaining balance and clarity of vision and action. In essence, this is a method that works well. There is however a subtle but definite difference between the concepts 'unattached' and 'non attached'. 'Unattached' seems to carry with it the meaning: "I could be attached to this normally but I'm going to choose to not allow that in this instance". Non-attachment, on the other hand, indicates a willingness to completely remove oneself from even the possibility of becoming attached to the event or thing in question. It allows one to process that which occurs from a distanced yet compassionate viewpoint.

It is probably even more difficult to maintain a Non-attached position regarding your personal relationships than it is when dealing only with self. The emotional loading of the relationship has the effect of placing its every nuance under the microscope of judgment and fear. It is only when you remove yourself emotionally from the process that the situation becomes totally clear. In many instances, I will recommend to clients that they attempt to perceive a situation as though it was happening to a complete stranger. Given that condition; what is the advice would they offer to that stranger and for what reasons? Perhaps that is the teaching that Spirit is offering you in the form of this word at this time.

It is important to remember always that all things are in Divine order at all times whether we understand them or not -- whether we like them or not. If we can maintain this understanding at all times it becomes easy to be Non-attached to the outcome. We always have the right and power to express and work toward our preferences if we can remain unattached as to the ultimate outcome. We almost always remain on the spiritual 'shortest path of greatest Light' when we live in our understanding of the event and the process's inherent 'rightness'.

It seems to be rather easy to remain Non-attached on the emotional level for many people. There is even a word for that state in its most common form. It is called 'denial'. What is sought here is the less common form. There is really not a single English word that describes this state. It is not 'above' or 'beyond. Perhaps 'observational' comes nearest to the state recommended by Spirit. One is in the situation but not of it; maintaining a slight attitudinal distance in the direction of Spirit so that instead of the short-sighted human point of view: ("My nose is in it and it stinks!") one instead perceives the situation from the soul or Spirit point of view. ("In this tiny, tiny moment of this tiny, tiny life experience in this eternity of existence, my nose is in it and I know it stinks, but I can see the pattern and I understand why this is happening, and it's OK because it serves my growth.").

Taken to its worst possible extreme, Non-attachment can evolve into abuse, neglect, denial, or apathy. None of these forms are recommended.

COMMENTS FROM SPIRIT:

When it becomes possible to truly become Non-attached in the material world one then discovers how completely and intimately one is connected to the fabric of eternity. Let go your training wheels, my Children, and fly beyond the stars!

Blessings.

HOPE

Hope is the triumph of awareness over fear. It is also a symptom of looking into the future with expectation rather than existing in the "now" of the moment. Hope is not necessarily a 'bad' thing so long as balance is maintained and the Hope does not become a crutch upon which you fix your attention. Its true purpose is as a tool to assist you in focusing upon the desired goal as part of your on-going process of co-creation.

It is a symbol of the desire that resides within each of us to control the outcome of situations that may affect our lives in what we think to be a positive way. One must never forget that all things are in Divine order at all times. This is true whether or not we understand or like that which appears to be happening or is about to happen.

There are two ways in which we can perceive something that happens in our world. The first is as a victim. The second is as a student.

The victim observes these happenings from an extremely personalized point of view; feeling at times that the entire universe is conspiring to assure their misery. This is what Spirit refers to as the 'human' point of view; best illustrated as "My nose is in it, and it stinks". It is this point of view that can benefit most, at least in the short term, from this thing called 'Hope'.

When we choose to perceive a situation from the viewpoint of the student we are choosing to observe from the viewpoint of Spirit. That is to say from a somewhat detached point of view that de-personalizes the happening and allows us to see it as though it were happening to a stranger. Think for a moment of how easy it is to offer advice to another and how difficult it can be to find our own way out of a similar situation when we find ourselves in it. That is the difference of which I speak. It simply makes the lesson clearer and more readily assimilated when we choose to be the student. The student always sees things from the spiritual point of view. Spirit says that this form is best illustrated by the statement "In this tiny moment of this infinitesimal life in this eternal existence, my nose is in it and I know it stinks, but I see the pattern. I understand why it's happening and it's O.K.

Personal relationships are almost always built on Hope. Because these partnerships are so often turbulent to some degree it is a matter of constant focus and intent in a worthwhile relationship that 'smooth it out'. That is 'Hope". The reality is that the only way for a relationship to 'smooth out' is for one or both parties to become a student in the situation and grow out of the place that has created the disharmony.

The same is true in our relationship with ourselves. Every thing we think, say, do or experience is happening FOR us – not TO us. It is our responsibility to see the value of these things. I have a good friend who was a chronic complainer and could not see the goodness in her life. I finally told her that she was the only person I knew who thought that every silver lining must have a cloud! Hope is the first step toward growth in a case such as this. If this sounds familiar to you perhaps that is the reason this word has come to you today!

Blind Hope helps no one. Neither does blind faith. Be aware of Hope for what it truly is -- a method to focus on the outcome that seems most appropriate and desirable to you. Rest assured that Spirit will direct you onto the path of experiences that will be most useful to you, regardless of your preferences. It is a mark of your attunement to the will of Spirit when what you Hope for comes to pass on a regular basis.

COMMENTS FROM SPIRIT:

Hope, Dear Children, is a bird straining to reach the sky. It is the nature of the form known as 'life' to strive to improve its lot. It is one of the most deeply ingrained instructions in your being for it is through this pathway that you will return to that place of glory that you have never truly left.

Welcome home, Beloveds. Welcome home.

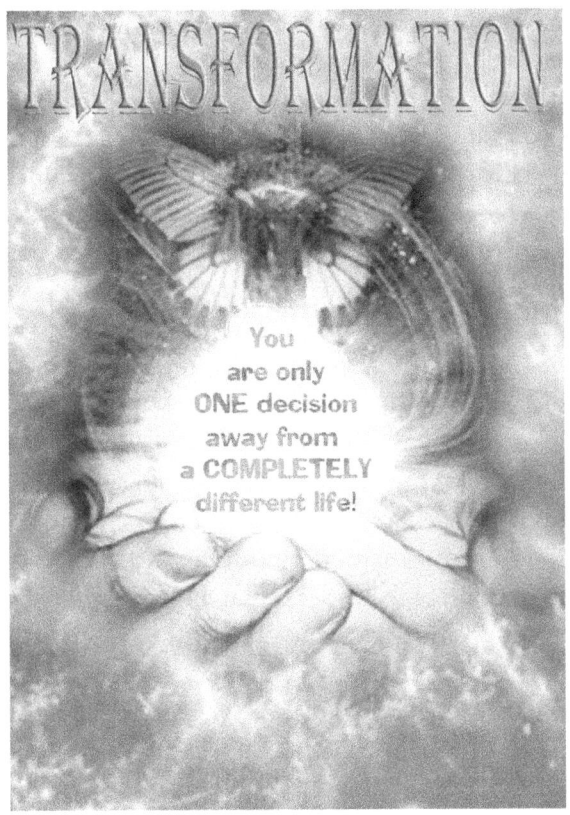

TRANSFORMATION

    The story of the butterfly is most often used to describe this process but that story is but a pencil sketch of the far-flung and remarkable aspects of this energy.
    Transformation can mean traveling from ignorance to bliss. It can involve the journey from fear to total acceptance and understanding. It can tell the tale of enlightenment or of physical death. What this word is telling you is that the world as you know it is about to change in a way that will forever change your perception of life in either a large or minuscule dimension. Think of this word as a certificate of completion or graduation. You have so satisfactorily completed a certain series of lessons that you have transcended the need to ever revisit them. You, or a portion of you, are being born anew at a

higher consciousness level!

Transformation of your personal relationship reveals that the time of the current stresses or lessons is over and that it is now time to move out of that energy and into a new level of happiness and contentment. This could be with or without your current partner; as the energy refers to you only in many instances. This is not a bad thing. It meant that this relationship has served its purpose in that it has hastened your growth and understanding to the point where you have learned the lessons involved. Quite often your partner will accompany you into the new level. This is indeed a joyful occurrence and a great blessing.

Some of the people we meet in our daily routine can appear to be quite abrasive. Some of the situations can seem intolerable. This energy in your life can be likened to a magic wand that will bring whatever it touches into harmony and balance. Don't make the mistake of trying to control the aspects that are to be touched but know that Spirit knows even better than your conscious self what lessons have been completed and what requires more understanding. Be grateful for what you receive for you have earned it. Always remember: Nothing can ever happen TO you. It is all happening FOR you!

Transformation of the self is the greatest of miracles. This is where the butterfly image is most often used and most accurately. Transformation many times will mark the transition from ignorance to knowingness. It many times is drawn to indicate movement into a higher plane or vibration rate. It can herald primary enlightenment or movement to an even higher level of spiritual awareness.

Transformation may sometimes carry the appearance of being unpleasant in some aspect but remember: there is no birth without pain and birth is what this energy brings.

COMMENTS FROM SPIRIT:

We invite you to experience this Joy called Transformation. Though you wear the body of a human, you are in every sense a member of the heavenly host; and beyond that the Creator. The limits that you have placed on yourself in order to experience and grow as a soul are those aspects that are shed one by one in this process called Transformation.

FOCUS

There are two parts to achieving Focus. The first and often most difficult is to wean away all of the distracting thoughts or influences until only the aspect one desires to Focus upon remains. The second part of the process involves sorting through all of the apparent parameters of the situation at hand until one finally arrives at the core of the issue or situation. Only when one is able to arrive at this point of single-ness in perception and thought can one truly be said to be Focused. If you have drawn this word to you today it is time to strip away all of the attitudes and emotional connections that blind you and begin to find the heart of the matter.

It is so very easy in any relationship but particularly in a personal partnership to allow oneself to be blinded to the true issues at hand and to see only those aspects that make one feel blameless. It is also easy and unfortunately common to attach oneself to the opposite extreme where the cry of "It's all my fault" is often heard. Step back so that you can see the issue as a whole; then go through the process outlined above. Find the one core issue. There is no right -- no wrong -- in anything we do. It is all a matter of intent and it is advisable to Focus on 'Being Love' in all situations. The other party's behavior or responses are not your responsibility. Do what you know to be right. Focus on being the highest and brightest reflection of the Light and Love of the Creator as you can be. That is the only Focus of importance in this dance called Life.

Many of those around us seem to have the agenda of creating chaos in the lives of those with whom they deal. This is nothing more than an attempt to cause us to lose Focus and become disoriented. This makes it easier for those others to achieve what appears to be control over the situation so that they can manipulate it to their advantage. Remain in Focus. See these activities for what they are and maintain your emotional distancing through using the tool of Spirit. The only time someone else has power over you is when you allow it, and speaking from the point of view of Spirit, any time that happens it is because you have requested that lesson to surface once more in your life in an attempt to understand it better.

It is important to Focus always on the positive for our thoughts and fears DO create our personal reality. That which you Focus on is drawn to you if only in your own mind and perception.

COMMENTS FROM SPIRIT:

Be still and KNOW that Thou art the Creator. This is the only Focus we would ask of our beloved Children. Be still -- set aside the cares that rule your life. KNOW that Thou art the Creator. We are all one, Children -- the same body – the same heart. The only true form of existence is Love and Thou art that.

Blessings.

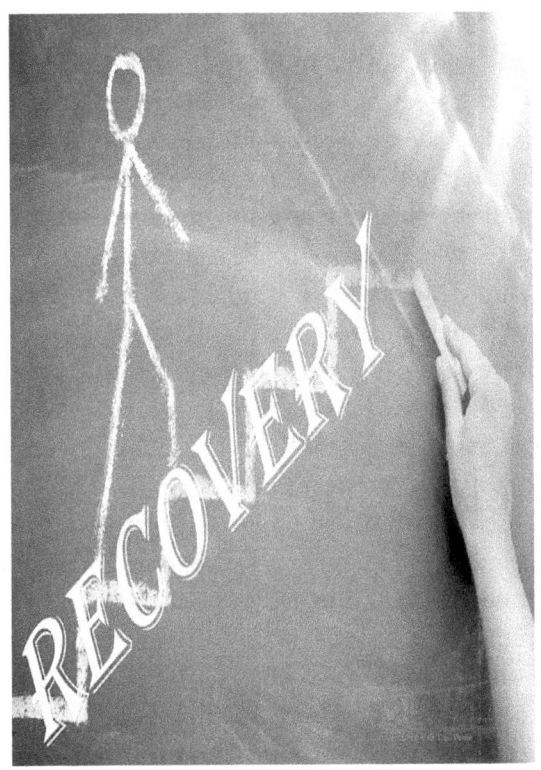

RECOVERY

Recovery is something that happens after one has lost their balance in some way. (Read the section on Balance for more information)

When one shares a life with another it becomes so easy to let down the guards that we normally keep up in 'polite' society. We expect more and allow less deviation from that expectation from our partners than we do anyone else with the possible exception of ourselves. This can have a detrimental effect on the relationship. Step back for a moment and see where the relationship is out of balance and what movement is necessary on your part to insure Recovery of the integral poise found in a healthy and growing relationship.

The outer world is for most of us a constant struggle for balance with its casual relationships that we share with hundreds of people each day. Nowhere is this more apparent than while driving. A sage I once knew told me that if I truly wanted to see a person in their purest form -- who they really were manifesting as in their innermost conscious being -- I should ride with them on the freeway for half an hour. If you have drawn this word today take a mental ride with yourself and see who you are allowing yourself to be. Is there room to Recover your balance? How do you refer to the person who just cut you off and made you miss your turnoff? How many times have you done the same rude act to others? Remember -- the things that irritate us most about others are usually those things that we have trouble admitting exist within ourselves. Every irritation is a gift and an opportunity to learn. Realizing that is the first and possibly most important step in Recovery.

There are many times in our lives when we feel totally disgusted by or deeply troubled with our thoughts and actions. This self-dismay can lead to emotional or physical abuse of self through words, deeds, or choices that we know will lead to painful repercussions. The objective seems to be to 'punish' oneself in order to 'atone' for our 'sins'. Not only is this a foolish and counterproductive activity, but it can also lead to further 'transgressions' and the perceived need for more 'atonement'. Should you find yourself in this position this word reminds you to step back, get a clear view and begin to Recover your balance.

COMMENTS FROM SPIRIT:

Recovery is coming closer to the Creator -- to eternal Love. If the distance seems to increase it is not the Creator who moved. Come home, Children. Allow yourselves to be Loved. Eternal love has eternal patience. We are always here for you.

Be at peace.

ALERTNESS

It is so easy to stumble through this thing called Life; to doze through class and 'get by' with an average grade. That is not what Life is for. We are here to discover and manifest our own Divine nature. That can only be accomplished if we become aware of and attentive to that still small voice within; the voice which says "be still and KNOW that Thou art the Creator." Alertness demands this of us. We cannot allow ourselves to be satisfied with that which 'everyone else' is doing or we become mired in the same traps and turmoil that hold everyone else.

Alertness is strongly recommended if one wishes one's personal relationship to thrive. We all know or have heard of a couple who have been together so long that they finish each other's thoughts and sentences. They are so comfortable with one another that they sometimes will spend an entire day together with only a few words necessary. This is as a result of years of Alertness to the tiny subtle signs that each gives the other. Over time, words that after all are a rather clumsy form of communication become redundant to the more delicate and exquisite non-verbal structure. This is not an overnight occurrence but a process involving attunement, commitment, and Alertness. It is this process that bringing this word into your awareness at this time is suggesting to you. You are invited to become more sensitive to the signals of your partner and more ready to believe that which you feel to be true.

Although the above-mentioned level of Alertness and attunement rarely occurs in a more casual relationship it is strongly suggested and can be very conducive toward what the world refers to as 'success'. When you are Alert to the details of an interaction the larger aspects seem to take care of themselves. In many cultures, business does not commence until the parties involved have sat together and have coordinated their breathing patterns. These merchants are both attuned and Alert.

Our awareness of our own condition, process, and progress depends on signals that can range from extremely blatant to extremely subtle. The more Alert we become to that which is happening within and around us the better informed we become and the wiser the decisions we can make. As an example: Someone I know is a highly evolved soul manifesting at what others perceive as a very high level. At times, this individual will find themselves using some of the more innocuous 'four letter' words. In an average person, this would not be cause for alarm but in this person it is one of the earliest warnings that a low-level entity is trying to attach to or affect them. Another warning sign that this person has grown to recognize is the persistent feeling of a cold draft on their left elbow. By being Alert and attuned this person is able to short-circuit the attempted energy invasion.

The ultimate in Alertness is to become all-knowing.

COMMENTS FROM SPIRIT:

Set aside the world, beloved Children. Focus your essence and core only upon All that Is. Become that which sees all, knows all, and Loves all. Become the God or Goddess that you always have been. Come home.

Sometimes the mere fact that you exist can lift another up.

HUMILITY

Humility is not the child of a poor self-image. It comes from strength in its true form. It is only when one owns who they truly are at their highest level that one can truly be humble. There is a song that was popular several years ago on the country stations. It had lyrics that said, "Oh Lord, it's hard to be Humble when you're perfect in every way". It is only because we are perfect in every way (whether or not we choose to manifest it fully at all times -- or even at all) that Humility can exist. Humility involves passing off the honors or accolades offered one for doing those things that ought to be done in the first place or for being that which we are. There is nothing there to be proud about. It simply IS, and IS as a gift of the Creator. Humility is simply placing the credit where it belongs. Whatever we do -- however we choose to manifest -- we are simply the glove on the Creator's hand.

Recognize that every personal relationship is an interaction and that whatever is accomplished requires two. The other person can validate you, assist you, or provide a firm resistance for you to push off in a new direction from, but it is always a partnership. One should always give credit where credit is due.

Nobody wants to hear how great you are. Show them instead. Drawing this word into your life in this moment indicates that perhaps you have allowed your ego to inflate to the danger point. Just as we can suffer from a poor self-image, so we sometimes forget our partnership with the Creator and forget what the source of our gifts and abilities are. Take a time out -- and remember.

False Humility is worse than no Humility at all. False Humility is an act of ego.

COMMENTS FROM SPIRIT:

Thou art God. Be Humble! The best leader is a dedicated servant.

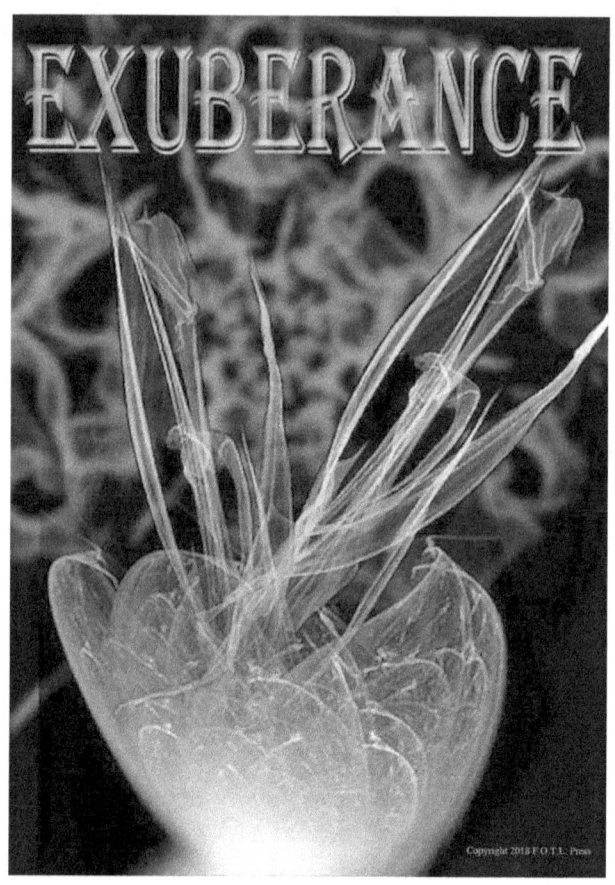

EXUBERANCE

Exuberance is the unrestrained expression of Joy. It is the heart at play and the psyche at rest. It is one of the most beautiful and unguarded of human moments and a distinct thing of beauty. It is complete freedom from troubles or woe. It is the antithesis of worry and care.

There are few more appropriate places to experience and express Exuberance within your life than with your life partner or family. Let yourself go. Re-experience the joyfulness with which your relationship was born, and the underlying love that holds it together. Alternately, if it has been a long, long time since you have experienced Exuberance in your partnership, perhaps it is time to explore the question of "Why". Is it time to seek/create a new relationship? Is the person you are currently with the one with whom to seek that new expression? Only you can decide. There is no wrong choice as long as everything is done from and with Love.

Spirit would remind you that forced Exuberance serves no one.

COMMENTS FROM SPIRIT:

Oh, delightful ones, Children of the Most High. Remember that all is yours -- all is provided in all ways at all times. Be care-free! Would you play the clod when you are the star? Rejoice in your true nature and fly on the wind of Love!

SPONTANEITY

Surprises around every corner! Nothing is as it was or as it will be. Don't plan on anything because nothing will transpire as you have planned. Spirit is playing with you and you'll both have fun. Go a little crazy! After all; look at the 'normal' world -- is that how you want to spend your life? This is a joyful invitation to break free from the humdrum and the mundane!

Expect the unexpected! Anything goes! Throw out the rulebook and write a new one. The energy of Spontaneity is Spirit's joyful jester - tumbling and romping through your life like a fresh strong summer breeze.

Do something unexpected for your partner. It's time to take a break from the daily routine. Surprise your sweetie. Take them out or ambush them in the hallway. Do something that they love but rarely have the opportunity to do. This energy invites a new level of closeness and playfulness.

Day by day we plod through the world. Step by step we travel the rutted road. Jump free! Break the patterns! Declare your independence from the rules of the material world. You live in Spirit and Spirit has different rules. Amaze your co-workers or business contacts by doing something completely out of the ordinary today. You'll be glad you did!
During the negotiations that occur in our day-to-day living experiences break out of the mold and move in a surprising direction. This is Spirit's suggestion when this word falls into your life. You'll be surprised at the results!

On a personal level Spontaneity invites you to let go of old and no longer needed patterns. We create for ourselves a comfortable perception of who we are and how we function in the world. Day after day we plod this road safely in the cocoon of our own illusion. Stagnation equals the death of our sense of spirit. Come alive and escape the walls you have built within. You are far more than you have ever dared dream and Spirit is here to assist you in discovering your own limitlessness. Become a new person in at least one aspect of your being. Break out of the old -- move into the new.

As long as you do everything you do from Love and with Love, you'll be fine. The only caution would be to be careful in the exuberance of Spontaneity to remember to always act in consideration of others.

This joyful jester has an evil twin named irresponsibility. Irresponsibility can always be identified because his actions do not take into consideration the welfare of others. Remember to act always with and from Love and this evil twin will not bother you.

COMMENTS FROM SPIRIT:

Living in the NOW is the essence of Spontaneity. Existing in the totality of the flow of the River of Life; giving no thought to yesterday or the morrow but trusting that all things are indeed in Divine order at all times gives you the perfect opportunity to be Spontaneous in your every action. This removes all restrictions from the possibilities in your life. There is no greater form of Spontaneity than total unconditional trust. Live in the Love of the Creator and manifest that Love freely to all about you.

Blessings.

SOLUTIONS

    The essence of all Solutions to be found regarding questions of a spiritual nature is: "It's simpler than that".
We have a tendency to complicate our lives and our perceptions as we observe all of the symptoms and think that they are the problem. Any time you feel yourself to be the victim it is only because you are not 'getting the message'. Any time you are confused about an issue it is because you have not stepped back far enough to see the problem as a whole. You are too close to the problem to see its shape; to feel its energy and texture. Once you truly know the problem in all of its manifestations it becomes a whole rather than a confusing conglom-

eration of parts.

An example might be a warrior battling a hydra.

Up close and personal it may seem a hopeless task. All of those heads with their hungry, angry mouths, and every time you cut one head off two grow to replace it. This is the way in which a problem or confusion can proliferate itself in our lives.

Imagine now for a moment that that warrior has the ability to vastly increase their physical size just as we can vastly increase our point of view by accessing our Spiritual self-awareness. Suddenly our Hydra is no longer a life-threatening problem but an insignificant and pitiful beast the size of a flea. The problem has found its Solution as you can with the help of Spirit now find yours. Take this moment to ask Spirit to bring you into alignment with the knowingness and understanding of the root cause of your confusion and questioning. Ask, if you are unsure of your own communication skills regarding spirit, that you be told or shown three times in the material world. You will usually find that in less than a day you have your Solution.

COMMENTS FROM SPIRIT:

The Solution to all things is to have sufficient Love. When you Love enough, there is no problem—no trial that may touch your heart. We Love you.

Blessings.

ACKNOWLEDGMENT

    Acknowledgment is one of the most important blessings to receive or give on this material plane. It is an affirmation of one's existence, growth, and value from those one encounters in this life.

    How long has it been since you have Acknowledged your partner as the pillar of your life experience that they are? Regardless of the nature or state of harmony of the relationship, it is important to remember that on a soul level your soul and the soul of your partner have agreed to be together for however long is appropriate. You are together in the physical in order to teach and learn important lessons from one another. Thanks are in order whether the situation has been grim or if the situation has been grand. Acknowledgement of their value in your life can only help.

This world; this western society (and, I suspect, many other societies) have forgotten how important it is to thank those who help us. We ignore the homeless person on the street, forgetting that they have needs and feelings too and that their situation is not necessarily their 'fault'. We have been taught and teach ourselves to become isolated islands of consciousness in an apparent sea of indifference. This path is exactly opposite to the path of Spiritual growth; of realizing and achieving One-ness with All that Is. All that Is includes the bum on the street and the 'enemy' of your nation. The more we Acknowledge that all of us are One the sooner we can begin convincing others to act that way also.

Be still and know that Thou art God. That is the most meaningful and important ACKNOWLEDGMENT we can give ourselves. The time will never be better than now. Be still....

COMMENTS FROM SPIRIT:

Throughout all life runs the thread of its own Divinity. Acknowledge this, and all is won. Blessings.

ENJOYMENT

Enjoyment -- the word seems common enough. Let's look at it more closely. It literally means not only to experience the Joy in a given situation; it also refers to the act of allowing yourself to feel that joy. We must all constantly give ourselves permission to be happy, as human nature and societal pressures seem to discourage it at every turn.

How long has it been since you have taken the time to really Enjoy all of the aspects of your relationship? Even if some aspects do not seem to be overly pleasant in the moment step back far enough to see and appreciate the lessons you are being offered. Enjoy those aspects that are overtly pleasant. Take the time to sit down and write a list of them and share it with your partner. After all, Communication is the life's blood of any relationship. Now do the same with the parts that seem to be less pleasant but take the time first to see the beauty in them also and share that observation of beauty with your partner. Enjoy the presence and company of one another. You are perfectly suited for one another in this moment of your lives.

Every being on the planet is the Christ in disguise. Admittedly, some of the disguises are extremely good. Look at those around you through your Knowingness of this fact and Enjoy the light within them whether they know it or show it, or not.

This word at this moment is a hint from Spirit to you to lighten up on yourself. Take a day off (or at least some time out) and do some of your favorite things. A trip to the coast, a day of meditation, anything that renews you, and your joy of life is called for when this word comes to you.

Make sure that the things that you Enjoy are not done in such a way as to disregard or lessen others. If these are things you Enjoy perhaps you should examine yourself and your motives in the light

of spiritual awareness and growth.

COMMENTS FROM SPIRIT:

You are invited to set aside your cares and re-enter the aspect of self that is of the universal soul. That aspect exists in a condition of the never-ending en-Joy-ment which is your birthright, your essence, and your core. Be at home in your heart and feel the Love of the Creator within and about you. There can be no greater en-Joy-ment.

Blessings.

GRATITUDE

    Drawing Gratitude reminds us to recognize that all things we receive and every experience that happens to us are gifts.

    It is easy to express Gratitude when things are pleasurable or otherwise appear to be going well. This word reminds you to remember to express Gratitude to the Creator and your partner for those situations that are not readily apparent as being positive for it is through adversity that most growth occurs. Because a personal relationship is the most fertile field for growth in the human experience (see Balance) we are liable to experience the greatest opportunity to exercise Gratitude in this context.

The expression of Gratitude in a casual relationship is very similar to that expression in a personal relationship although quite often diluted and spread over a wider base of experiences. Simply remember that you have called all experiences to yourself in an effort to grow in spiritual awareness and understanding. Those who have agreed from the level of Spirit to assist you (like that reckless driver who just cut you off on the freeway) are deserving of your sincere Gratitude for the insight and lessons they have offered to you. Remember that the things which irritate you about others are almost always found to some degree in oneself!

There are many times in our lives when we make choices and decisions or take actions that we recognize as 'wrong' within our own set of moral codes. This recognition usually carries with it a period of remorse and resolution not to repeat those activities. That is good. Unfortunately, many of us continue to 'beat up' on ourselves past this point. That is foolish. We have received an opportunity to change, reviewed our options, and decided to make an effort to do so. Gratitude to yourself and the Creator would seem to be the appropriate response. This word invites and supports that response.

There are no harsh aspects to Gratitude as long as it is not overdone. Some people have a self-image so impaired that any kindness transforms them into a slave of the person who offered the kindness. They do this in an effort to 'be worthy' of the kindness already given. If this is you, STOP IT! You ARE worthy!

COMMENTS FROM SPIRIT:

Gratitude is another human concept. It arises from the misperception of not being worthy of all gifts and experiences. When one truly recognizes themselves as an integral part of the Creator and as the flow of Life and the Universe; one is all things, all times, all experience. There is no separation, there is no gift and there is no owing. There is no need or function for this thing called 'Gratitude'. There only is...IS. Walk in the glory of your own be-ing-ness.

EAGERNESS

Eagerness occurs when we decide to try to accomplish joyful things on our own schedule. Try to remember that all things are accomplished in Divine order and according to the Divine plan. Many times while counseling a 'client' I have found myself saying to them: "You have arrived at the growth level necessary for this thing to occur in your life. This material existence is like a jigsaw puzzle, however, and all of the adjacent or similar pieces have to be identified and placed in the same general area in order for us to start assembling them. It is the same in your life right now. You are ready but there are some elements that are still becoming. When they are you will be there. In the meantime, be patient and trust."

A personal relationship is a delicate thing and must be nurtured constantly in order to grow. One of the most important elements of this nurturing is patience. Eager as we may be for a new level of intimacy; physical, emotional, or spiritual, it will come in its own way and in its own time. Eagerness is the positive side of the coin whose negative side is called worry. Neither side provides any positive function and when carried to extremes can actually make the situation worse.

Any astute businessperson will be glad to tell you the hazards involved in appearing Eager during a business transaction. Once again, patience is the watchword. Eagerness occurs when you are 'trying' to accomplish something. Trying is an aggressive, acquisitive, controlling, and manipulating process. I would suggest that you allow and encourage rather than 'try'. When used in this context 'allow' brings with it a mental picture of a large, clean nest; deeply padded with huge soft pink feathers and waiting for something to be lovingly placed in it.
Which of these two descriptions more nearly matches your impression of the nature of Spirit?

Which would you rather manifest, and which ARE you manifesting?

COMMENTS FROM SPIRIT:

Children: -- you are Eager only because you do not realize that all things ARE. There is no time, there is no process and there is no journey. There is only an arrival. Welcome home. You are already here. We love you.

FLEXIBILITY

The wind blows. The trees sway to and fro. The hurricane comes and while the smallest trees are whipped and their leaves are stripped from each branch, the tallest trees stand stiffly and proudly in the face of the tempest. Suddenly, the air is shattered by the tremendous sound of splintering wood. One of the proud giants tumbles out of the sky, moaning out its painful destruction for the world to hear. The lesson is clear. Bend to the winds of change or perish. This is the lesson and energy of Flexibility.

Every relationship suffers its ups and downs in the normal course of things. We make one adjustment and things change again requiring yet another adjustment. On and on this process of change and adjustment goes in a never-ending cycle of change. Is this not growth? This is what relationships are for. Drawing this word means that help is on the way; either to ease the adjustments or to help you focus on the need for Flexibility.

Flexibility as it refers to self also has to do with the ability to move within oneself to a new position of understanding; a new point of view for both internal and external issues.

A word of caution here: it is possible to bend over backward so far that people mistake you for a doormat. In your quest for Flexibility, don't forget to honor yourself.

COMMENTS FROM SPIRIT:

Flexibility is an integral part of the balance we all seek. Static balance is precarious, at best. As a living balance, this Flexibility is able to respond to the shifts in the reality we perceive. To move is to grow. To stop moving and growing is the end of existence.

COMMITMENT

Commitment is a two-edged sword, capable of cutting in both directions. It can be one of the most difficult things in the world to achieve, yet once you are 'there' it can be a great strength and true joy.

There is an old story of a master and a student who were discussing the difference between involvement and Commitment one evening. As it was late, the master suggested that the student come to the master's house for breakfast and to continue the lesson the next morning.

They discussed the concepts over a breakfast of ham and eggs, but the student still unsure of the difference.

Finally, gesturing at the now empty plates, the master said: "The chicken was involved – the pig was committed".

In a personal relationship, it would seem that Commitment to that relationship is of the utmost importance. It is indeed of importance but even greater should be your Commitment to self and to the Creator. On the human level, Love is easily defined and recognized. It is marked by the simple event of consistently putting the health, happiness, safety, and comfort of another above your own. Commit yourself to the continuation of this pattern but beware 'locking yourself in' to a particular relationship blindly. Each relationship (see 'BALANCE') has its own purpose and will last as long as both partners are willing to have it last. Be totally Committed to the concept of partnership if you wish, but realize that your ideal partner may not be the same person (physically or emotionally) throughout this lifetime.

Commitment is closely aligned in most minds with the concept of 'honor'. That is to say: keeping one's word and acting in a way so as not to hurt others. The statement that covers all of these bases is: "BE LOVE, in every word, in every thought, in every deed, in every prayer". Bringing this word into your circle this day invites you to re-evaluate your situation and to re-Committing yourself to being the highest being possible in each moment.

Personal Commitment is closely aligned with the concept of 'integrity'. It requires you to do those things that you know to be right in each moment, regardless of the apparent and temporary cost or discomfort to yourself. Jesus of Nazareth was Committed. So was Buddha.

As with most other concepts, this one can have its dark side. Make sure that the things you are Committed to are of and in the light in all ways and at all times.

COMMENTS FROM SPIRIT:

The glow of Love that surrounds all; embraces all is the mark of Our Commitment to all our Children. Infinite Love has infinite patience. We are Committed to seeing you through your growth and welcome you home with an open heart. Blessings

PERSPECTIVE

    This is one of the most important concepts in Spirituality. It encompasses the reasons that we get angry and why we grow. It answers the question of how so many religions and sects within those religions form. It explains why we are often misunderstood when we try to communicate with another those things dearest to our hearts. Perspective is the means through which each of us creates our own reality. As this thing that we call reality unfolds around us, we each (usually unconsciously) manipulate our perceptions in a way that supports our inner agenda. An insecure individual will find a slight where a secure one would only see a joke. A person who needs to be surrounded by enemies would see a darker purpose -- perhaps even a conspiracy (it is easy to ignore working on 'self' when one is busy battling dragons -- and if there aren't enough dragons, one can always create more!). The point is that we create our own reality on an ongoing basis by how we choose to perceive it!

There is a wonderful story that illustrates this point:

> Once upon a time, there was a bird who told his friends when it came time to fly south for the winter:
>
> "I don't think so. It's been a warm dry fall and I think I'm going to save myself a lot of work and just stay here this winter."
>
> His friends argued and argued with him but the little bird was adamant. He would spend the winter in the northern climes while his friends flew south for the winter.
>
> About three weeks later the weather turned distinctly chilly and before long the bitter freezing rain and sleet arrived. On the first day the bird thought to himself:
>
> "This is just a fluke. Tomorrow will be sunny and warm."
>
> The following day the snow began before dawn and steadily worsened. By noon the bird knew that he had made a grievous error and began the long, lonely journey south by himself.
>
> After several hours; just before dusk, the little bird's wings were numb with cold, and fighting his way through a sky full of snow and slush had worn him to a frazzle. Each beat of his wings was a tremendous effort. Finally, he could fly no more and tumbled, beak over claws, out of the sky.
>
> Kerplop! He fell, semi-conscious, into a farmer's field. He lay there amidst the gathering clumps of snow and felt his strength and his life ebbing from his numbed body.
>
> Suddenly a passing cow decided to relieve itself. With a deafening 'plop' the bird found himself encased in a fresh cow pie.
>
> "Great! How humiliating! What a horrible way to die. I can't think of anything worse", he thought.
>
> A few minutes passed. As he lay there he realized that the cow pie was quite warm. And, you know -- it really didn't smell all that bad -- kinda sweet as a matter of fact. Maybe things were going to work out after all!

He could feel the warmth soaking into his little body and the strength returning to his once numbed wings. He was going to make it!

His joy was too great to contain. He broke into his song of joy.

The farmer's old gray tomcat was making one last tour of the cow pen before going in to lie before the roaring fireplace. He was a fierce old soul; the victor of many a battle, a mighty hunter, and as curious as ever a cat could be. He had seen about everything that a field cat could see on this farm but the one thing that he'd never seen -- never even imagined -- was a singing cow flop. As he marched across the field toward this curious thing he racked his memory for something like it but to no avail. When he got to the musical cow pie he stood and just looked at it in amazement for a while. Finally, curiosity overcame distaste and he gingerly began prodding the mass with his paw. Imagine his surprise when he discovered the little bird!

In a trice, it was over. The little bird had become a light snack and the old tom retired to the fireplace to wash his paws and nap; to dream of this curious occurrence.

The morals of this story, my children, are these:

1) Not everyone who poops on you is your enemy.

and

2) Not everyone who rescues you is your friend!

As you can see, the bird and the cat had vastly different versions of the same reality yet that did not keep their realities from interacting. It is in exactly this way that our own Perspective gathers from the universal experience those lessons that support it or even those which challenge it, in the way that our soul has chosen, in order to learn and grow.

Perspective makes all of the difference in a personal relationship as indeed, it does in our total existence. Whether we choose to view ourselves as a victim or a student determines whether we are going to feel happy (or at least understand what is going on; why, and choosing to grow from it) or be totally miserable. (See WISDOM) Bringing this word into your awareness at this point in time carries with it this message: if you are unhappy about how things seem to you, change your point of view. They are all happening FOR you, not TO you!

Many of us, especially in our youth, get caught up in maintaining our image -- what we wish the world to see. As a result, we strut around like little Banty roosters and take offense at the slightest hint of adversity. (We all know of course that as adults we would never do such a thing). If we were to change our Perspective to align more closely to Spirit and realize that all beings are us and are mirroring us for our benefit there would be nothing to pretend about, and nothing to defend. We would recognize ourselves as innately perfect and live accordingly as dedicated servants of the Creator in Loving conscious co-operation with one another.

It is so very important to remember in all circumstances that all things are in Divine order in all ways and at all times. This is true whether we understand them or not and whether we like them or not. If we feel that we are being victimized it is only because we have shifted our view from this Perspective. When you allow your Perspective to be that of Spirit the function and value of each experience (both positive in the moment and negative in the moment) become readily obvious and there is nothing to be excited about. Remember: no one can ever truly cheat or harm you -- they can only cheat or harm themselves. This word in your life in this moment reminds you of these things. Chill out! It's all O.K.

The harsh aspects of an unbalanced Perspective are obvious. The feelings of anger, victimization, and fear that we all experience from time to time are manifestations of an unbalanced sense of Perspective. If these are too much a part of your reality, this word coming to you today is your invitation to change your mental stance.

COMMENTS FROM SPIRIT:

The only totally true Perspective is that all beings -- all things -- are totally One with the Creator of all that is. There is no separation of being-ness or purpose. The only Being is God. The only Purpose, regardless of your often-limited perception, is Love. Trust us, Children. You have never been more Loved. You have never been safer. All things in this universe exist for only one purpose and that purpose is to Lovingly guide you into a full remembrance and acceptance of your Divine nature within the Mother/Father God.

We Love you.

Blessings.

INVOLVEMENT

Involvement speaks of grabbing hold of life with both hands and your teeth. It refers to a full participation in making a difference in the world around us through how we manifest in the world. It is not enough to simply observe. You must enter into life in all of its aspects, wade into the stream and make yourself known. Involvement is YOU, facilitating change. It is you taking action to manipulate the worlds around you as much as is possible, hopefully from a Spirit-filled and Lovingly balanced point of view.

Personal relationships are simply not possible without the concept of Involvement. Personal relationships are intended by Spirit to be Involvement of the most intimate and powerful kind. This word coming into your awareness at this moment suggests that perhaps it is time to pay more attention to your partner and the relationship.

A non-intimate relationship is usually a little less intense although it can become more so. When it does, though, it is no longer a casual relationship but becomes a personal one.

To be Involved with self is the most intimate and the most difficult of the forms of Involvement. To truly be Involved with ourselves we must recognize and own who and what we are and where our current path is leading. We must be willing to accept responsibility and co-create our experience of existence in every situation in every moment and in every way.

Involvement with the intent to improve is a wonderful thing. One must be extremely careful not to allow the specter of Ego into the mix, however. It is vital to remain non-attached to the outcome as you work with the concept of Involvement. Remember: Spirit usually knows what is best in every situation far more accurately than we do. Trust and allow yourself to hear Spirit and you will never be led astray.

COMMENTS FROM SPIRIT:

Dearest Children: we invite you to relax and enjoy this gift called "Life" that you have chosen. This gift has but one purpose and that purpose is for you to become totally immersed and participatory in the material realm and the lower vibrations so that you will more readily understand the nuances of the higher. You are the ladder you climb and you await yourself at the pinnacle. Have faith in yourself and in the All-One that you are. We Love you.

Blessings.

ACTUALIZATION

Actualization means to bring something forth into this physical reality; into our consciousness. Knowing that there is something that should be done or a change that must be made within our perceptions of ourselves is not enough. We must set about to allow this thing to manifest. This is the energy of Actualization. It is not enough to accept the need for a change. We are being invited to co-create in order to birth it into our reality.

Those of us who have an ongoing personal relationship recognize the frequent need for the relationship to change; to grow into a new space and in a new direction. Actualization takes place in the moment in which we allow and facilitate those changes. Drawing the energy of this word into your life at this time suggests that it is time to stop thinking about the changes that ought to be taking place and simply support their birth into your reality.

We are all aware of how our day-to-day interactions can be improved by living our higher belief systems on a daily basis. Drawing this word at this time invites your greater attention to exactly that process. It is not enough simply to 'know' that you 'should' do such a thing. You must choose to do it and allow Actualization to take place.

All of the above is true on the personal level, but there is more. Self-Actualization is called for here. Reach down into your doubts regarding self, grab hold of your spiritual bootstraps and pull yourself up to your full potential by allowing yourself to limit less. Remember; spiritual progress is never a matter of growing more -- it's always a simple matter of limiting less!

Actualization can sometimes take a different direction than we thought that it would -- or should. Don't try to 'second-guess' Spirit. Don't expect and you'll never be disappointed. Above all; resolve to view everything that happens in your life from the point of view of a student -- not a victim!

COMMENTS FROM SPIRIT:

This adventure that you refer to as 'life' has but one purpose. That purpose is to allow each of you the opportunity to fully Actualize as the spark of the Creator that you are. As you grow, so grows the whole. As you become One in totality, you assist all other living beings in their similar quest. Allow yourself to be touched by the loving hand and heart of the Creator. Become and observe the intense beauty of all that you are.

Blessings.

YIELDING

Many martial arts are based on yielding to an opponent, and in so doing, utilizing the energy which seems directed against you in such a way as to serve the ends you desire. Done skillfully and carefully, it is almost always successful.

Because you have drawn this word to you today there is an indication that there are forces that seem for the moment to be working against your desires and plans. This word is suggesting that you bring forth your strength of awareness of the "rightness" of all things and step aside so that that which must take place will be allowed to. In the process, never allow yourself to forget that ALL things are in Divine order in all ways and at all times and that even the most distasteful experience is a gift from Spirit and it serves your spiritual growth. It is only because you have ignored previous versions of the lesson that it has evolved to the point that it has. Remember that the tree which bends in a strong wind often survives undamaged while the proud giant which stands firm and strong may well be destroyed. Now is the time to be flexible in every way.

Personal relationships are full of crosswinds and unexpected up-and-downdrafts. Because we allow ourselves to be so completely exposed in a personal relationship these forces often affect us more strongly than the same disruption would in a general relationship where we are generally more guarded. We are reminded to BE with the situation rather than trying to DEAL with it or even worse, to fight against it. This word coming to you today is a strong suggestion that this is a time to 'be small'.

Yielding to the wrong things can bring lessons in swarms. Spirit will often Lovingly offer us surprise reviews of recent and not-so-recent lessons. Yielding to the temptations offered to you will assure a review of the lessons not quite learned as yet.

COMMENTS FROM SPIRIT:

Beloveds, Yield only to the Divine Love that permeates the multi-verses. Yield only to your own Divinity and infinite worth. Yield to the flow of Love that is your essence and Yield to the One-ness of all things and the Yield of your efforts will be immeasurable.

VITALITY

    Vitality is a measurement of the amount of Life you are allowing yourself in this moment. If you have drawn this word today, your level is evidently an area of concern to Spirit. How much are you allowing yourself to participate in Life and to be aware? How are you blocking your access to the energy; the power, the Love of All that Is?

    We all know or know of couples who stay together out of sheer inertia; Newton's third law of motion: "A body at rest tends to remain at rest". This, my friends, is not living. This is not living – this is barely existing. You and your partner both deserve more (See

Delight). This word is asking you to change your patterns. Communicate with one another in body, mind, and Spirit. Learn to enjoy one another in all of these forms.

Vitality is not usually a concern in General relationships but perhaps it should be. Vitality in our very essence is the goal and that should probably extend into every aspect of our lives in every moment. If we become Vital people we touch all around us with that Vitality.

COMMENTS FROM SPIRIT:

Vitality -- the expression of the life force -- is a human concept. It is only measurable because it is often manifested at less than its full potential. We urge you to allow full awareness and manifestation of the life force; that force called Love that surrounds and permeates you and all about you. It is only through your choice and your fears that it appears to be limited. Be Love, and Be in total Vitality at all times.

We Love you.

ABANDONMENT

Abandonment is the sense of being unhappily alone. It occurs when another person does not adhere to one's expectations of what that other person should be, say or do. A sense of Abandonment cannot occur except in an atmosphere of control and expectation.

Abandonment is most often experienced in a personal relationship situation. It is easy to project our wants, fears and hopes onto our partner; making him or her responsible in our mind for the success or failure of a particular set of circumstances. We give away both our power and our responsibility when we invite in the feeling of Abandonment.

Much the same occurs in a general relationship. However, in order to truly feel Abandoned (betrayed), the general relationship must first transform at least partiallyintoo a personal one.

While at first glance it may seem to be impossible to Abandon oneself it is actually quite a common practice. The form in which it most often manifests is that called 'denial'. If you have called this energy into your awareness this day, perhaps it is time to inspect yourself for the imbalance of denial. What are you not willing to look at in yourself and your life and with whom do you place the blame. Remember; we choose every experience on the Spirit level in order to give ourselves an opportunity to learn and grow. There is no 'blame' and regardless of how it appears to the material world, the responsibility rests squarely upon our own shoulders. As long as you feel yourself to be a 'victim' there can be no resolution or growth accomplished.

The sense of Abandonment is one of the greatest fears many people have. This level of fear (the absence of Love and understanding) empowers Abandonment far beyond its normal strength and can create or promote aberrant thoughts and activities. Should you feel Abandonment, you might want to stop, ground and center; step back from the situation and observe it as though it was happening to someone else. Can you see the root cause of the feeling and the suggestion that you would make to the party involved? Spirit suggests that you not become hope-less, but rather, faith-full.

COMMENTS FROM SPIRIT:

Beloved Children ... please know that Our heart is yours forever and that infinite Love has infinite patience. If ever you feel Abandonment from Spirit, know this: it was not Spirit who moved further away.

Blessings.

DENIAL

"I don't believe I pulled this word. I won't read it. I'll put it back and pull another one that I'll like better."

"Everything is going just fine at home. Sure, my partner gets a little rough on me (there are almost limitless ways to manifest this) from time to time but I'll heal. Besides, they really love me. I just know it"

Denial is rampant in our personal relationships. Many of our relationships are based on Denial realities such as that just illustrated. This word coming to you today is suggesting to you that you step back and look at the situation as though you were hearing about it from someone else, then determine what you would say to that person about his or her situation. (See Perspective)

Possibly the only positive use of Denial is to give someone else the 'benefit of the doubt' even where there is really no doubt. Who knows, your faith in them might just be the key to helping them turn themselves around! Just remember: "Fool me once, shame on you. Fool me twice, shame on me!"

Ah! Now we get to the root of the situation. The only true form of Denial is Denial within the self. Self-delusion is the track that the trains of many of our lives (if not all of them) know best. We each do indeed create our own reality by what we choose to perceive (or ignore) and the way in which we modify the actual events and facts in order to support the point of view that best serves our purposes. In doing so we are in total Denial of the entire and literal truth. I have yet to meet a single person who does not indulge in this activity at least occasionally, with the possible exception of the Dalai Lama. This word is inviting you to look at the frequency and scope of your self-delusion and reality manipulation. Now would be a good time to start.

In spite of what was written above, there is actually no instance in which Denial is strictly a positive. Spirit has told me: "Darkness is required to hide something. All things are made visible in the light." This word is your invitation to exist in the light in all ways and at all times.

COMMENTS FROM SPIRIT:

Denial of anything is a repudiation and rejection of yourself and your Creator. Remember that all things are given to you in Love, with Love, and from Love. All things are ultimately to the benefit of your soul and further your growth toward your ultimate awareness of Self as God.

Blessings to you in this journey.

TOUCH

Touch can be a noun or a verb. It can refer to having a definite affinity with something or someone (She has a real Touch with horses), or to actually reaching out at some level to interact with that something or someone. See 'Involvement'.

To Touch and to allow yourself to be Touched is the essence of a personal relationship. Drawing this word encourages you to open your heart and your defenses to your partner so that they might Touch you at a deeper and more intimate level. It is also speaking of your need to attempt to be much more sensitive to the needs and desires of your partner on every level so that you also may reach out and Touch them all the more deeply. It is only fear that restricts our ability to open ourselves and fear is only the absence of Love and understanding. Because all things are One and that One is Love, nothing can ever harm us regardless of how it may appear to our human senses. It is a common reaction to the unknown when we forget that all things are in Divine order at all times.

A commercial message used to urge us to "Reach out and Touch someone". Indeed, that is what this thing called Life is all about. As was mentioned above; all are One but we have chosen to manifest as apparently separate beings in order to increase our understanding of our selves at every level. Thus when we interact with 'the world' we are but Touching ourselves. Self is often the most slippery of items to try to truly Touch. Let us try to always do it with Love. Most of us have spent a lifetime learning to hide from ourselves. This word coming to you in this moment encourages you to try to 'get in Touch' with the 'real' -- the innermost -- feelings. It is at that level that we can most readily help ourselves. Meditation -- going within in quietness and peace -- is an excellent way to accomplish this.

Many fear-oriented people can take even the most genteel and compassionate spiritual or physical Touch as an imminent threat. It is sad that they live in a world that requires a fear response but that is their prerogative. Try always to be aware of the response your offer to Touch generates and be prepared to withdraw it if that is what seems indicated. Remember: there is only one ultimate commandment and that is to BE LOVE. Love never goes where it is not invited. Simply because you really wish to help someone does not create a responsibility on their part to allow you to do so.

COMMENTS FROM SPIRIT:

Touch the heart of your neighbor with Love. Allow the harmony of All that Is to manifest through your very essence and you will be the Divinity that Touches all about you in a healing and Loving way. Healing, Teaching, Loving. These are not things that you DO; these are things that you BE. Be Love, Dear Children, and you Touch all about you with the hand and heart of the Creator.

Blessings.

RESULTS

    While it is true that intent is everything it is always nice to see that intent bear fruit. When that occurs, that which we observe is the Result of our projections. It is also important to remember that all things in our experience are Results of all things preceding them. There is nothing in the material realm that is not the Result of pre-existing energies or patterns.

    Drawing this word into your life suggests that you look at your personal relationship from two points of view.

    1): What condition is this relationship in, in this moment, and what are the causative factors. As nothing in a partnership is caused by only one of the partners (at least in the spiritual sense) how have you contributed to the seemingly positive or the seemingly negative?

2): How would you like to see the relationship changed in the future? Having the Results in view now, how do you need to change your energy input to achieve those goals?

What you perceive in this moment is the harvest of the energies you have been planting for a long time. If you don't like the Results it is never too late (in the spiritual sense) to change the pattern you put into it.

Remember -- nothing happens at random. Spirit is very aware of the lessons your soul desires to expose you to and will do everything in its considerable power to assist you. When a complete stranger enters your life in a seemingly disruptive or traumatic way please remember that that event is a direct Result of Spirit acting in your behalf.

All of us desire to improve ourselves at some level; to grow in some dimension or way. Simply wanting to is not enough. This word has come to you to remind you that commitment and patience must become your handmaidens and constant companions if you want Results.

Remember -- not all Results are immediately obvious as positive but as the old saying from the Orient tells us, "That which does not kill you strengthens you". All experiences are designed and intended to help us in our return to the heart of Spirit.

COMMENTS FROM SPIRIT:

Once again we find a concept held only by those in the material realm. When you come to that place of total One-ness there is no time, there is no space, there is no better, and there is no worse. There is only BEing-ness. There are no "Results" because all things simply ARE and always have been and always shall be. What you call Life; this constant struggle with self, is but a divertimento of your own soul; an attempt to discover in a way that cannot be forgotten your own eternal and limitless self.

Blessings.

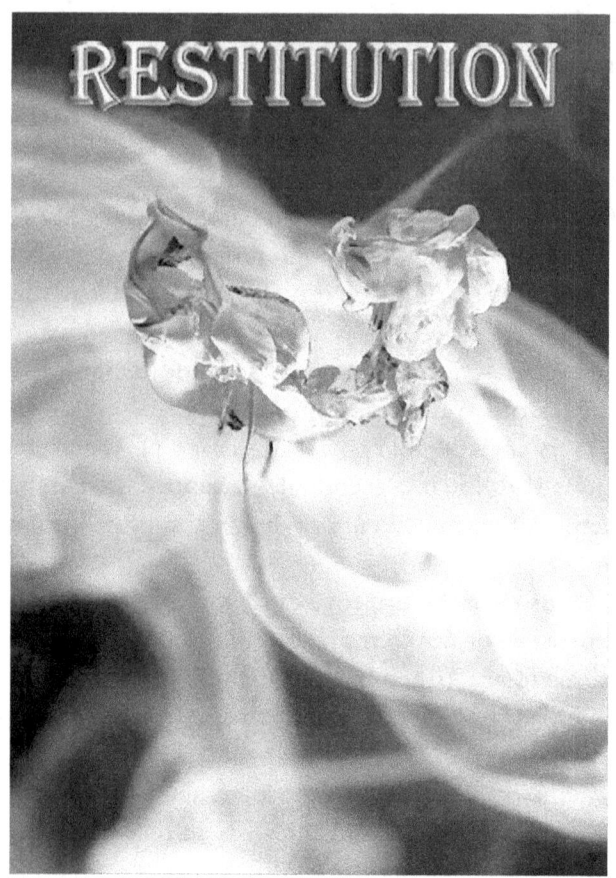

RESTITUTION

    Restitution means literally to repay; to replace that which has been depleted. It is related to and most likely a contraction of "re-constitution" -- recreating something that was but is now less than whole.

    No matter how hard we try to always be in balance in our personal relationships there are always those moments when we 'slip up' and cause our partner to experience distress. While this too is in Divine order, on the human level we often feel the obligation to 'make it right' with an apology, roses, candy, and so on. The greatest and most sincere form of Restitution is to become more aware; to injure less and less often. Bringing this word to yourself this day invites you to do just that.

There are times in our lives when the perception of others differs from our own. This seems to happen quite frequently in the public sector. One result of these types of misunderstanding is the feeling of another that we have wronged them and owe some sort of Restitution. Try to remember this; all things; even the most blatant lie, have at least a particle of truth in them. Remember also please, that all things are given to us as lessons and as opportunities to learn and grow. The gentle (and genteel) path is that of understanding and of least resistance. You do not have to prove yourself 'right' even if you know that you are (from your own perspective). Do what seems reasonable to accede to the demands of the others involved but remember also to honor yourself and the Creator. Restitution given when it is not 'owed' is only payment in advance.

Some of our biggest 'debts' are to ourselves. We constantly underestimate our own power and importance or we overestimate it by the same amount. Either way creates indebtedness in the context of this word to the balance that we all seek. You are encouraged by this word to try to see yourself as you really are -- in all of your glory and with all of your warts and wrinkles. Neither really matters. They both simply are.

Spirit says that most of us have a tendency to do 'two cents worth of damage, and make twenty dollars in Restitution'.

At the soul level, we are all Loving and concerned beings; compassionate and caring. When something occurs in the physical for which we feel somewhat responsible on the conscious level our conscience and our soul conspire to 'make up for' that 'error' with a concentrated and sometimes prolonged (over many lifetimes) series of lessons and Restitution. This can even often take the form of physical ailments. It is when we have learned our lesson but have forgotten why we were studying it that the illnesses continue. Often at this juncture, a 'healer' is brought into the picture to assist you in releasing the imbalance created by the 'over-payment'. When that is done there is no reason or energy for retaining the physical symptoms; thus a 'miraculous' healing occurs.

COMMENTS FROM SPIRIT:

Beloved ones; how can you owe anything when you are All? Seek balance in your pattern called life, and you will never perceive a debt or the need to repay another.

WEALTH

    This is perhaps one of the most misunderstood words we use. Each of us has a concept of the meaning of the word and indeed many of those individual meanings are valid. The variety of Wealth we shall describe here is that of balance, understanding, and peace within oneself. This is the greatest form of Wealth one can ever experience and is consciously or unconsciously sought by all.

    A true and loving partnership is another form of Wealth that nearly everyone seeks. Having this word brought to your attention today suggests that exactly that is on its way to you either in the form of a new relationship or a shift in your current one. Congratulations!

For many years prior to my spiritual awakening, I felt that I was a lower-level person and a misfit in the world. In any casual transaction, I was uneasy and sought ways to gain power or control in order to feel better about myself. With my awakening, I came to realize my own true value to myself and to those about me. With this Wealth; this self-worth and self-awareness, I now enter and consciously face the world as a peer to all those around me and as both a student and a teacher. The peace of mind that has accompanied this transformation is indeed Wealth of the sweetest kind. If you have not yet accepted your Divine nature please allow yourself to do so now. Remember that a truly balanced individual realizes that they are both Divinity and dedicated servant. Being able to move through the world in this state is a sign of great Wealth.

Wealth in the contexts of which we speak has no harsh aspect. Remember, though, that on the physical level, whatever you cannot give away owns you!

COMMENTS FROM SPIRIT:

True Wealth, Beloved Ones, comes simply with the realization of who you truly are. There can be no greater gift to self nor to the world. BE LOVE in all ways and at all times, and you approach this level of conscious existence.

Blessings.

PROGRESS

A few years back one of America's corporate giants had a slogan that stated, "Progress is our most important product." While some of us may feel that profit was intended to be their most important product the sentiment makes a good rallying cry for all of us. Progress is what this thing called life is all about.

Every personal relationship offers us tremendous opportunity for growth (another word for Progress). According to Spirit, personal relationships provide the most fertile field for growth in the human experience. Spirit then added, "Of course, you know what is needed in large quantities to make a field fertile?" Aren't you grateful for the opportunities you have received now and in the past in this regard?

Stop now with that answer still in your mind and look back at those 'tough' times. The times of greatest turmoil are often the times of greatest learning and growth -- in other words, Progress!

Regardless of the path we take, those of us who have consciously entered the realm of growth in Spirit have a responsibility to the rest of the world. Our responsibility is to show through our actions - not our words the difference that our connection with Spirit has made in our lives. As each of us learns and grows the entire world is slowly brought forward toward its ultimate state of conscious grace in the Loving Heart of All that Is because all beings are One. Bringing this word into your awareness today invites you to, in the words of another giant organization, "Be all that you can be!"

Ultimately this is the only form of Progress that exists. In spite of that which was stated above, we cannot make anyone else do anything including grow. We are responsible only to and for our infinite selves. Because most of us act as though we are separate beings from those around us on the Earth plane our major focus and concern should be the Progress that we personally appear to be making on this particular journey through Life. Because there is no time in Spirit and because all times are now, who or what you feel that you were or will be makes absolutely no difference. It is whom you choose to manifest as in this instant that determines who you are. It is the positive change from whom you manifested as at an earlier 'now' within this lifetime that determines your 'Progress'.

It is only when we choose to believe our selves to be Progressing while we have gone back for even more lessons in a particular area that we may be out of touch with our immediate reality. That is always a dangerous position.

COMMENTS FROM SPIRIT:

Progress is another human perspective. While it may seem important to be able to measure your passage through the material realm, never forget that your home and your greater self exist eternally in total Oneness and Balance.

Blessings.

CONFIDENCE

Once again we must dissect a word to find its true meaning. When someone Confides something to someone else there is understood in the word the potential of whatever it is that is Confided to be embarrassing or damaging to the one who first tells it. Therefore one must trust the people to whom one Confides. Confidence, then, means to place or have trust in.

No truly personal relationship may exist without trust (Confidence). This is the second most important place to have trust. Given the particular circumstances of each partnership, the level of trust is an accurate indicator of the (human) love in the relationship. When there doesn't seem to be sufficient trust in your relationship it can be either from a lack of sufficient love to overcome the circumstances or because one or both partners have decided at one level or another to terminate the relationship.

Whether it is on a daily basis or once in this lifetime Confidence in those we deal with casually is an integral part of the successful living of life. A certain degree of trust is imperative every time you eat a bite of food that someone else may have touched and every time you start the engine of your vehicle and pull out into the road. The more at peace you are with yourself and with the Creator the more you will understand the unity of everything that happens. All things that occur in our life experience have but only one source and one goal regardless of how we filter them in the moment. The purpose is always growth and the source is always Divine Love. That source alone should be enough to give anyone all of the Confidence they will ever need.

Self-Confidence is probably the most important form of Confidence. This is not human self-Confidence but rather Confidence in the Divine self; that part of us that purely reflects the Creator within and will never lead us in any way except that which we have chosen to tread in order to better understand ourselves and grow toward total reunion with the Creator of all things.

It is possible to have what the world calls 'misplaced' Confidence. When someone has repeatedly demonstrated a lack of ethics or concern for others one would be foolish to give them the keys to a new car or a bank vault. Discernment is also one of the lessons to be learned in the material realm.

COMMENTS FROM SPIRIT:

The ultimate in Confidence may be obtained by connecting within to the glory of Eternal Love that guides your every step and your every breath. We guide you home to the Heart of Hearts; to the Love of all Loves. Be here now and in each moment of your Earth-walk as we are always with you. BE Love!

CONSISTENCY

It is not enough to manifest your highest nature once in a while or to do a good act twice each day that you think of it. Drawing this energy to you indicates a need for a deeper level of commitment and devotion to those ideals that you pay lip service to. Talk is cheap. Action is what is called forth by this energy. Live your beliefs Consistently. Walk your talk on every path on which you place your feet. Service to Spirit and to humankind is not a part-time job. One cannot speak holy phrases with one breath and curse with the next and still be in integrity with oneself.

There is a great need in any personal relationship of quality for this thing known as Consistency. Consistency is perhaps one of the most desirable qualities most of us search for in a partner. Partnerships are traumatic enough for most of us without having to guess who or what your partner is going to emulate tonight. Reverse that thought now and see how important it is to your partner in life that you are Consistently who you are. Another aspect is referred to as constancy. This is generally understood to mean that you remain Consistent and trustworthy in your emotional bonding as you both understand it and agree that it 'should' be. It is a cornerstone upon which trust is built and trust is the foundation of the relationship that grows. When this word comes to you it is a suggestion that you look at your recent thoughts and actions. Are they Consistent with what your partner has grown to expect of you? Are they in alignment with who it is that you would like to think that you are? What do you need to do to resolve the issues around your behavior and its causes? Spirit will be there by your side to assist you in this repair.

In non-personal relationships such as business dealings, Consistency translates to the concept known as 'trust' or 'respect'. A Consistent person is said to be a 'straight shooter' and to generally give those who deal with them 'a square deal'. If this is not how the world views you perhaps it is time to change those behaviors that have given you that outer image. Consistency is also important in the mundane world as we all have to work with one another on a daily basis. There are certain levels of behavior that we can generally expect of the stranger on the street. For example; a stranger is not going to suddenly walk up to you, stick his thumbs in his nose and yell "Boogedy boogedy"! Well, not most of the time anyway. The point is that we have built our lives around certain assumptions regarding the people we are going to interact with each day. That is why reports of random violence affect us so deeply. They show us that perhaps the level of Consistency that we expect from our fellow humans is not being met. It is important to maintain our own personal Consistency in order to provide stability for society as a whole.

All Consistency is internal. A certain balance achieves it within oneself. The place of balance can be anywhere on the emotional or spiritual spectrum. It simply is where you are at this point in your development. Some people are balanced at the level of drugs and drive-by shootings. Some are balanced in total dedication to service and to Spirit. If the gang-banger were to suddenly become a Holy Roller that would be in-Consistent with his/her previous pattern. If the servant were to shoot heroin into his/her veins that would be in-Consistent with who they have previously been.

Change is a good thing. It is what life is all about. Sudden and unexpected change often makes life uncomfortable for those who have come to depend on us to be a certain way. This is not always a bad thing. If you are ready to give up some of the patterns that you no longer are comfortable with Spirit will be glad to assist you starting right now! "To thine own self be true."

There is no harsh aspect to Constancy even if the Constancy is performed in a way that is uncomfortable or unpleasant for you. At least you know what to expect most of the time. It is possible to be Consistently an agent of disharmony, disruption, or chaos. Just ask any two-year-old child.

COMMENTS FROM SPIRIT:

Consistency of the heart is the only Consistency we ask of you. Fix your mind upon the Heart of Hearts. Be in the heart of Love in every moment of every lifetime. Come into the light and glory of your own essence and experience the Consistency of All that Is. Consistency is Balance in its highest form. To live in the heart of All that Is; to exude that tranquil balance in your every moment and word. That is Love at its finest. We invite you, Dear Children, to allow yourselves each and all to manifest your Divinity in this manner in each moment of your existence.

Blessings.

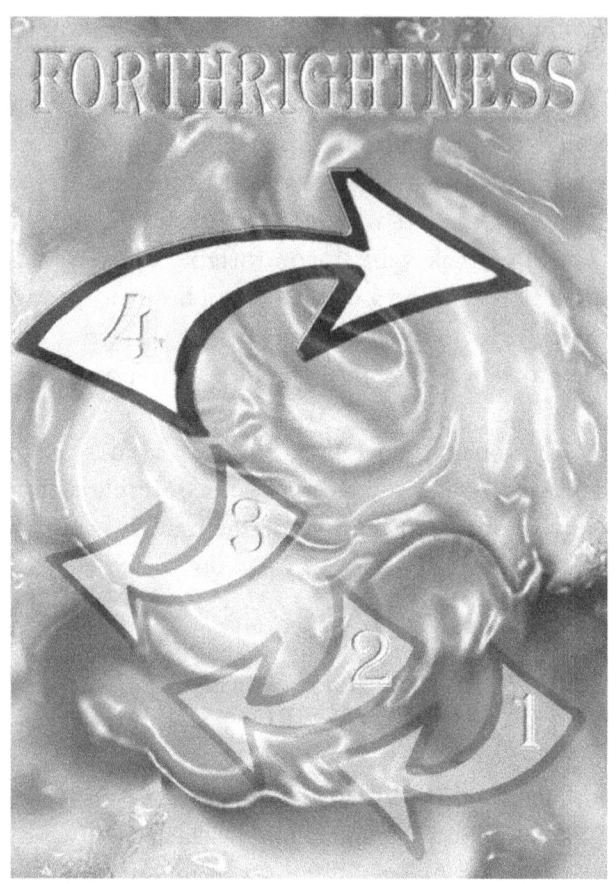

FORTHRIGHTNESS

Express your true feelings openly. Extend yourself past your comfort level in service to the truth as you understand it. This is what Forthrightness commands of you.

Many times we tend to gloss over those things that truly bother us about the situation or about our partner's behavior in our personal relationships. As a short-term solution, this sometimes seems to work. Unhappily this solution is only temporary. The underlying problem will remain and will continue to chafe until you choose to become Forthright with your partner. Calling this concept to you today advises you that perhaps that time is here. Many of us 'bite the bullet', waiting for the problem to go away by itself. How is it going to if you do not communicate it to your partner? Even the most psychic of partners cannot read your thoughts and emotions in every moment. As a matter of fact, would you want them to? This leaves only verbal and written communication. Often as time goes by and the situation (that we have not fully discussed with our partner) seems to become intolerable so we do the human thing and blow up at our loved one who hasn't the slightest hint where all of this vitriol has come from. Talk now -- there'll never be a better time!

Apply the above to your business and casual relationships as well. When done with and from Love, you'll be amazed by the results!

As always, the person we try to fool most often is ourself. It is only when we can become fully Forthright with ourself that we can begin our Spiritual growth.

It seems to me that I've heard somewhere that the wise man builds his house on a base of stone and a foolish person on sand. Build yourself on the stone of Truth and your structure will be sound and will last for the time that you need it.

Forthrightness is often best served with large portions of

tact. Not everyone is willing to hear the naked truth.

COMMENTS FROM SPIRIT:

Living in the Light; living in the truth that IS precludes any necessity for Forthrightness. It is only on the lower levels that the option for anything but total truth exists and it is only your choice on a day-by-day basis to exhibit anything less than that total truth that gives meaning to this term.

Live in the light of your own Be-ing, Children, and know that you are Loved beyond measure, whatever your choices.

Blessings.

READINESS

Readiness is a tricky word. It means to be in a state or condition of preparedness for anticipated events in our lives. What it means in the context of a reading is generally the state or condition of preparedness for whatever Spirit may throw at us next. It deals much more with spiritual preparation than emotional, mental, or physical. When one is wholly attuned to Spirit even the biggest surprise is but a ripple in the pond of our tranquility.

A good relationship is the essence of Readiness. I will tell you some of the events of the past two months within my own relationship to illustrate the point:

1) After holding it off for 8 years, I finally must file for bankruptcy.
2) My 20-year-old daughter's marriage collapses and she returns home with 4 cats (and we already had two cats). We now call it the 'house of hair'.
3) I have to cut my mid-back length hair and Santa Claus beard for the first time in 10 years in order to take a 'real' job to keep the family afloat financially. I give up my freedom of movement and time as well.
4) I take a visitor into my house to help him get re-started in life – he stays for 2 weeks, then helps himself to a week's worth of my pay and several valuable items from our collection of 'stuff' as a parting gift to himself.
5) My daughter's health seriously deteriorates. Many trips to the emergency room result.
6) My health seriously deteriorates.
7) Our 15-year-old cat dies.
8) My daughter's soon-to-be "ex" arrives unannounced on our doorstep at 11:15 P.M. with unreasonable demands at the top of his voice while my daughter is in the emergency room. The next morning he meets with her and screams, threatens, and intimidates so much that I step in and throw him off our property.
9) …. And about a dozen other things ….

And on it goes……

As my partner and I look back over these two months we are amazed at the events but not overwhelmed by them. We are able to see the purpose for each event and the amazing choreography and timing of each one and of all of them together. We move on into our joint future at peace with the universe, our lives, and one another. We have learned not to ask "What could possibly happen next!" because Spirit is only too willing to show us. We walk, live, and Love in faith in every moment. This is Readiness at its finest.

Living and walking in faith is simply another way of stating that one eats, sleeps, and breathes the awareness of the Divine balance to be found in every event and thought. When one is intimately aware of this sublime 'rightness' there is no event public or private that can or will catch us with sufficient surprise to throw us even momentarily from our path.

The only possible form of Readiness is ultimately personal Readiness. Be spiritually prepared for anything and everything in every moment and you will constantly and consistently be at peace to such an extent as to set an example for the world around you.

COMMENTS FROM SPIRIT:

Readiness, Beloveds, is simply a matter of being in your Creator Consciousness in every way and in every moment. Step outside the human doubts and fears and simply be aware of the eternal flowing of All that Is as it passes within you and appears around you. Blessed indeed are those who reside here, for eternal tranquility is their realm and their domain.

Blessings.

WILLINGNESS

It is one thing to hear the voice of Spirit. It is one thing to know the will of the Creator. It is quite another to be Willing to follow that lead immediately, totally, and without question. Trust is involved in this process as well. Willingness involves unquestioned total intention and action aimed at accomplishing those goals regardless of the apparent cost or discomfort on a personal level. It is only through Willingness that the Creator's work is advanced on this plane.

Willingness reflects in a personal relationship an intentional choice to work toward and allow positive changes to occur. Sometimes the process or even the steps along the way can seem to be unpleasant or confusing. Trust: there is no other path. Open your heart to the Creator and let Love guide you.

Be Willing to follow the lead of Spirit wherever it may bid you travel. Spirit never will lie to you nor lead you astray. Follow with all your heart and you will go far.

If you have drawn this word in response to a question regarding self, know that everything I have written here is all especially true and pertinent in that context.

COMMENTS FROM SPIRIT:

Willingness is the natural state for one in Balance and in total attunement with the Creator and with Creation. Love is always giving. Giving is the heart of Willingness. Think not that you give but to the Creator and yourself, whatever the form. Be Love. There is no effort or discomfort in this matter nor could there be. Walk in Balance always.

Be at peace.

HARVEST

After all of the work; after all of the planning, the tilling, the planting, the nurturing, and the weeding; after all of the tending, the overseeing, the patience, the prayer, and the toil, comes the Harvest.

Harvest is the reason and the reward. Harvest is the incentive to return to the field one more time with hope in your heart. Harvest is the gift we give ourselves.

As we sow, so shall we reap. This is more than an in-the-moment fact. When we find ourselves in an extremely painful relationship or an extremely good one or anything in between for that matter, it is important to remember this: ALL THINGS ARE IN DIVINE ORDER IN ALL WAYS AND AT ALL TIMES, WHETHER WE LIKE IT OR NOT AND WHETHER WE UNDERSTAND IT OR NOT!

The relationship you find yourself in is both the Harvest of the past and the seed of the future. There IS a reason for every detail of the happenings within this partnership and that reason is always Love of the highest order. If your experience seems harsh and abusive it is because in this life or another you have been harsh and abusive to those who depended on you for nurturing and support. This experience is both a reminder and self-imposed 'payback' for those deeds and an opportunity to realize how it feels to be on the receiving end of such treatment so that you will determine at a deep level never to do such again. That does not mean that it needs to continue nor that you should tolerate or remain in an intolerable situation nor an untenable relationship. We as individuals have the right – indeed the duty to ourselves – to say when enough is enough and that we need a break from experiencing certain unpleasant lessons in our lives. It is our responsibility and ours alone to modify the environment as it appears to us in the moment. Once again we find: "Perception creates Reality". What's yours?

If you don't like what you are experiencing this word invites you to change your point of view from that of a victim to that of a student. Once that is accomplished, the pain, anger, and distress of any situation will fall away effortlessly, as it is not happening TO you but FOR you.

It is possible to reap a bitter Harvest only if we are bitter people. If we understand that the true intent of every experience is to assist us in understanding ourselves as Creator, not Man, there is absolutely no experience that will be seen as negative in itself or in the greater context.

COMMENTS FROM SPIRIT:

Harvest, Dear Ones, can only occur when seeds are planted and attended to with Love, attention, and devotion. You are the seeds; you are the soil, you are the rain and you are the sun. Each of you is a seed of

Myself Lovingly cast forth into the universe to grow; each in your own time and each in your own way. You have all of eternity for this growth and there is no way to fail. The husbandry you offer yourself is the only variable. Love yourself enough to blossom and bear fruit and ye shall soon become the Harvest and your Love and your works the fruited seed.

Blessings.

GENTLENESS

Gentleness is the essence of Love made tangible. It is the whisper of Love in the ear of need. It is the warm sweet breath of a mother upon the sleeping cheek of her newborn. It is the loving touch of gnarled fingers as they stroke away an infant's tear. It is an act of kindness, a word of warmth and support in a time of distress. It is Love held in the hand of action.

Nowhere except with ourselves is Gentleness more often called for than with our life partner. As the days wear upon us; as the world seems to rest its weight upon our shoulders we often share our burdens harshly with the one who is closest to us in our life.

In our selection of this partner, most of us did not place a requirement upon them to be a whipping post yet that is often how we use them as we vent our frustrations and anger on the one person we know will have to bear it. Share instead your love for that partner and then merely mention your problems in passing. Listen to yourself as you do so. Hear the pettiness and the whining child in your speech. Is this who you truly are? Is this the face you would turn to the chief love and support in your life?

Gentleness, friends; Gentleness.

How often we see cruelty toward one another as we observe children at their play as a means of obtaining the appearance of the 'upper hand' in a given situation. When we as adults see this we see right through the simulated reasoning to the core issues of power and control of others engendered from ego alone.

As we observe ourselves in our lives how often do we see cruelty toward one another as a means of obtaining the appearance of the 'upper hand' in a given situation? When we see this as spiritual beings, we see right through the simulated reasoning to the core issues of power and control of others, engendered from ego alone.

Gentleness, friends, Gentleness.

How often do we see cruelty toward ourselves as we observe ourselves in life and living, as we constantly battle with our diminished sense of self-worth and then move consciously and un-consciously to validate those feelings? When we have the consciousness to observe this we see right through the simulated reasoning to the core issues of giving our power and control to others, engendered from fear alone. It is much easier to abdicate our power and with it, we assume, our responsibility.

Even in those moments where it appears that someone else is gaining power or control over us as a result it is important to remember that no one can ever harm us but ourselves!

COMMENTS FROM SPIRIT:

When it comes to pass that all Love one another as I Love you, then Gentleness shall reign. Leave fear, need, and desire outside your heart, for there is only space enough for the Gentleness of Divine Love in the heart of the awakened. Bless you, one and all.

COURAGE

Courage is the internal strength to stand firmly behind whatever you know to be 'right' regardless of the cost to your personal comfort or situation. Courage is often (and erroneously) measured by physical action. In truth, it can be reflected in all aspects of human endeavor. Courage is also often associated with compassion.

Courage is shown in a personal relationship when you take responsibility for all of your actions and thoughts. Total honesty, beginning within, and the strength to recognize and deal with all of those unbalanced aspects of any relationship require a great deal of Courage.

When dealing with the daily injustices of life in public, Courage refers to remaining steadfastly in the truth of a given situation. If something seems 'right' then do it or support it. If you honestly feel a situation is not in the highest interest of all concerned you may choose to do everything you can to nudge it toward balance. The result is not nearly as important as the sincere effort.

Personal application of Courage usually indicates that you are or are about to experience a challenge to your ethics and/or your spiritual standards. The good news is that this usually marks a 'final exam' for a certain area and level of learning. If you successfully complete this 'test' you will be ready to move on to higher levels in this area. If not you will have the opportunity to review the lesson more intensely in the immediate future.

It would be very easy to indulge in what you believe to be Courage while actually supporting a position of stubbornness. The difference is Ego. When you steadfastly maintain a position in an effort to protect your previous or current stance and ignore any new input this is simple stubbornness. This is not an act compatible with spiritual growth. New lessons will make this clear.

COMMENTS FROM SPIRIT:

Courage is a word that has no counterpart in Spirit. It is a human concept in that it presupposes conflict. When one flows as part of the River of Life there is no conflict but only eddies in the greater flow. All falls within the Divine pattern and all is in harmony in that Whole.

ASPIRATION

    To Aspire is to lift up our sights until they match our hopes. It is to step beyond our current sense of limitations and through the veil of our fears into the light-filled realm of infinite possibilities. It is to dare to dream and to further dare to make those dreams our reality.

    A personal relationship is ideally a study in Aspirations. Each person comes into the relationship with hopes and desires for a better life as a result of their new status as partner and beloved. If this word has come to you today perhaps it is time to review your level of Aspirations regarding your relationship. Are you settled into the rut of the daily grind? Have you given up on improving your relationship through improving how you choose to perceive it? Take a moment; go back in your mind and heart to the time that your relationship was new. Allow the hope, the faith, the trust in yourself, the Creator, and your partner to rekindle and light your days with hope. It's never too late!

Aspirations can have high and lower forms as can all other emotions. It is sometimes easy to let the lower forms rule when dealing with others in the business or workaday world. Avarice, control, and jealous manipulation are all potential directions of the lower energies of Aspiration. Monitor your thoughts and actions for the next few days. See exactly what your motivations are and what the desired results may be. Is this the energy you wish to put into the world? If so, congratulations! If not — change it!

Aspire is another of those words that is always and ultimately personal. If we cannot hope to better ourselves then we cannot hope to better the world. As above, so below. As within, so without.

When allowing oneself to Aspire it is important to do so from the heart, not the ego.

COMMENTS FROM SPIRIT:

Beloved Ones: You fear the depth of your hearts. Focus instead upon the lofty heights of awareness and participation within the Heart of Hearts that all beings share as their birthright. You are born as a being in the heart of the Creator and there you reside for all of eternity. You – each and all of you - ARE the heart of All that Is. Let your Aspiration be to recognize yourself in every moment regardless of what the mirror of the material world would have you believe. Thou art God. Aspire to that.

Blessings.

STEADFAST

    This is a word whose meaning is apparent at first glance. 'Stead' implies Steady, unwavering, trustworthy, and strong. 'Fast', as in holding fast or in hand fasting means still, rooted, bonded, dependable, and unshakable. The combined word: 'Steadfast' represents all of these elements and is a high compliment when applied to oneself or another. It is also a daunting challenge to achieve should one not already have this attribute.

    Sometimes in a personal relationship, the events of the moment can seem so daunting and insurmountable as to make the thought of discontinuing the relationship quite attractive. Sometimes this is indeed the next logical step but much more often it is simply that our inability to see the events as the lessons that they are has allowed us to slip into 'victim' mode. A Steadfast belief in our partner, in Spirit, and in the Divine order of ALL events in our lives regardless of how they seem when filtered through our doubts, fears hopes and agendas will see us through to the successful completion of this particular lesson. (Not that there is any way to complete it un-successfully)

Used car salesmen have a certain reputation. So do door-to-door vacuum cleaner or magazine salesmen. They are frequently thought of as 'flaky'. The lesson here is that when we as individuals or as a group are less than Steadfast in our business or personal integrity it creates an energy field around us that puts others at dis-ease and dis-trust. In order to be a truly successful member of society, it is imperative that the utmost integrity is upheld with the ultimate in Steadfast-ness. Drawing this word to you in this way suggests that perhaps this is not the current mode of operation in your life. Remember, Spirit will always be happy to show you how it feels to be on the receiving side of your actions.

As William Shakespeare said in "Hamlet": "This above all: to thine own self be true; And it must follow, as the night the day, thou canst not then be false to any man". Steadfastness extends from our own inner self and strength into the cosmos and the material world about us. This is simply one more illustration of co-creation.

There comes a time, a place, and a situation for all of us where we simply have had enough of a given lesson for now. It is our right to put down the tools and excuse ourselves from the classroom for a break. It would be foolish however to think we will not have to go back at a future date, review what we have gathered thus far and continue the lesson until we 'get it'.

COMMENTS FROM SPIRIT:

In the realm of Love, there is naught but Steadfastness. Love simply IS. There is no wavering, no thought of lessening or ceasing the flow. It IS and in its IS-ness founds and supports all that you might think, feel, hope and fear is 'real'. All that is 'real', Beloveds, is LOVE. There is naught else in the cosmos and naught else in your heart of hearts. Steadfastly maintain the Love that you -- and all about you – are. Hold this awareness regardless of the apparent discrepancies to be found in your experience and in your mind. BE LOVE in all ways and in all things, and you manifest the Love of the Universe, which is the being you call GOD, which is you in your greatest form.

Eternal Blessings.

EASE

    This word is used in many forms but they all boil down to different aspects of one meaning: A lessening of pressures perceived or effort required. Ease is a period of relaxation in body, mind, and spirit. It is a situation resolved or a chance to lean back, take a deep breath, and an even deeper sigh of relief. Ease is the heart at rest for a moment.

    When things go right in a relationship – especially when they have been troubled for quite a while – there is a palpable release of tension in the household and in the atmosphere. The walls you weren't aware you had built to protect yourself suddenly become perceptible as they begin to soften and wilt. The 'tap-dancing on eggshells' aspect of day-to-day life is over for now and it's OK once more to be yourself without fear. Relax.

Entering into a new situation in the world can be stressful. The expansion of an old situation and the addition of new constraints or parameters in an old matrix creates an entirely new situation that might seem dangerous. As we move through our own insecurities, expectations, and fears into an acceptance and understanding of the cosmic 'why's' of the lessons we are offering ourselves we come to a place of relative Ease with the new or changing situation. Bringing this word to yourself today reinforces the message that relief is spelled SELF-UNDERSTANDING. Enjoy!

Each and every one of us is our own harshest critic and worst enemy. We allow our emotions, reactions, and fears to rule our lives on a moment-by-moment and day-by-day basis. It's easy to say, "Even though one can see the mountaintop that doesn't mean that one lives there" as an excuse. In actuality, it does fall within the potential of every human to live on that spiritual mountaintop. All it takes is a total and absolute understanding of the Divine nature of EVERY experience – without exception – and a willingness to ever be the student – never the victim. Living on this mountaintop is the epitome of Ease from the human condition. That is not to say it is an easy thing but it is a very simple one.

Ease is a contrast word. Without stress there cannot exist its opposite; Ease. If you are experiencing this thing called 'Ease' be aware that you have been out of balance in some way and that you will likely be so again. Don't ever give up but neither allow yourself to be disheartened when the next lesson appears.

COMMENTS FROM SPIRIT:

Children: Beloved Children of Mine. Release the fears, the hopes, the agendas, and the schemes. Simply BE LOVE. If, as and when all beings consciously participate in the simple act of Be-ing what and who you are this world will terminate as the class will graduate and the material experience will now be complete. Ease is simply a lack of stress.

Stress is a gift of dubious value that each of you brings upon yourselves as a learning tool. Ease – true Ease – eternal Ease – lies in simply Being the being I have created you to be. BE Love, and be completed.

I give My Love.

SEXUALITY

This is without a doubt, from the human level, one of the most powerful words in this series. Sexuality is the humanization of the material realm's most powerful drive: the drive to perpetuate the species. Humans have discovered the pleasure/power of this drive and have raised it to new heights and lowered it to new depths with mental and 'moral' manipulation.

Sexuality is neither good nor bad. As with all human emotions, it simply IS. It is only the slant and perspective we bring – our desires and our fears – our ego and our willingness that can make it seem to be a positive or a negative. For further information in-depth on Sexuality from a spiritual viewpoint as opposed to a religious one, I suggest reading "Sex, Sexuality, Spirit and Appropriate Behavior" which can be found in the book "A Few Easy Lessons", also by Mani Pureheart and available at www.ManiPureheart.com.

In many but not all cases an intimate personal relationship is either built upon or directly derived from a Sexual one. Sexuality is the magnet that draws beings together. It is the promise of ecstatic pleasure that is the drug above all drugs and which can become the addiction above all addictions. It is not inconceivable (no pun intended) that in a life or Sex situation (where to take one action would assure life while another choice would in all likelihood forfeit life but result in a Sexual experience) quite a number would choose Sex in that moment. It has been said that the act of Love is as close as two souls can come to one another while wearing their mortal forms. In its finest form, it is a total merging, melding, and blending into the Divine One-ness of our highest selves. It is not in error that many belief systems have used either Sexuality or the control of Sexuality as a main tenet of their belief systems and practices.

Sexuality is impossible in a general relationship. Any time one relates to another from a Sexual space an intimate emotional and spiritual connection is formed between the participants. A Sexual relationship does not require the verbalization or action of the thoughts or feelings (doesn't the Christian Bible say that if one lusts after another 'in their heart' that it is the same as having committed adultery?) but only the perception of another as an object of Sexual interest even if that interest is of the basest nature.

One's Sexuality is one of the most personal of one's aspects in the material world's view. This is not necessarily as it 'should' be in an ideal world. It is simply what we have been taught through centuries of repression and guilt around the possibility that we might find something we enjoy more than the Church and its rules. How you relate to yourself as a Sexual being – be it with shame and humiliation or with comfort and joy – says a lot about your spiritual nature. It has been my observation that highly evolved spiritual beings in material bodies are most often totally at ease with their own Sexuality and the Sexuality of others. They will almost without exception immerse themselves in it, joke about it, and celebrate and revel in their joyous sharing when it occurs. At the same time, they are not consumed by it or by thoughts of it. It is simply another aspect of their totality.

Sexuality is such a powerful tool that it becomes easy – even tempting for some – to misuse it for the benefit of one's ego. This usually occurs at the expense of another's self-worth.

Think of your Sexuality as a scalpel. In the hands of a skilled and caring practitioner, it can literally save lives. In the hands of another …

COMMENTS FROM SPIRIT:

ENJOY
In Joy,
enjoy!

DESIRE

Desire is both a noun and a verb. We shall examine the verb's characteristics.

Desire is a step beyond simply wanting. To want suggests a temporary feeling of lack. To Desire indicates a more lasting focus ranging from benign to obsessive.

Desire is often a programmable emotion. We can Desire a smooth relationship path or greater understanding of our partner and ourselves. Calling this word to you today suggests that it is time to take the upper hand in the paths your Desires take. Look at your areas of focus and intent. Are they of your highest self? How could you improve and uplift the process? Spirit is here to assist you in achieving that if you will allow.

Desire is above all a personal expression. It is the inner self recognizing or demanding the 'right' to be valued; whether by the conscious self or by the world at large. It is the small sense of 'self' wanting to add on from that which it perceives around it in order to be 'more' than it has previously allowed itself to be seen as and understood.

Desire is often intimately connected with obsession and can easily slip from the first state to the second without our notice. There is an old saying: "The road to Hell is paved with good intentions". Desire is often the road crew that does the paving work. It can also be an uplifted shining goal if we can only allow it to be, observe that it is, and detach ourselves from the results. At this point if it can be maintained, Desire serves us by providing direction in our lives and growth.

COMMENTS FROM SPIRIT:

Desire reflects that which you feel you need or want but do not have as yet. Know yourselves, Dear Ones, as an intimate and integral portion of All that Is. Know that there is nothing; no one, no experience or goal that lies outside of your greater self as you already exist! Desire only Love of Self sufficient to recognize this truth of Being.

Blessings.

BLESSING

Blessing is a human word expressing a human view and human needs. Blessing is that which supports and nurtures. It is also that which challenges and promotes growth and learning. It can be a verb, an adverb, or a noun. It indicates that the words, deeds, or thoughts of another being or entity augment one. It is a sop to our innate insecurities and at the same time a statement of honoring and respect much as the word "Namaste" which means: "The Creator within me recognizes and honors the Creator within you". A Blessing offered is succor, Love, aid, support, condolence, and alignment. It says: "I may or may not totally agree with you and where you appear to be in the moment but I sincerely offer the greater you non-conditional Love and fervently hope that whatever greater powers there are in the universe will assist you in seeing this event or situation through in a way that you will find to be positive as it occurs."

We shall focus on this human interpretation of the word.

No matter how 'good'; no matter how 'bad', every personal relationship is a Blessing. No other format in the human experience has the potential to support and challenge us to the degree that an intimate relationship does. Whether we are able to perceive the events as a Blessing in the moment of their occurrence is determined exclusively by our choice of perceptive 'windows'. In a reversal of the phrase "what you see is what you get" I would state "what you think you are getting is determined by how you choose to see it." All things are Blessings. ALL THINGS ARE BLESSINGS. It is only our 'small self' centered material world focus that can sometimes make things seem to be less than a Blessing.

COMMENTS FROM SPIRIT:

Beloveds; there can be no greater Blessing than to anoint your own brow with the light of your greater self; to open that eye that sees only Divinity in all. Bless yourselves in this manner and you Bless your world. Be it so.

PARTNERSHIP

    Partnership is a word of many contexts. It can be temporary in the human perception or life(s) long in duration. It can be supportive or challenging. It is the 'you' in another form that comes forth to mirror and guide you in your quest for self.

    Quite often in this text, we have used the word 'Partner' in the description of the meaning of a word or concept in a personal relationship. Partnering at this level includes letting down one's protective walls so that the facades and false faces of public life disappear. As a result, this is the one arena of life involving others where we allow ourselves to become most exposed, most vulnerable, and most ready for growth and change. For this reason, a personal relationship with your Partner requires the utmost trust and openness in order to function well. You and your Partner, be they husband, wife, teacher, lover, brother, mother, aunt, grandparent, or simply an extremely close friend, have entered into a cosmic, karmic agreement to dance the intricate dance called life in this imaginary experience; to play 'let's pretend' on the material plane. The resulting bond is one of the most powerful possible to those in body and has the potential of being one of the most profitable for all concerned. Remember always to see it from this point of view in order to maximize the 'positive' aspects of the experience.

It is both extremely important and extremely difficult for most of us to remember and to live our understanding that all beings are One and that we ARE that one. Thus every interaction you ever will have or have had with 'another' is simply You playing 'life' with you. All beings, entities, and energies are your Partners in this experience. Most are thinking and feeling that they are separate and unique and that 'stuff' is happening TO them instead of FOR them. You, of course, know better than that. You are Partnered together just as the warp and the woof of a fine fabric depend on one another for support and contrast so that a pattern may be formed and completed. You are Partnered together just as the warp and the woof of a fine fabric depend on one another for support and contrast so that a pattern may be formed and completed. The ones to which you choose to open your most intimate thoughts and feelings are the loom and the shuttle of your process. Their supportive pressure and guidance as well as the limitations and challenges they present are the parameters of the world experience you have chosen for the moment. If you feel too tightly constrained perhaps it is time to reconsider the loom you find yourself attached to or the way you choose to perceive it. If you feel lost in the vastness of the process allow yourself the time and opportunity to weave yourself into your full potential. Either way is perfect.

Although some of the events associated with Partnering as seen from the limited human perspective can seem harsh or unpleasant in the moment, they can be recognized without fail as the blessing that they are when viewed from the greater or spiritual form

COMMENTS FROM SPIRIT:

My Dearest Beloved Children,

I constantly invite you to see yourselves and the Universes as the singularity of Beingness that I AM. There is none but I and no reality other than your Self as Creator. The 'IS'ness of your existence precludes Partnering with any but your as yet unrecognized essence that is I. I AM that I AM. You are that I AM. Partner then with the Love that is All; with the permeation of the imaginary material realm with the illusion of permanence, of solidarity with ALL aspects of self, and the total rejection of any possible restriction or limitation. Partner with All that Is, for beyond your wildest imagination lays your stark Genesis.

Blessings.

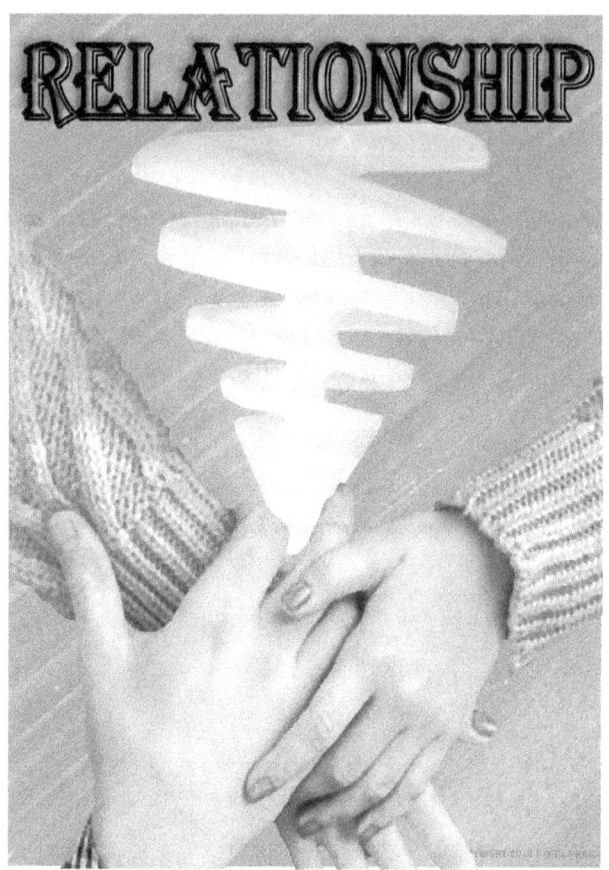

RELATIONSHIP

Relationship has the root word 'Relate' as its basis. In order to consciously Relate to a person or thing, we must at least temporarily place our consciousness 'outside' ourselves in order to observe how 'we' and this 'other' revolve around one another and the effect each has or could have on the other. These effects and the extent to which we allow and/or encourage them are the measurements of this thing we call "Relationship".

Personal Relationship is the single most powerful Earth-plane tool we have for the encouragement and facilitation of spiritual and personal growth. It is the magnifying glass through which we may see our problems most magnified and thus most clearly. We would only remind the reader that those things that trouble us most about another are but a mirror of those things within ourselves that we fear or dislike most.

The crux of the matter is this: our single most powerful personal Relationship is first and foremost with ourselves. We are the ones whom we most often try to fool. We are the ones who are most apt to believe our own lies. We are the ones who demand the most of us and the first and harshest to criticize when we 'fail'.

It is only when we come into the balance of truthfulness and understanding within ourselves (after all, there is never an apparent need for forgiveness when there is true understanding) that we attain true spiritual growth and inner peace.

Bringing this word to yourself today indicates that this is an area that Spirit feels is ripe for more improvement.

Although Relationships (especially with others) can seem extremely harsh at times it is only presented to your senses in that manner because you have neglected a basic rule of spiritual growth: "All things are in Divine order in all ways and at all times." It is only our understanding (or lack of it) that makes us feel that we are being made a victim when in reality every experience is offered to us as a gift of the greatest Love and at our soul's request. It is only an opportunity to learn and grow. If it seems harsh it is because we have been offered the same opportunity many times before and have not responded with understanding or growth. As an example of this:

A teacher tells your class, "Two plus two equals four". Everyone seems to understand it except you. "TWO PLUS TWO EQUALS FOUR", the teacher repeats. If you still don't 'get it' she may have you come up to the blackboard and write it ten times. If that doesn't work she may demonstrate the principle with blackboard erasers. If you still don't get it she may give you the homework assignment of writing the equation one hundred times. If you still don't understand you may have to stay after school in a study hall. If that doesn't get through to you, you may have to attend summer school. If that doesn't work you may have to repeat the class.

Spirit tells me, "Infinite Love has infinite patience". We can keep coming back as often as we want -- or need -- to get a particular lesson. Every time it is offered to us and we don't 'get it' it travels around the wheel of our life once more and approaches us from a slightly different angle – and with greater intensity. This process continues until we finally 'get the message' or until the message is coming to us so loudly and with such force that all other aspects of our life must take a back seat until that particular lesson is learned (becoming a student). This is the reason that it sometimes seems that our entire life has gone to heck. It is only Spirit Loving us enough to offer us an important lesson in a way that we cannot ignore. As soon as we get the message, Spirit (the teacher) offers us another one built upon the last but offered in the gentlest of fashions.

"Two plus three is five."

COMMENTS FROM SPIRIT:

Beloved Ones; We invite you to enter the heart of hearts: go within to the ultimate degree and find yourself in the greatest form within. In this manner, you find and become one with All in the greatest possible Relationship. This is the Divine gift We offer.

FORGIVENESS

If one is truly at peace within and truly in the flow of All that Is it becomes obvious that all things are always in order and there is never anything to Forgive.

So much for the ideal.

Most of us are constantly in a condition of being upset with ourselves, our partner, the world, or all of the above. The energy of Forgiveness might better be called 'understanding' or 'attitude adjustment'. This word invites us to look at our own out-of-balance condition which somehow causes us to perceive ourselves as victims. The resulting self-generated anger, righteous indignation, and frustration are what cries out for 'forgiveness'. This condition, Forgiveness, occurs when we abandon the 'victim' stance and assume that of the student!

Regardless of whether the difficulty is personal or general in nature, the cause is the same: failure to truly understand the situation from the spiritual point of view. The resolution, in either case, is to shift our perspective and understanding toward the spiritual level.

There is no harsh aspect to this process. Don't forget to tactfully share your new point of view with others involved.

COMMENTS FROM SPIRIT:

Forgiveness is a tool of the human psyche. It is a useful bridge over which one may pass in the journey from 'not in balance' to 'in balance'. It often eases that path as well as shortening it.

Blessings.

PLEASURE

Believe it or not, there is absolutely nothing wrong with this thing called Pleasure. Perhaps it should be spelled 'Play-sure'. It is closely associated with the concept of 'Joy'. It is a method of celebrating life and living. It can only occur when one is totally in the moment and is in fact one of the best ways to bring oneself totally into the moment. This is one of the reasons that ancient cultures based many of their spiritual practices on bringing or giving Pleasure

One of the greatest potential sources of physical and emotional Pleasure available to us lies within our personal relationships. If you are not experiencing sufficient joy and Pleasure in this format you must then ask yourself why. What is blocking your Pleasure? Hint: regardless of appearances, it is always you. What lessons are present that you refuse to recognize at this time? If the identical situation were happening to a friend, what would you tell them to do and why?

Life is to be lived and enjoyed, not tolerated and suffered through. The choice is yours and only you can change your attitudes. It is those attitudes that can turn ignorance and pain into understanding and peace.

There are two great teachers in our lives; two main paths to learning: One is pain; the other Pleasure. Most of us seem to choose to learn from pain most of the time. Which is your teacher? Which would you prefer to have as your teacher? What do you need to change in order for that to happen? The answer is simple and the answer lies within your patterns of observation and reaction.

There is a sick and sad bastard brother to Pleasure. It is the Pleasure born of ego. Its henchmen are vengeance, insecurity, arrogance and greed. To achieve the appearance and feeling of Pleasure at the expense of another is a manifestation of Evil as defined by Spirit, who says. "Evil is the misuse of Ego". Whenever you put your needs or wants above those of another for whatever reason you are indulging your ego (your small sense of self) as opposed to your Divine self; that which is associated with the Creator.

COMMENTS FROM SPIRIT:

Dear Ones, Come home within your hearts to the Love that never ebbs; never faileth. Come home to the Pleasure of eternal peace; eternal Love for you and for all of Creation. This is the ultimate Pleasure; never to be sullied by lesser thought. Come home now. We Love you.

Blessings

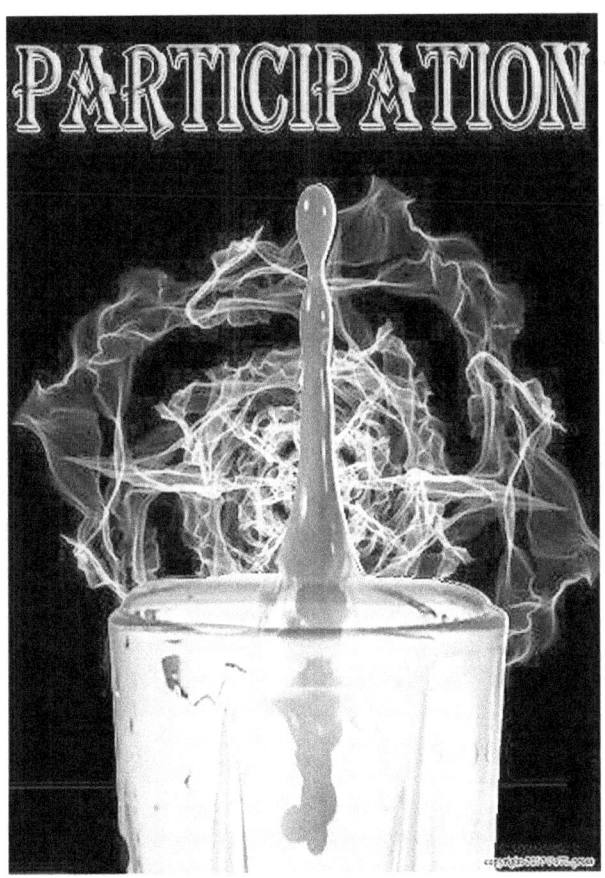

PARTICIPATION

    Life happens all about us in each moment whether we Participate or not. It is only when we grab life in our teeth and hang on for the ride that we truly experience all that which we came to this plane to Participate in.

    A relationship does not just happen by itself nor is it self-perpetuating or self-supporting. It is up to each individual to come forth in Participation to feed, nurture, co-direct and learn from the experiences of which the relationship is made. Lack of Participation is the best way in the world to bring about the end of the relationship as an openly positive force in your life experience.

The same is true of casual relationships. To steal a phrase from the world of computers; "Garbage in, Garbage out"; or in this case; nothing in, nothing out. Time and effort are never wasted; they are only invested. How much are you willing to invest in your life process?

Here we come to the crux of the matter. Are you willing to Participate in your own life? Are you willing to take some responsibility for the events and emotions of living or are you content to simply let life happen to you -- to be the victim? There is a saying from the Christian tradition that it is good to remember: "God helps those who help themselves." Bringing this word into your consciousness today suggests that it may be time to 'get off of your duff' and help yourself a little. If you simply sit there long enough you may just rot.

It is important that you Participate in whatever it is that you Participate in only with and from Love.

COMMENTS FROM SPIRIT:

Beloved Ones. Participate fully in this opportunity referred to as Life; for within it lie many of the lessons of Spirit that you have set forth for yourself. Do not let fear or lethargy hold you back. The lessons

will hold forever that you might experience them. Play at Life and do it NOW! There will never be a better time.

Blessings to you, each and all.

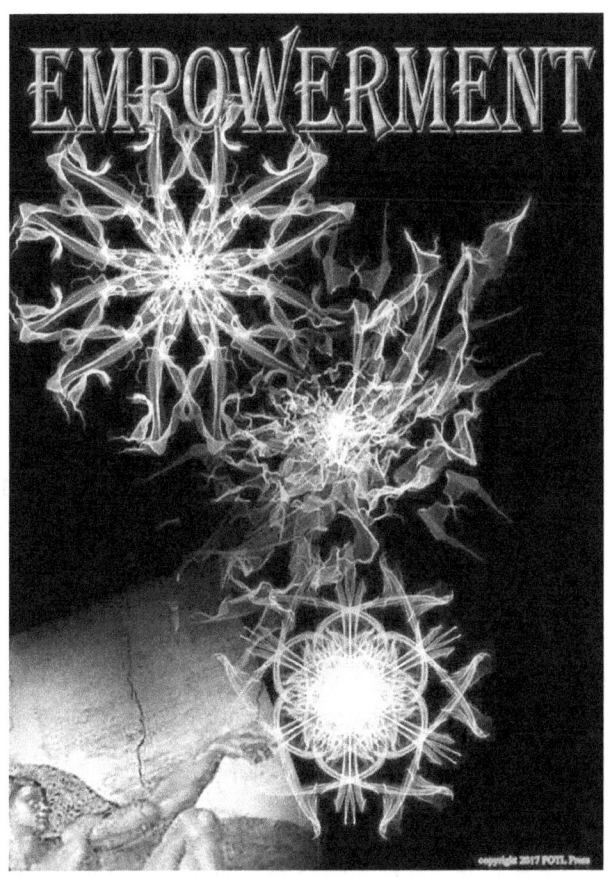

EMPOWERMENT

How often in our lives do we feel ourselves to be helpless? Perhaps we feel ourselves to be the victim of events or people who seem to have taken control over us.

This is all illusion. The only being that ever will or ever has had control over our lives is the Creator and ourself as an aspect of that Creator. Empowerment is simply realizing that we ultimately are the ones in control from the level of ourselves as Spirit. Remember; no one loves us more than ourselves in the non-judgmental form of our own soul. Our soul will do everything in its Divine power to ease our path while giving us the lessons that we have decided that we need. Empowerment is achieved by simply realizing and utilizing this in our daily life. No one else has any power over us except that which we choose to give him or her. All they can do is to make a tiny portion of this life unpleasant or uncomfortable. As an extreme, they can end this lifetime. So what.

All things are in Divine order at all times and in all ways whether we understand it or not and whether we like it or not. Other than overcoming our own fears (gee, perhaps that's one of the lessons), where is the problem in apparently cutting short one visit to the material realm? It is roughly akin to waking up earlier than we had planned. We may temporarily regret the end of the dream but we move on into the reality of our day-to-day living only to once again visit the world of dreams when we choose to do so. My very wise partner, Kim, summed this up nicely at the beginning of our relationship. She said to me when it appeared that this might not be the lifetime for us to partner, "I, too, am forever". Remember please that this so-called material realm life is but the dream of a dream and other than what we learn while we are here means absolutely nothing.

Some of us have chosen personal relationships that are oppressive in nature. There are lessons to be learned even in these distorted conditions. One of the major lessons is self-Empowerment from a place of Love, not anger. The object is growth; not vengeance. The partner who is the oppressor is living his or her own Karma day by day. That is punishment enough. When it is time to get out, do it! Remember to always do everything you do with and from Love. Bailing out simply because the relationship is uncomfortable or inconvenient won't do unless you have learned and accepted the lessons involved. It is extremely important to put yourself into your partner's experience and make whatever transitions must occur as gentle and loving as possible. That which you do unto others ...

Do not let someone else walk all over you. Remember that you always have a choice, and sometimes you have to travel through brambles in order to find the true path.

Self-Empowerment is the only Empowerment that is. You have never been without power; only without the awareness of the power you wield as part of your Divine birthright. Others such as I may tell you of your power but only you can allow yourself to own or use it on a conscious level.

There is a school of thought that seems to feel because of its innately poor self-image that the only way to build oneself up is by tearing others down. While this may give the impression of self-Empowerment, it actually has the effect of lessening one because all beings are One. This practice is an exercise of ego and should probably be avoided by the serious student of Spirit.

COMMENTS FROM SPIRIT:

Empowerment is a human term; a human concept. When totally within the heart of the Creator one is all-powerful in all ways at all times through the power of the Divine Love that has created all realms and all realities. There can be no Empowerment as there is no illusion of being less than All that Is.

Blessings.

FUN

Fun occurs when we joyfully place ourselves in the moment and only in the moment. When you forget all of the could-have-been's, should-have-been's, and ought-to-be's that the world and others, as well as ourselves, place upon us Fun is all that's left.

What better way to experience our partnership than in playful joy? We always have the choice of learning through pain or joy. Which sounds like more Fun to you?

There is no reason in this world why we cannot have enjoyment and Fun in every moment of every day. It all depends solely on our own mental attitude and outlook. If you simply refuse to see anything but joy and growth in every situation then there is absolutely no room or reason for anything but Fun. Enjoy!

It can be so very difficult for many of us to allow good things into our lives. Bringing this word into your consciousness at this time is a hint from Sprit that you are long overdue for a self-generated break from your daily grind. Only you can do this for yourself. See joy and Fun where you had only found drudgery and set yourself free!

Fun in its pure sense harms no one. Be careful not to acquire your Fun at the expense of another. That is an exercise in the misuse of ego. Misuse of ego is Spirit's definition of evil.

COMMENTS FROM SPIRIT:

Beloveds -- how can you not allow yourselves the wonderment and joy of All that Is? The wonders of the universe are your playthings, your toys, as you move through your childhood into the full grace and glory of all that which you are. Have Fun! The universe is your playpen!

Blessings to you all!

AWARENESS

Imagine that you place yourself in a sensory deprivation tank; floating in a bath of saltwater that exactly matches your body's specific gravity and temperature; in absolute and total darkness and silence. There is not a single thing in your universe but you -- the essence of 'self'. This is the beginning of Awareness. One can spend as much effort as one wants directing attention into the material world; even to the point of becoming a 'success' in that world and yet never becoming Aware in the slightest. Look within you will find the multiverse!

Each relationship has a life -- a persona -- of its own. It is up to each of us to learn to tap into that persona, to feel its pulse, judge its health or illness and act accordingly for the best interest of those concerned. When we become silent within ourselves in Awareness we make this task much simpler. Perhaps this is a good time to do just that.

It is only when we allow ourselves to move beyond mundane perception that we become Aware of the true nature of things. At that point, we recognize that all things are in Divine order at all times and in all ways whether or not we understand or approve. When we find ourselves in this place of understanding and acceptance we find our lives to become simple and joyful experiences.

Awareness ultimately involves an inner journey; an inner understanding and allowance and an inner peace. It is no mistake that this word has found its way into your world today. Take the time to recover the Awareness that you left behind a little at a time over many years. Come home to yourself. You'll find a loving landlord awaiting you and a sumptuous table of rewards spread in celebration of your return.

At times becoming Aware brings us into touch with aspects of ourselves that we have pointedly ignored for months -- or for years. This is not always a pleasant experience but it is truly a blessing. Once we become Aware of those areas of ourselves that we do not like we are free to remove them from our life pattern. Good luck!

COMMENTS FROM SPIRIT:

Let down your guards; let go your fears. Forget your apparent limitations and allow yourself to have the Awareness of your Divinity; your God-self. Manifest in the world as the god/goddess that is your inner and true self. Self Awareness is Divinity.

Blessings.

ENTANGLEMENTS

As we move through our lives, the ideal is to seek the 'shortest path of greatest light'. Unfortunately, because we so often listen to our human fears and desires, that path becomes ever more convoluted and confused by Entanglements. This is not necessarily a bad thing; it simply indicates that further lessons are required in certain areas. With all Love, we are providing them for ourselves. As we reach clarity and understanding within ourselves regarding a certain pattern or behavior the Entanglements associated will simply fall away. Thus the goal is not to attack the Entanglements but rather to seek further understanding and awareness of our self so they no longer exist in our experience.

Entanglements in a personal relationship can easily involve more than an interest in someone not already your partner. It can involve a goal or interest that takes away from your primary relationship. It can also relate to a loss of interest in that relationship. An Entanglement is anything that appears to complicate that which seemed to be running more smoothly before the advent of the Entanglement.

We always strive to have every aspect of every interpersonal relationship go as smoothly for us as possible. It can be very irritating when things become complicated to us. Remember please, that these are only lessons we are offering ourselves from the level of Spirit and when we decide to 'get the message' the lessons and Entanglements end in that area.

Entanglements are almost always an interpersonal phenomenon. While it is possible to misdirect and complicate one's life with things, most of us are too aware to allow that to happen to excess.

As with many concepts, Entanglements appear initially to be a negative. However, as we move through our lives we discover that the times of greatest pain and turmoil are also often the times of greatest growth and learning. Thus, even the most (apparently) negative of circumstances ultimately serves the Light, and us.

COMMENTS FROM SPIRIT:

There is but one Entanglement in the Universe. That is the Entanglement of One-ness from your heart to the Heart of Hearts; from your soul to the Soul of Souls. This Entanglement is Love; the greatest force in the Universe, and the greatest gift it is possible to give or receive. It is gladly given without restraint or limitation to each of you and to all of you.

Blessings.

REASSURANCE

    Every parent remembers the time after their child's first steps when the child could only walk or would walk better only when holding the parent's finger, a blanket, or a favorite toy. The mental reinforcement and strengthening that children (including ourselves) extract from an apparently outside source is a good definition of Reassurance.
    The more intimate the relationship on the emotional level the easier it is for us to let ourselves feel hurt or insecure. This is an unconscious return to the level of childhood outlined above and a cry for our loved one (parent) to give us their undivided loving attention

and (emotional) support. This is often a destructive pattern for both our relationship(s) and us.

This situation rarely manifests in a general relationship simply because at the point where one seeks and accepts Reassurance from another the relationship becomes a personal one. This is quite well illustrated in the common phenomenon wherein one person starts telling another (a friend) about their problems with their partner. As the communication progresses the two people are drawn closer and closer in their roles of infant and Reassuring parent until they often bond as a new partnership. The problem with this form if it is entered into unconsciously is that it sets the pattern for the relationship to come into being as a co-dependent relationship. Eventually, it's going to get very old to the 'parent' who is always carrying the majority of the load and who is liable to feel 'trapped' in the situation. The other pattern to be found here is that the 'child' is someone who is normally fairly self-sufficient but who felt insecure during the dissolution of the previous relationship. As they regain their composure and self-assurance in this instance the forced 'infancy' of the original contract begins to grate on them. This causes a great deal of stress in the new relationship. In either case, unless the cause is seen and consciously modified by both parties the new relationship would appear to also be doomed.

Ultimately, the only form of spiritual Reassurance that is not harmful (in the short-sighted human understanding) is the Reassurance one finds at the deeper (higher) levels within oneself. As we become closer within ourselves to the Ultimate Source there is an innate Reassurance that resides always within. Those who are not so developed spiritually will quite often see this as ego.

COMMENTS FROM SPIRIT:

Beloved children, so insecure in your Divinity; so unsure of your own worth; know ye that ye are the spawn, the seeds, the body, the heart, and the very soul of the Creator of all that exists. You seek Reassurance as the infant lion, king of beasts, seeks Reassurance from its parent. You, as does that cub, slowly and eventually grow in your own time into an innate awareness of your mastery; of your value to the cosmos. This is not a matter of Ego but simply is. Be Reassured. This is truth.

Blessings.

REJUVENATION

Rejuvenation comes from the root word juvenile - in Spanish; joven, and from the original Latin; juvinis. It refers to recovering a state of less than full maturity (in the eyes of the world). It refers to returning to a state of mind that refuses to take things as seriously as others would like us to. In other words, recovering the ability to laugh and play.

Things can become so very serious almost without warning even in the best of relationships. Rejuvenation: recovering one's youthful point of view, can often result in a rapid and gentle de-escalation of these situations. When we learn not to take everything so seriously we don't feel the need to posture and preserve our dignity. We find a middle ground much more easily.

However, there is a possibility that your partner might feel the need to maintain the posturing and might become very agitated and angry if you drop that need and 'act childishly'.

Used judiciously this energy can often return the relationship itself to its livelier and more playful youth.

Business and other relationships can sometimes benefit from a Rejuvenation. Sometimes, a playful attitude when one is least expected, offered in a non-abrasive way, can bring new life into an otherwise dull and boring situation

Day by day we plod through our lives; always grinding deeper ruts through which we travel until we have dug ourselves so deeply into our established paths that we can no longer see the options. "I can't do that because ---". "That won't work because ----". And so forth. Rejuvenation of self literally uplifts us to the point where we regain options and regain hope. Drawing this word into your awareness today suggests that you strongly contemplate this option and your need of it.

There is a huge difference between being child-like and childish. One can maintain a sense of responsibility and care for the welfare of others while enjoying oneself in life.

COMMENTS FROM SPIRIT:

It is only when one allows oneself to be out of touch with the Infinite that one feels weary or tired. Thus, the perception of the need for Rejuvenation is simply a reflection of the state of being that you have created the illusion of for yourselves. Return home to Love, Sweet Ones. That is all the Rejuvenation your Spirit could ever desire.

Blessings to you, each and all.

SIGNS

"Hi, honey! What's your Sign?"

"No trespassing."

Signs are just suggestions that when followed thoughtfully can make our lives much gentler and our paths much smoother. They can also be 'red herrings' intended to misinform and misdirect.

Many of our communication Signs in our intimate relationships are on the level of unconscious communication. This is sometimes seen in its extreme form with couples who have lived and/or worked together for decades. They can work side by side for hours with only an occasional nudge or grunt by way of communication. This may be a bit too much to expect for most of us but the fact that this particular word has found itself in your awareness today suggests that perhaps you have been ignoring some of the Signals and Signs that your partner has been displaying. Maybe that's one of the major reasons that relations are becoming a little more strained between the two of you. Take the time to really watch your partner's body language. Find the Signs that you have been missing and act on them in an appropriate way.

Our world is absolutely full of Signs: Street Signs, advertising, and warnings. We find that we ignore these at our own discretion and risk. Exactly the same is true of the Signs that Spirit provides for us in each interaction and every moment. Ignorance is no excuse. The lesson will come to you whether you are paying attention to the Signs or not. It's just that events are generally a lot more pleasant and easier if you are forewarned of their direction, purpose, and advent.

Pay attention to the Signs provided by the casual contacts found each day. Pay attention to these little things and you will find that the bigger things are far gentler for you.

Look now at your own life. What is going smoothly? What is not? Why isn't it? What would you tell someone else if the exact same thing was happening to them and they came to you for advice? Many times this is the easiest way to get a clear view of a situation regarding yourself. When you extract yourself from the equation it suddenly becomes much easier to see and understand the Signs in your life.

No Sign can serve you if you close your eyes or refuse to learn the meaning of it. It is your own blindness that causes you to travel other than the 'shortest path of greatest light'. There is absolutely nothing wrong with this. It simply indicates that you require more experience and learning in a particular area or areas and it probably won't seem to be quite as pleasant a journey as you might have experienced had you been more perceptive and receptive.

COMMENTS FROM SPIRIT:

No matter the Sign; no matter the apparent path, remember: there is no journey; there is only an arrival to that place you have never left. Never forget, Dearest Ones -- all paths lead you Home and limitless Love awaits you here.

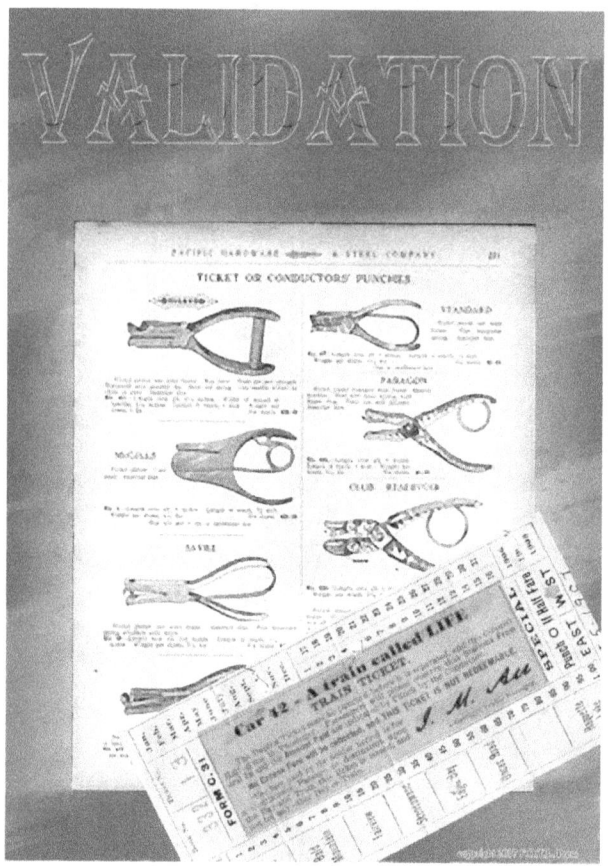

VALIDATION

Chackata, chukata, chackata, chuckata. The train of life chugs and rumbles on down the track of time. Some get on and others get off at the many whistle stops in history. Once on board, most everyone takes their assigned seat and waits patiently for the authority figure dressed in his celestial conductor's uniform to come along and ask for their ticket and their passport for this ride called life. Swiftly and expertly taking the paper in hand; he perforates it in the approved manner, in effect telling the passenger that it's O.K. to be alive - to be on the train.

Drawing this word today indicates that you are (at least in

some areas) doubting your right to life as you would like it to be. You are looking outside yourself to someone to whom you have given up at least some of your power. You are waiting for them to tell you that it is O.K. for you to be alive. How much simpler it would be if you kept your own power and KNEW that all things that you think, do, or say are in Divine order.

We consciously re-enter our childhood every once and a while when we feel the need to be nurtured and taken care of. We assume the 'helpless' persona, silently inviting our partner to Validate our neediness by assuming the 'nurturing parent' role. As long as both parties are conscious of and consent to what is going on (even though they would never talk about it) and it does not become as common as to set a rigid pattern it probably does little harm. It is important to remember that our only true strength comes from within ourselves and every time we reach outside we are in-Validating ourselves.

At times, we can become so demoralized (off-center) that we reach out wildly; grasping at straws and trying to find something -- anything -- that will buoy us up in the stormy seas of existence. When we come to the place of seeking Validation from the population at large we have reached this abyss of self-worth and we can expect Spirit to reach in with some rather heavy lessons to help us bring ourselves out of it. Hang on!

The only Validation that is of any worth is self-Validation. You are hereby invited to do so. As with so many other things, intent and focus are everything.

COMMENTS FROM SPIRIT:

You are totally Validated in every moment by the simple fact of your existence. Each and every one of you is a creation of the Creator by the Creator. There can be no greater nor can there be any further Validation. All that is left to do is to Validate yourself by recognizing and allowing all that you are to become evident in every moment. We Love and Bless each and all.

Blessings.

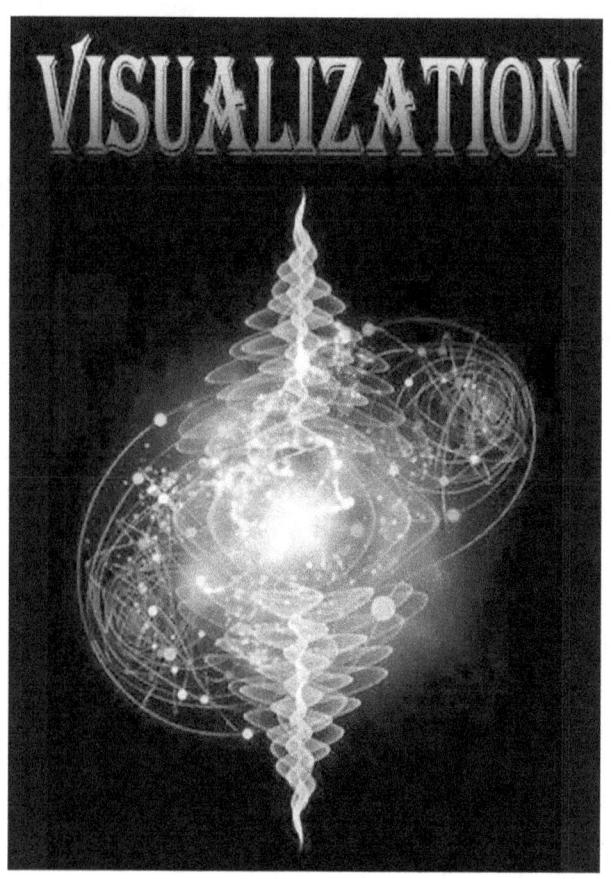

VISUALIZATION

    The first step involved in creating our physical reality is to create that reality in our minds and hearts. The more intimately we know and understand our creations before they manifest in the material world the more easily we can consciously co-create our world, our experiences, and our lessons. Visualization is the process through which we achieve that intimate awareness. If you are not already consciously entering this state might I suggest the practice of deep meditation as being an appropriate and powerful doorway leading to it?

    Visualize your perfect partner. Picture your perfect relationship. How do these pictures differ from what you experience everyday as your reality? What would you need to change besides the way you choose to perceive these things in order to more closely approach your idea of perfection? Drawing this word to you this day is an indication from Spirit that you have the power and the right to change your reality, and that Spirit is available and willing to help you to do so.

How is that promotion coming? Would you like a better job or better conditions in the job you now have? Does the neighbor's dog keep you up all night? Are those crazy kids down the street throwing wild all-night parties again? Visualization is one of the remedies for these and other aspects of your general relationships. While there are other tools every bit as powerful this is the one we are discussing at present. While in a meditative, centered state; create the scenario you would like to see in your inner vision. Nurture it within yourself and allow it to abide within you even after the meditation has ended. As we have all heard, "as above, so below; as within, so without" As we create the reality that we desire within our inner awareness; nurture and live in it, it begins to affect and change the material world around us.

Visualize yourself in total harmony within and without. Picture yourself living in total Christ Consciousness in every moment of every day. Why not? You are totally limitless. You have spent a lifetime Visualizing yourself to be the person that your parents and other authority figures have told you that you need to be or already are. Would you rather be that limited, helpless 'sinner' or would you rather be the individualized expression of All that Is that is your birthright? The choice is yours and the time to choose is now.

When you verbalize, pray, think, or Visualize, your thoughts are creating reality. Be very, very aware of this in each moment, and remember to BE LOVE in every moment and in every way. Also, be aware that the law of Karma states that "What goes around comes around." That which you create with your intent shall come back to you. Be careful what you Visualize for it will be part of your reality even if directed toward another. Let another's Karma take care of itself. It is not your job and you will only be demonstrating your own need for further lessons in a particular area.

COMMENTS FROM SPIRIT:

That which you Visualize -- IS. You are the co-Creators, Dear Ones. Yours is the gift of Vision and Creation, tools of your learning process. Whatever you create is for your own benefit, and is a gift of Love from your soul and from All that Is.

Blessings to each of you as you discover the reality of your infinity.

RECOGNITION

    Have you ever stared at a photo or the television screen, knowing that there is a distinct image that you are supposed to be seeing, yet your eyes refuse to connect with your brain? Suddenly and with a silent 'click' the connection is made; the image is found and locked into the visual center of the mind. Now, try as you might you cannot return to that place of not-knowing that had existed before. That is the essence of Recognition. It is that instant of 'getting it' after which you can never go back to the place of not understanding.

    There are a couple of areas of personal relationships that should be mentioned here.

The first is that magical moment when you first meet someone who has been in another lifetime or who is about to become in this lifetime an important partner to you. That magical moment when your eyes first meet and the spark of recall passes between you is Recognition. The eyes truly are the windows of the soul. You are peeking into each other's windows to see who lives there. Imagine the pleasant surprise when you find that it's an old friend and confidant, come back to help and Love you.

The second is a multiple occurrence. There are times when your partner is trying, consciously or unconsciously, to communicate their feelings or needs to you and you just don't 'get it'. Sometimes we can be so dense. Over and over the communication is attempted. Finally! That instant of Recognition comes, and the circuit is completed. Now, something can be done to change the way that things have been.

When we are dealing with the world at large it becomes very important to do so from a place of conscious participation. That is the only way in which we can consciously co-create. We must be awake and aware of what is happening around us. We must Recognize the patterns and reasons for these things and the lessons that these things are about to offer to us. The sooner we "get the point" or Recognize the lesson the more gentle is the learning process and the sooner we can move on to the next level of learning.

Here is the crux of the matter; the key to Recognition is to truly Recognize ourselves. For most of us, this is like so many areas; a matter of continually 'peeling the onion' of our own mis-perceptions of 'self' until we finally begin to approach the core of our reality, our god-self.

The only apparent harsh aspect of true Recognition might be when we fool ourselves by creating a false reality that supports our ego-needs then fool ourselves into accepting that as 'reality.

COMMENTS FROM SPIRIT:

Still, your mind, hush your fears. Feel the Love, and Recognize that you are; and that you are All that Is in an individualized expression.

Recognize that the only limitations you need express are those that you accept in that moment. Recognize that you live in the Love you require. It is up to you to open yourself to receive it. BE LOVE, Dear Ones, but BE LOVE first to and for yourself for you are the center and the reason for the universe as you perceive it. When you have understood this in its totality, you have just begun to Recognize yourself.

Blessings to you. BE LOVE.

UNIQUENESS

"How do you catch a one-of-a-kind rabbit?"

"That's simple. You 'neek up on it"

One of a kind. Each of us is a Unique and individualized manifestation of All that Is. Each of us has chosen an apparently different path, all of which are intimately interconnected in the fabric of what we call 'reality -- but that's another book. These many paths appear to be leading us helter-skelter into the unknown that we call the future.

If you were to take two Unique things and combine them intimately, creating yet another Unique entity, you would be creating a perfect example of a personal relationship. Regardless of appearances every situation and every experience is different in at least some degree from anything you have ever experienced before. Drawing this word to your consciousness today is inviting you to enter the moment of IS. Be present in the Uniqueness of the moment, of the company, of the situation, and glean from it all that it has to offer.

You are the most Unique thing in the Universe. So is your neighbor. So is your spouse and so are your children. At the same time, we are all facets of the Gem of Eternity: All that Is. Even though we are all one In the wholeness of that One-ness each face is distinct from every other and has its own characteristics and perspective. Never forget your Uniqueness and never forget that all are related in the most intimate way. Love your brother/sister as yourself, for you are One.

There is only one harsh aspect of Unique-ness. That is the aspect called loneliness. This occurs only when you lose sight of the

One-ness of all beings.

COMMENTS FROM SPIRIT:

Beloved ones. Do you not know that Uniqueness exists only in your own perceptions? All beings are aspects of All that Is. This is a bond that will never terminate. In your Earthly form, you feel and have the appearance of being Unique; as that is one of the major tools of your spiritual development. Use it wisely.

Blessings to you.

DISCOVERY

There it is! Look fast, before it gets away. Discovery can take a lifetime yet happens in an instant. To Dis-cover something means to remove from it that which has been disguising its true nature.

Personal relationships are a voyage of Discovery of self, of life, of partnership, of many things. As we have discussed at length in other sections of this book; relationship provides the most fertile field for growth in the human experience. Discoveries wait around every corner as you move through your intimate relationship experience.

Every transaction with every person in our experience has

within it the seeds of Discovery. Not only do we experience Discovery regarding the other person or persons involved but as we inspect our own actions and the reasons for them and as we view our reactions and the reasons for them we Discover deep secrets we have hidden from ourselves.

The core of the meaning of this word is Discovery of self. Once more we must peel the infinite layers of the onion of pseudo-self. As we do away with layer after layer of false and illusory notions of self what remains is the self we are creating.

Sometimes, the things that come to light during the process of Discovery are not things that are immediately pleasant to view or experience. That does not mean that the thing is not a good thing. Now that you can see the true nature of it, it can be dealt with quickly directly, and with Love.

COMMENTS FROM SPIRIT:

Beloveds, we invite you to Discover the Creator of All that Is within yourself, and yourself within the heart of All that Is.

Blessings.

CONTRIBUTION

Imagine that everyone decided that a mountain was needed where none existed before. The government wouldn't help but said that the people could have it if they would build it. Men, women, and children gathered. Each picked up as much rock and dirt as they could carry and they marched one after another to the site of the mountain. Each one dumped their burden and over a period of years and generations, a mountain grew where before there was none. Each of these people had made a Contribution to their common goal and as a result, that goal was achieved.

Every personal relationship can be classified as a partnership.

It is two (or more) persons who have consciously come together for the purpose of supporting and assisting one another in their growth. Each one makes their Contribution to this process and in turn, is the recipient of the Contributions of their partner(s) in life.

Whether apparently pleasant or unpleasant every interaction that we experience each day is a Contribution to our ongoing education and growth in this material realm. Please remember to remain aware of this fact as it marks the difference between being a victim and a student; between 'getting the message' and having to repeat the lesson at a more intense level.

The world; indeed the entire Universe exists to Contribute to the spiritual growth of each one of us. Remember this and open yourself to allowing and accepting these gifts on a moment by moment basis

Intent is everything. The intent with which you Contribute and the uses to which you put that which has been Contributed to you determine the (apparently) positive or negative effects that result. Don't forget -- one person's positive can seem to be another person's negative. Perception CREATES reality!

COMMENTS FROM SPIRIT:

As each grain of sand Contributes to a beach. So each one of you Contributes to the life experience of your brothers and sisters. Together then, you approach awareness of your oneness. The grains of sand find themselves to be a beach. You find yourself to be God/Goddess and All that Is.

Blessings.

LISTENING

    There is a huge difference between Listening and hearing. There is just as great a difference between Listening and not-Listening. Drawing this word to you this day is a statement from Spirit that you are not paying attention to the message being offered and you are missing something very important. Wake up and pay attention!

    Has your spouse ever exploded at you, yelling: "Darn it, you never Listen! I've been trying to tell you this for months now and you still don't get the message." If it hasn't happened yet pay attention or it may become part of your life soon.

What are you not getting? What are you not seeing? The harshest aspect of the word 'Listening' happens when you don't. There is a 'still, small voice within' trying to talk to you at all times. Are you Listening? Are you sure?

COMMENTS FROM SPIRIT:

Delightful beings of light, dressed in human flesh: Listen with your inner self; hear your own inner voice; the voice of the co-creator that you are. When you Listen to the material world or those in it you condemn yourself to perceive and operate from that level. Lift yourself beyond the farthest stars, Dear Ones. Come Home within yourself. Listen to the God/Goddess within and become what you hear.

PRACTICALITY

In an infinite universe, all things are possible -- they have already happened in fact. However, our material world selves exist in a distinctly finite manifestation of that infinity. This is due to our own sense of limitations and our buying into the 'laws' of physics and society. Given those limitations, Practicality often comes into play. Without them, it does not exist.

Practicality means: "Gosh, I'd really sorta kinda like to do something but it's more difficult/expensive/trouble than I'm prepared to face at this time so forget it." There are, of course, different levels of difficulty and different levels of determination, but what it boils down to is that the individual involved is not residing in their god/goddess self and/or is being lazy. They are living their limitations to the fullest. If you have drawn this word to you today, it is time to take a good, long, hard look at the stranger in the mirror.

COMMENTS FROM SPIRIT:

Practicality is your own determination of what you deserve from the Cosmos. When you arrive at the place within of knowing that you are an intimate part of All that Is, you will realize that All that Is, is you and is yours for the asking. There will be no need nor will there be any question of Practicality, for all things already are.

GENEROSITY

Generosity is another human concept. It refers to sharing freely that which you appear to own with someone who appears to need or require it. We are all one being in truth and that which you appear to give is only being transferred from one pocket in your trousers to another. There is no gain or loss. There is no gift or giving. There is only a balancing of apparent negative with apparent positive.

Many so-called 'primitive' cultures had a tradition of giving away those things that an individual valued most highly as they made the most meaningful gifts yet there was never an expectation of reciprocity.

How Generous have you been with your time and your affections toward your partner recently? Are you consciously or sub-consciously withholding these for some selfish reason? This word coming to you today suggests that that may be the case. Try to become more consciously aware of your partner's needs and make an attempt to fulfill them. After all, yours is the most intimate of human relationships - the most fulfilling and the most frustrating. Whatever you can do to make it run more smoothly benefits you also does it not?

How much does it cost you to let a stranger go through a door while you hold it for them? How much time do you lose if you let someone in ahead of you in a grocery line when you have a full basket and they have three or four items? Generosity is a simple matter. It is nothing more than a state of mind. It is the honoring of all as though they were another aspect of you. Another way to put that is: "Do unto others as you would have them do unto you." Wow! What a concept!

Generosity begins at home. Be generous in your Love of self. Do not scrimp in your recognition of your Divinity nor hold back your innate joy. Give yourself a day off -- a day of self-indulgence and pampering of body, mind, and spirit. Begin and end the day with deep meditation. Include an herbal steam bath and a full body massage. Listen to good music; gaze upon beauty.

When operating from the limitations that almost all of us cling to it is possible to be 'generous to a fault'. This refers to giving so much that either the recipient feels distinctly uncomfortable (what is your motive for giving -- what is their hang-up about receiving?) or you give away that which you need also; creating an apparent hardship in your own life. Listen to that 'still, small voice within'. It will tell you unerringly how much, to whom, and when.

COMMENTS FROM SPIRIT:

Generosity flows from an open heart. When you learn to truly Love all those about you there is no alternative than to share openly with them those things that have the greatest meaning -- the greatest value -- in your life. How can you not give to your Loved ones all that, that you are capable of sharing, when they appear to be in need? Have I not given to you All that Is?

RESOURCEFULNESS

Resourcefulness is a simple matter of using that which is available to you. The more far-sighted you are the more you will perceive is available to you. The more self-confidence and self-worth you have the more you will attempt to use and the more you will accomplish.

More is available to you in a personal relationship than in almost any other human endeavor. More lessons, more love, more challenges, more rewards, more support, and more intensity. What a gift!

General relationships provide a tremendous variety of experiences in which to be Resourceful. Any problem carries within itself the seeds of its own resolution. Be Resourceful!

COMMENTS FROM SPIRIT:

Behold, my Beloveds. You bear as your birthright every aspect of every plane of every reality and every universe. There is no Resource that you do not already own and yet there is but One, and you are that One. Be still, Beloveds, and know that you are Gods.

OPEN-HEARTED

    A closed fist cannot accept a gift nor a closed mind a new idea. To be Open-hearted indicates that you are willing to give and receive Love. A truly Open heart does not restrict the Cosmic flow of Love in any way but becomes transparent to it, simply being present in the flow; nurtured by it, and reflecting it into the world for the benefit of all.

    It is only when you can be truly Open-hearted with your partner; showing everything within exactly as it exists that you have a partnership in balance and in order. This is an extremely rare state for one person to achieve. When both partners achieve it and hold it you have conquered personal relationships.

Can you allow yourself to be vulnerable enough in the world to be Open-hearted in your day-to-day dealings in the world? Are you confident enough of your Divinity to let the world see the true you without the armor and the facade that most people carry as their public persona? Because you have been given this word today it is perhaps time to look at that aspect of your self and see how to improve it. Spirit is there to help.

As with so many other words and concepts, the most important, and the most difficult person to truly open your heart to is yourself. We hide so much of our true nature -- both positive and negative -- from ourselves. We pretend that we are less than Divine. We listen to the echoes and rumblings of our egos. Open your heart to all that you are and all that you can become if you only will allow yourself to do so.

There can be no harsh aspect to Open-heartedness. From time to time, others may seem to take advantage of you but that is their problem; not yours. No one can ever cheat or hurt you. They can only damage themselves and assist you in learning your lessons.

COMMENTS FROM SPIRIT:

To be Open-hearted is to throw open the doors of every church, every monastery, every cloister that ever has been. These structures try to contain the Creator. Each person who is truly Open-hearted sets the Creator free to walk among the material world. BE LOVE Dear Ones. Throw open the doors of your hearts and let the world see the Creator within!

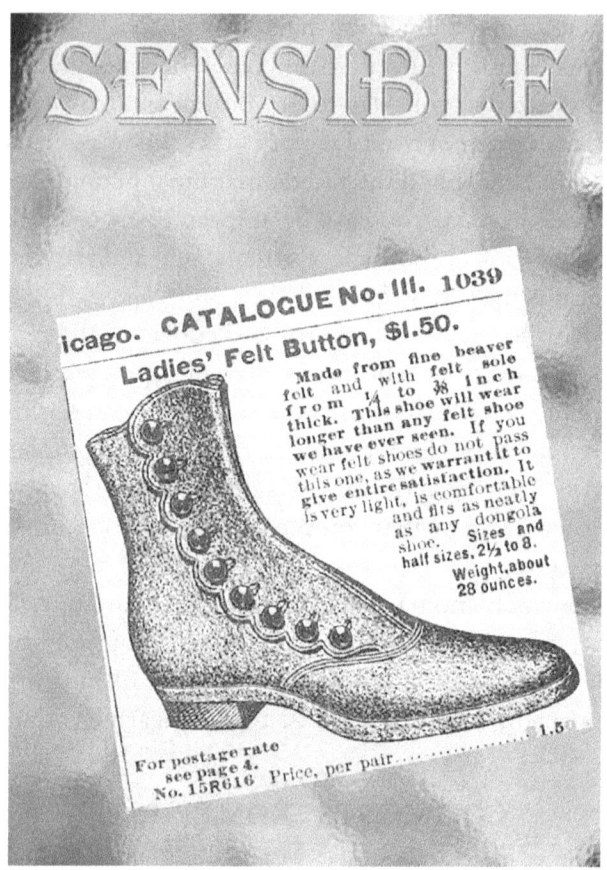

SENSIBLE

Usually what the speaker really means when we hear the phrase "be Sensible" is that they think you would be smarter to see things their way. To be spiritually Sensible is to always follow that that you believe to be the shortest path of greatest light in any given situation. This is not always the (immediately) gentlest path nor is it often the easiest path. The 'Sense" in Sensibility is a combination of (here's an oxymoron for you) 'common' Sense and our innate Sense of 'right' ness and 'wrong' ness. When you are attuned to and honor these Senses, you are truly being Sensible.

To be Sensible in a personal relationship it is necessary to constantly be attuned to the thoughts and patterns of your partner. It is not enough simply to hear that which is spoken but to become aware of those unspoken needs and concerns that are surfacing and to act upon them in a gentle and honorable way. Perhaps this is an area in your life that could use some fine-tuning. There must be some good reason that this word has come to you today. Ask Spirit. Help awaits you.

Being Sensible in general day-to-day activities simply involves acting from your highest awareness in each situation. Whether you are dealing with a homeless person or a bank president remember that each one is a manifestation of All that Is; perhaps under distressing circumstances and pronounced challenges; and treat them accordingly.

COMMENTS FROM SPIRIT:

Beloved ones. We ask you to search your self for those highest of Sensibilities that reside within. The knowingness of your intimate and pervasive connection with one another and with Divine Spirit represents all that you are and all that you strive to become. We Love and support you as you explore the realities of your own creation and as you climb once more into the heavens of self. Blessings.

CURIOUS

Curious is a Curious word. One can either BE Curious (odd) or one can possess a Curious nature and thus be Curious. Are you Curious as to which of these meanings apply here? Well, wonder no longer. While you may be the first, we will proceed to explore the second meaning.

One of the major tools that we have in our growth experience is a Curiosity as to what would happen if....?
When one of these 'what ifs' calls us loudly enough, we follow it into a whole new level of learning opportunities and experiences. Curiosity is what brought us into our intimate relationship. Never

underestimate the power of Curiosity. It is one of the hidden powers of the material universe. Curiosity is many times the compelling and propelling force that leads the relationship into new directions and dimensions.

Many times when Curiosity about your partner or your partnership wanes, 'the magic' can be perceived as being gone from the relationship.

If this is the case in your life it is not necessarily a bad thing. Certainly, you can try to revive the relationship and many times this will happen; carrying both partners to a new level of growth and understanding. Be aware, however, that each relationship is only a tool to help us move forward and that every tool has it's own built-in limitations. When you reach the limit of that tool's ability to assist you and continue to use the tool it becomes a crutch and holds you back. Only you will know if it is time to move on and then only after you have tried to move things up and into that new level without success. When it is time to move on; do what you must do. Do it always from and with Love, but remember you do no one a favor to drag it out.

Many people still feel that they 'have to stay together for the kids'. They have forgotten that we all select the parameters of our lives before entering our bodies and that we choose our parents based on the experiences they will provide for us as well as other aspects. Thus; if a separation appears to be in your best interest, remember the children also have chosen that decision and the consequences of it.

Along with necessity, Curiosity and laziness are the mothers of invention. These three concepts have been the leading forces in the technological growth of the human species. Be Curious about your world. Explore it top to bottom, side to side. Look at it under a microscope and from a weather satellite. How does it affect you and how can you best affect it? The more Curious you become the more answers you will find (and the more questions). The more actively you peruse life the more you will learn to live.

Curiosity regarding self takes two forms. The first and generally least important is Curiosity regarding the physical self. The second and most important is Curiosity regarding the inner self. You may take this word's appearance in your reality today to mean that you are cordially invited to participate in an inner safari to the site of 'darkest you'. It only appears dark because it is unknown to you. As you enter these remote areas you will find that you bring Light with you. There are only two forces in the world. There is Love and there is Fear; the absence of Love. We tend to fear those things we do not yet know. Use your Curiosity and get to know the inner you, and the fear that begets low self-image and diminished self-worth will be defeated.

As the saying goes, "Curiosity killed the cat". Luckily none of us are cats. As with every other tool, there is a Divine warning label urging you to use common sense while operating the equipment. Do all that you do from love and with love; mind your own business first and foremost and there will be no harsh aspects to Curiosity.

COMMENTS FROM SPIRIT:

Curiosity comes only when you forget your true Divine nature. When you connect with that Divine nature fully you are one with All that Is. There is nothing that you are not intimately involved with or cognizant of. Thus, Curiosity has no place other than in the material experience.

Blessings.

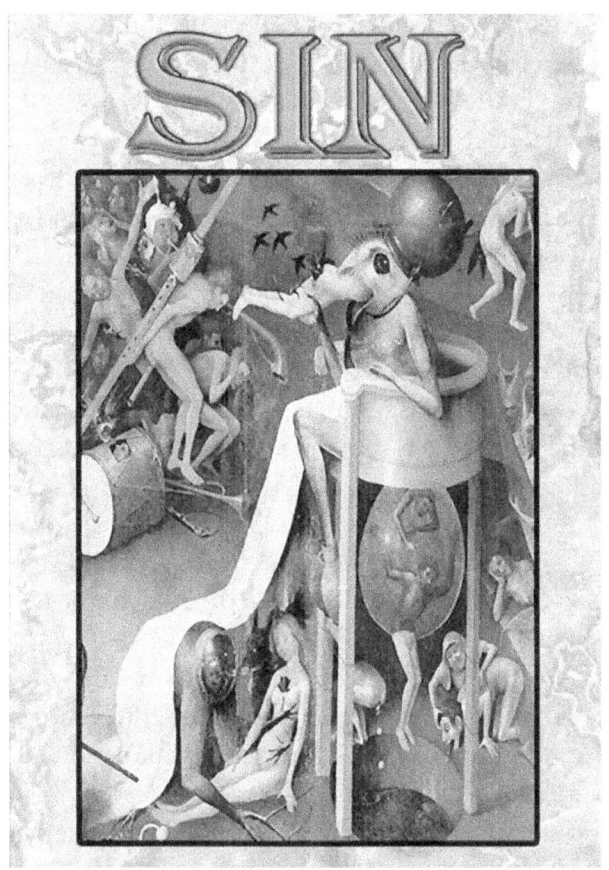

SIN

    This word has had one of history's worst P.R. jobs done to it. The origin of the word 'Sin' comes from the practice of Archery. A shot was either a "hit" or a 'Sin'.
The word used to describe when the archer shot an arrow at a target and missed was 'Sin'. To Sin meant only that you have missed the mark. There is always another chance to do better; to come closer to the mark.
When those archers 'Sinned' they would walk downrange; retrieve their arrows and try again. That is exactly the same thing we should do when we have 'Sinned'. We recognize that we did not accomplish

that which would have been the best possible in the circumstances. We gather ourselves up and, armed with our new awareness, prepare ourselves to do better next time. That's all there is to it. No fire. No Hell. No brimstone. No everlasting torment.

What kind of a Supreme Being would allow torment for all of eternity for one small error of omission or commission -- kinda seems like overkill to me.

The concept of Sin is strictly a creation of religion -- not of Spirit. It has been used since time immemorial to control the 'faithful'. Spirit has told me the following:

1) "Religion is Man's manipulation of Man in the name of God. Spirituality is each soul's recognition of their One-ness with that Creator".

2) "The definition of 'Evil' is the mis-use of ego".

3) "Given that definition, the organized religions of the world are also the greatest Single source of 'Evil' in the history of Mankind.

That which is a 'Sin' in a relationship is defined on a moment-by-moment basis by you and your partner. If you make every attempt to honor your partner as yourself in every moment there will be a minimum of perceived 'Sins'.

Probably the worst 'Sin' is to go against your own sense of 'rightness'. If you can live in your integrity, there will be no 'Sin' against self. The worst aspect of 'Sin' is that it can be used as a weapon against ourselves.

Remember, please, that everything (yes, EVERYTHING) that happens in our lives is a gift of Love and an opportunity to learn and grow. All things are in Divine order at all times WHETHER WE LIKE THEM OR NOT; WHETHER WE UNDERSTAND THEM OR NOT!

COMMENTS FROM SPIRIT:

Beautiful ones; Children of my heart. Do you not know that there can be no such thing as 'Sin'? There is only growth. You all grow in your own way, in your own path, and at your own rate. But remember: There is no time and all times are now. There is no separation and all beings are One. There is no journey but only an arrival. We welcome with open heart all those who have never left. Dream your dreams, Dear Ones, as you sleep soundly on the pillow of My Love.

Blessings to you, each and all.

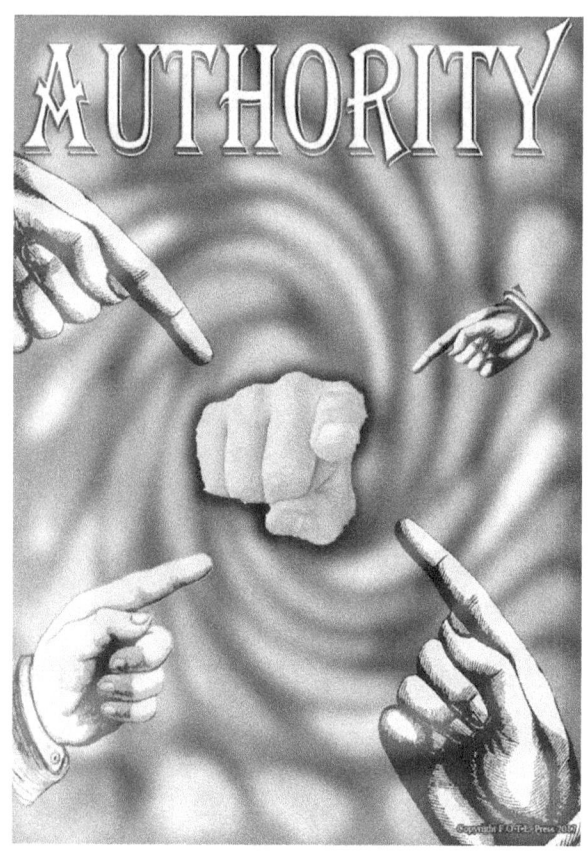

AUTHORITY

    Authority is a tenuous thing. Some folks think that they have it but don't. Others don't give it a second thought and as a result, seem to have it in abundance. The reality is that the only true Authority in the universe is Love. We filter that Authority through our integrity. Anyone who pretends to have any other Authority is exactly that: a pretender. There are those who may appear to have or seem to feel that they have Authority over you as a result of their position in the societal hierarchy. People such as parents, bosses, police, and other Authority figures will do all that they feel they can get away with in their attempt to control all or part of your life. It is up to you to determine how much of your autonomy and self-reliance you are willing to give up in each circumstance and for how long. You are the ultimate arbitrator of Authority in this incarnate form and ultimately on a karmic level, you are the party responsible for your actions and inactions.

It is quite often the case in a personal relationship that the partner with the stronger personality overshadows their partner on a day-to-day basis. This can take place in decision-making, conversation, and in other ways. What has happened is that the subordinate partner has abdicated their Authority. The only way for one person to gain Authority over another is for the second person to give away their power and integrity. The word 'Buddhism' means among other things: 'the middle path'. It is strongly suggested that if you recognize your relationship in the previous sentences you communicate with your partner about the situation and seek together that middle path. You have come together into a relationship for mutual benefit; not for the glory and comfort of only one of you.

Everywhere we turn in this low vibration material world there are those who would steal your Authority over your own life. As always the choice is yours. I suggest that you re-read the previous information before you let them have it, though.

The Creator delegates Authority and that Authority is delegated to and through our own souls. After all; who knows us better than our own soul which is intimately connected with Spirit? Our soul oversees our life experience and we are the gods of our own existence. At the soul level, we are the immediate ultimate Authority for our own lives and have total responsibility for our actions.

Authority is another word for power. There is an old and very true saying regarding the material plane. "Power corrupts, and absolute power corrupts absolutely". The more apparent Authority any person or governmental entity has the more likely it is that they (or it) will become twisted in integrity. Power is an addictive drug. The more one has the more one wants -- at any cost. Just say NO! The only Authority that you need is yours as your birthright.

COMMENTS FROM SPIRIT:

There is but one Authority in the entire cosmos. That Authority is the Authority of Divine Love. It is without beginning; without end. It is without limits and without malice. It is yours, Dear Ones. It is the essence of you. There is none above Love. There is none above your highest self that is that Love. Blessings of the universes fall upon your heads and overflow your hearts. The ultimate Authority is YOU!

Blessings to you.

REALIZATION

Realization is just a fancy way of saying that someone has finally 'gotten the point' and is now ready for the next lesson in the series; whatever it may be. We continually build upon the ramparts of that which we have already accomplished. That is why it is so critical that we build our foundations soundly; Realization after Realization.

We work constantly with our partners to achieve ever greater levels of understanding of ourselves and our greater nature. Some of the lessons seem to come effortlessly while others drag on and on until finally; with a metaphysical blinding flash, Realization hits and the background music swells to a crescendo.

The same is true in casual relationships except usually the lessons are smaller and the music isn't quite as loud.

Self-Realization is of course the ultimate Realization. To truly see and recognize our greater -- our god/goddess -- self in every detail and aspect of our lives and in every moment is Realization in its highest and most important form.

Although we don't always appreciate what we learn when we achieve a Realization; we would do well to remember that it is all for our benefit and it's all from Love.

COMMENTS FROM SPIRIT:

Quiet your mortal senses, Beloveds. Travel to your innermost, innermost. Be still now and KNOW that you are All that Is. There is no greater Realization.

Blessings.

LAUGHTER

Laughter is most often what happens when the joy you have within bursts forth from the boundaries of your physical being as sound. It is the exuberance of unfettered youthfulness and the glory of a new dawn all rolled into one. It is the Creator's Love made audible.

Laughter is often the glue that holds a relationship together. Imagine a relationship without Laughter. It's a pretty grim picture, isn't it? If there is no healthy Laughter in your relationship you are living a lie. Change it TODAY!

Laughter is also a wonderful thing in our daily lives. Unfortunately, most people in the material realm are so deeply insecure that your Laughter is often perceived by them to be a put-down or a threat and they respond with aloofness or anger due to those insecurities. Laughter in the stream of life is much like that popular gelatin dessert; there's always room for it. Just be sure to Laugh in such a way that even the most distanced and insecure person feels comfortable with it. This is just one more manifestation of BE-ing Love. When you Laugh from your inner joy you brighten the world about you.

Step back a few paces and take a good long look at who you have allowed yourself to become. Look at the walls you have built; the limitations that you have accepted and endorsed. Look at how you may have hidden the light of your being under a bushel basket of material world cares. See all this through your limitlessness and see and feel the joy of the lessons you have set for yourself. See the growth that awaits you. You can choose to learn either through joy or through pain. Choose joy, and let Laughter lead your way!

Laughter can be a double-edged sword. It is one thing to Laugh with pure loving joy. It is quite another; and quite dangerous in many ways, to Laugh at the situation or condition of another. Just remember -- what comes around goes around. By Laughing at another you are demonstrating that you do not yet understand the reason for the lessons that they are experiencing. Spirit of course, with all of the Love in the universes, is going to assist you in gaining the necessary understanding. (This comes under the heading of: "Be careful what you ask for because you will get it!")

COMMENTS FROM SPIRIT:

Dear Ones,

> *The skies are filled with Laughter,*
> *The earth resounds with joy.*
> *The firmaments are your plaything;*
> *Eternity is your toy.*
> *The path that you have chosen,*
> *The life that you now live,*
> *Is a creature of your notions;*

*A place designed to give
You all that you need to grow to God.,
    Now sprout the seed of who you are
And who you think you've been.
    And shout your joy -- with Laughter sing!
As you come home...
        ... where you've always been.*

Blessings.

CALM

Calm is the condition one achieves just before entering serenity. It is the suburb of serenity so to speak. Another suburb is peace. To refresh your memory, here is what Spirit had to say regarding serenity:

"Go to that place within you where the Creator resides. Feel the warmth, Love, and abiding peace that is your due; your birthright. Lay down all fears, all troubles, all doubts, and immerse yourself in total Love. Welcome to Serenity. Welcome home."

Calm is the last stop before this place. It is the inner self at rest; untroubled by rent payments or screaming children. It is the innermost temple where all who enter are silent in meditation and prayer. It is who you are when you set the world aside and become your higher nature.

Calm, placid behavior is of great benefit in any relationship. While there are those couples who seem to thrive on antagonism and chaos this is not a recommended course for those who would choose moderation in their lives. No one wants to come home to a shrieking harpy or an angry blowhard after their day's work in the world.

We find the heart of Calmness (literally) lies within. Calmness, like charity, begins at home. The only way you will be able to face the world or your partner in a Calm and balanced way is to actually be Calm and balanced within yourself. Because you have drawn this word to you today there is a strong suggestion from Spirit that perhaps you have lost that center somewhat; that you have become less than Calm in all aspects of your life.

Consider this to be an engraved invitation on a silver platter:

"You are cordially invited to get back into harmony with yourself and with your inner peace. Hosts of elevated beings eagerly await your participation in reclaiming your Calm. Your attendance is strongly urged. RSVP"

I'd pay attention if I were you.

COMMENTS FROM SPIRIT:

The greatest turmoil; the loudest chaos is Calm and silent when viewed from a great enough distance. Should you find yourself in not-Calmness simply detach from the human view and come home to the view that knows no imbalance; that hears no Discord. All things are in Divine order at all times. It is the way of all things; there is no other. All that you perceive with your mortal senses is illusion. Come home to clarity. Return to your native sense of Calm. Be here now. We await you.

Love.

REJOICE

    Rejoicing is the celebration of unbearable joy. To draw this word to you today indicates that things in your life are about to take a remarkable turn for the better.

    The problems or difficulties that have plagued you in the recent past are about to explode with a flair of trumpets a flare of skyrockets and a burst of confetti. Surprise! This is simply a manifestation of the beauty that has always remained within them. The lessons which they were are simply gifts of Love from you and to you; not the problems which you sometimes perceived them as.

    Expect to hear some very good news in the near future. In

some particular area, things have never been better! It's all true, and it's all a gift from All that Is directly to you. Isn't it nice that other people get to share in it, too?

How could there possibly be a harsh aspect to Rejoicing? Just remember that not everyone will understand or wish to share in it. That is their choice and no concern of yours. You cannot force joy on anyone, so don't try.

COMMENTS FROM SPIRIT:

To Rejoice is the heart of Be-ing. Understand yourself and your place in the universe, and you will have no choice but to Rejoice. Blessings to you, Dear Ones. Our Love for you knows no bounds; no limits.

Blessings.

JOY

Joy is the blending of extreme happiness, peace, and Divine Love. It is transformational. It changes all those whom it touches. It is often a direct gift from an angelic presence. These powerful occasions are often marked by a perpetual grin and helpless tears of happiness. Joy is one of the greatest blessings offered to humankind. You must indeed be in a special 'place' if this energy is offered to you this day!

Joyful personal relationships are a rare and beautiful thing. You are being offered the opportunity to move toward that goal. There are many ways to do so. Listen to your heart, and follow. Spirit once asked me to tell a student: "Follow your heart, for your heart knows your soul."

Joyfully interacting in a general relationship is a very rare occurrence. Enjoy this gift and study how it comes about so that you might generate this opportunity for yourself in the future. In most cases, it is impossible to experience this Joy in a casual relationship without it becoming at least to some degree a personal and intimate connection.

Inner Joy is an ideal 'place' to live your life. Start now.

COMMENTS FROM SPIRIT:

Joy is the natural state of being-ness. It is the highest vibration life is capable of sustaining in the material plane. It is one of the higher vibrations in the etheric and is a medium level harmonic of the vibration of Divine Love; the vibration of creation. Any state less than Joy is incomplete and crippling. Live in Joy -- let it radiate from your heart, your eyes, your very being! Let this energy be your calling card and touch others with Joy at every turn.

Blessings.

HUMOR

    Spirit loves to Laugh. Humor is one of the greatest teaching tools used by Spirit. The nice thing about the humor of Spirit and the point at which it departs radically from human Humor is this: The humor of Spirit does not rely on the embarrassment or pain of another for its 'kick'; whereas most human Humor does.
    Knowing when to Laugh and when not to Laugh has marked the survival or demise of many a relationship. Laughing at the wrong time can easily be fatal to a relationship (sometimes to an individual as well!). Please remember that you are in a relationship in order to be mutually supportive -- not mutually destructive. Laugh with one

another and at yourself.

When healing is needed; Laugh together and be healed.

Laughter (again: with -- not at) can smooth over those tense moments we seem to find in our day-to-day living. Let's say that a blankety-blank individual rushes up to the line in the grocery store one step ahead of you. They have a full basket and three non-stop screaming children. You've got a loaf of bread and a package of frozen Brussels sprouts and ten minutes to get home and start dinner. The 'normal' reaction would be one of irritation and/or anger. Take a second to see the situation through someone else's eyes. See the humor in it. You'll find that your whole attitude (and often the situation) has changed for the better.

Laughing AT someone is not the act of an enlightened being. Compassion and understanding would probably be a more appropriate choice. Having the strength and insight to Laugh at yourself is a great power. When something appears to go wrong in our lives it is only because we have chosen to receive a lesson and/or healing in that area. How we choose to perceive the situation determines how difficult it will be for us to move through it. Once we arrive at the mental point of being able to Laugh at our selves for getting into this situation we have defused it to a manageable position in our life. Humor is a great healer. Don't be afraid to use it.

COMMENTS FROM SPIRIT:

Joyful Laughter is God's Love made audible. It is the singing of the angels, the music of the spheres. Laugh long, loud, and heartily -- with Love and from Love. When you are done, you are nearer the heart of the Creator.

Blessings.

PROSPERITY

As many other people have, I have had my battles with Spirit regarding Prosperity and my perception of its distinct lack in my life. After several years of dedicated service to Spirit; never charging a penny and just barely squeaking by month after month, year after year, I finally blew up. "Spirit", I yelled "I am sick and tired of never having enough money to pay my rent on time. I deserve, demand, and expect Prosperity in my life, starting now!" Spirit answered with a smirk: "Sure; no problem. Oh, by the way, do you know what true Prosperity is?"

Uh oh.... think I'm in trouble...

"I think so...." I said.

"Prosperity is freedom from want"; Spirit informed me "and you can work on it from either end of the equation. You can have more which can give the impression of Prosperity; or you can learn to be happy with less; which is true Prosperity. When you are happy with less and not in need you are ready to receive more. At that time; if it lies within your life plan you will be given more."

Gee...Thanks...I think...

Like the old song says; "You don't always get what you want (but you get what you need)".

Prosperity in a personal relationship occurs when your joint cup runneth over with satisfaction and joy. This is a rare occurrence in many partnerships and merely uncommon in many others. It is truly a rare couple who maintains this feeling of partnered Prosperity a majority of the time. If you are one of these; blessings to you. If you are not it is a wonderful goal to pursue together.

Most of the people we encounter in our daily lives have a much different perception of Prosperity. They view Prosperity as the value of your house, your car, your clothing, and the beauty or monetary worth of your partner. These are totally fallacious values; temporary and shallow. True Prosperity occurs when your life is a rich broth of resources and experiences in which you consciously immerse yourself., in an effort to learn and grow.

Prosperity is what you decide it should be. As with every other aspect of our existence, the way we choose to perceive our world (and ourselves) creates our reality. What does your reality look like right now? In this moment, do you have clothing on if you need it? Are you starving? Do you have a roof over your head?
Chances are that in this moment you have all that you require. That, my friend, is Prosperity.

The only harsh aspect to Prosperity is when you expect too much of it.

COMMENTS FROM SPIRIT:

Prosperity; Dear Children, is in the same mind that perceives lack. They are the two ends of the same stick and that stick exists only in the human experience. Forget the stick for you are -- you have -- you own, All that Is. How could you measure a proportion of everything when all there is, is All there Is?

Blessings.

TRIUMPH

Triumph is another of those 'material world' concepts. In order for there to be Triumph, there must first be conflict and an enemy. To be in total balance seems to be totally unachievable and seems to be an unattainable situation for most of us most of the time. Given that state of awareness (or is it non-awareness) Triumph is a very real concept. It is our conquering of that area in our life that appears unbalanced and seems to challenge us. The true challenge, of course, is almost always fear of one sort or another.

Personal relationships provide endless opportunities for Triumph. The opportunity for Triumph over large and small temptations is a daily occurrence. The temptations are not just those of the flesh but also the temptation to be short-tempered; to put your own comfort or pleasure above your partner's 'just this once'. It can be as simple as eating that last cookie before your partner gets home even when you know that it's their favorite. And the list goes on.

Get a large sheet of paper. Write down all of the ways and all of the opportunities that you have in large ways and small; both in general and in one-to-one situations, to gain advantages over others in the material world.
Don't do them.
That is Triumph. Our 'enemy' is ego. Our 'foe' is greed. That which we seek to conquer is our own lower-level instincts.

The only Triumph possible is Triumph over self. Since this word has been given to you this day it is obvious that you are experiencing challenges in your life involving struggles with self. It may be that you are feeling like a victim rather than being the student. It may involve your sense of your own integrity. Whatever it is; Spirit has noticed and is here to help you (whether you like it or not) by offering you a series of concentrated lessons involving your challenges in order that you might conquer them. Good luck! Remember to remain the student and the process will be quick and painless!

Do not set your sights so blindly on Triumph that you attempt shortcuts to arrive there. Might does not necessarily make right. In fact, it usually leads one astray from 'right'. Do not let your ego lead you astray. After all; it is exactly that which you are seeking Triumph over.

COMMENTS FROM SPIRIT:

Beloveds; the greatest Triumph; indeed the only Triumph is Triumph over self. The Triumph of the soul over the darknesses of the human spirit and psyche is the challenge you have given yourselves and it is the victory you seek. We Love and support you as you grow toward the wholeness that you are.

Blessings.

HEALING

Healing brings us back once more to the concept of 'balance'. The only mode of existence that requires Healing is one that is out of balance in some way. Healing is simply bringing an out-of-balance situation nearer to its Divine center. Drawing the word 'Healing' assists you in becoming more balanced in one or many areas in your life.

Living together even with the best of intentions we constantly bump and scrape one another emotionally. This is normal and even desirable for we learn through this process what to do and what not to do to achieve and maintain harmony in our household. Sometimes we lose track of the purpose of all those little nudges we give and receive. At those times it becomes easy to be angry with your partner or with the situation. Call Healing energy to the rescue in order to move your perceptions and attitude nearer to the balance of center. The energy represented by this word is here to help you do just that.

Drawing this energy to you in response to a question about general relationships is unlike many of the other energies that are more dilute in a general relationship than a personal one. In the personal relationship, the discord is mitigated by the strength of the partnership and its romantic love acts as a buffer; softening the impact in most instances. That aspect is not present in most general relationships; making it easier to become irritated and out of balance. Reactions to perceived indignities are generally quicker, stronger, and held longer. Invite this energy of Healing to be your buffer as you work through these situations. Remember -- center is the place of least turbulence. This makes it easier to regain your balance and perspective.

Healing in response to a personal question can deal with your response to outside stimuli as outlined above. More commonly it has to do with our out-of-balance view of our actions and ourselves. The energy of Healing invites you to go within and see yourself from the viewpoint of Spirit. You are created of the Creator by the Creator. Thus; you are a part of the body and Spirit of the Creator.

How could the Creator not be worthy --?

How could the Creator not be Loved --?

How could anyone judge the Creator as being in error --?

Even seemingly gross errors or 'sins' are opportunities to learn not to repeat your actions and thus are in Divine order. Learn to Love yourself at all times -- without hesitation, without reservation. This is true Healing.

COMMENTS FROM SPIRIT:

Healing consists of returning your focus to existence within the heart of the Creator. No more. No less.

Blessings to you.

DARING

The true meaning of being 'Daring' is to go beyond what those around you consider 'politically correct' or 'safe'. It also means 'to extend yourself beyond someone else's concept of comfort'.

Because personal relationships are so much a vehicle for personal growth and awareness there is a constant opportunity and indeed; demand for Daring acts and Daring thoughts. These do not have to be confrontational. In a solid, high-level relationship they rarely will be.

Dare to follow your integrity. Dare to allow yourself to manifest at your highest level in every transaction in every situation. Dare to go against the 'dog eat dog' flow that most of the world seems to float upon. Be the essence of Divinity that your inner self has always been. It is not always easy. It is not always comfortable. That is why it is Daring to do so.

There is an old saying: "Consider the turtle; it never gets anywhere without sticking its neck out". Spirit is telling you through the messenger of this word in your awareness today that it is time to stick your neck out; to exceed the boundaries of propriety and safety that others would like to force upon you and step out decisively in the direction of your dreams.

The only harsh aspects of true Daring are temporary and ultimately of little lasting consequence. You may be temporarily embarrassed or even scorned but that is a small price to pay as you have lived your integrity.

COMMENTS FROM SPIRIT:

Daring is another of those human concepts that have no correspondence in Spirit. When one is all things there is nothing that is beyond one's abilities. There are no situations where one is not Lord of all they perceive. Blessed ones: feel the strength of your nature; your innate and

indwelling self. Allow yourself to manifest as the king of your world, the queen of your life, the Creator of your reality. All these things are true. Do you Dare to allow them?

Blessings to you.

INVENTIVENESS

Some people say that necessity is the mother of Invention. If that is so the aunts must be laziness and greed; for they are responsible for as much Invention as necessity ever was. In reference to this word in a reading; we are speaking of assembling the serendipitous parts of our lives in a previously unused way.

Other than the obvious physical aspects Inventiveness in a personal relationship helps to keep it alive and growing. Nothing is more stifling or deadly to a relationship than day after day; month after month; year after year of dull sameness. Change the way you greet your partner at the end of the day. Try new television programs or suddenly escape with your partner for a day in the mountains or the beach. Try a new food or a new restaurant. Change is part of the life's blood that nurtures both personal and partnered growth.

The same general meaning holds true for our daily interactions outside the home. There is a sameness that creeps into our lives; nibbling away our interest and vitality in undetectable segments until there is nothing left but gray. Inventiveness is the road out of this rut. Receiving this word today is not only an invitation but a strong recommendation to do something unexpected and out of the ordinary!

On a spiritual level, this life is meant for one thing: to re-Invent ourselves in every moment of every day.

To quote Spirit:

"Each of us creates our own reality as we travel this path. This reality is both gift and trap, for it is something that is intended to be transitory and changing as we grow. Many of us come to a wide comfortable spot in our road; lie down and wrap ourselves in the dream, halting all forward motion. Do not fear change. Rather look for it; study it and accept that which seems "right" for this is the growth we all seek."

As with so many concepts, it's very possible to twist something through the use of ego into an apparent negative. Don't you hate it when you outsmart yourself?

COMMENTS FROM SPIRIT:

The concept of Inventiveness is a step along the path to the recognition of your own value in the universe. To be able to create on even the smallest scale; something that did not appear to exist before is the first of many steps toward consciously co-creating all that exists in your perception and much of that which you do not yet know of. As you use your gift of Inventiveness, we welcome you to the ranks of Creators.

Blessings.

FRIENDSHIP

Friendship covers a wide gamut of emotional ground. Basically, it means: 'an affinity toward, a predisposition of well-being'. You can be casual Friends with someone or have an intense life-long commitment to one another above and beyond all else in your life. Sometimes Friendship is slow in developing and remains rather tenuous for a period of time before finally solidifying. In other instances, it is immediate, unshakable, and powerful. Friendships of the latter sort are almost always continuations of relationships that have existed for many lifetimes.

The single most important person to maintain a Friendship

with other than yourself is your spouse. Without that Friendship, you are two strangers who grudgingly share a domicile. We all know of people who have allowed themselves to travel down this road. It is not a pretty sight. It is providing exactly what those two individuals need, however, in the way of spiritual lessons.

I met a woman once who told me that she would never seriously date a man until she had arranged to go somewhere on the freeway with him driving. I asked her why this was and was astonished by the understanding of human nature that she evidenced with her answer. She told me that it had been her observation that people's real personality comes out when they are behind the wheel of their car in a stressful situation. She was able to see in an instant what the men's true level of inner peace and enlightenment was. Well, I was forced to take a good hard look at my own behavior and I wasn't real pleased with the 'me' I saw manifesting. As a result, I have made a point of teaching myself to refer to even the most irritating of drivers (Isn't it true that the things that irritate us the most about others are those things we need most deeply to look at in ourselves?) as 'Friend'. An example would be: "Can't you go any faster, Friend?"

I found that as I changed the word I used to refer to the other drivers as I changed the way I felt about them. Instead of outraged anger, I found a kind of warm fuzzy parental concern type feeling (in most cases) toward them. This has since translated into non-driving situations. I suggest that if you ever find yourself having distinctly un-Friendly feelings toward someone you try referring to them in your own mind as "Friend". You'll be very surprised at the difference it will make in your perception of the world. It takes you out of the 'victim' position and puts you into the 'student/nurturer' position.

We do not get anywhere by 'beating up' on ourselves over some perceived mistake. The most important Friend you can have is yourself. The most important person to be a Friend to is you. First and foremost Love yourself. Let your Love flow outward from the overflowing core of your being. Otherwise, you are but an empty shell and serve no one.

COMMENTS FROM SPIRIT:

Friendship is the Creator's hand in yours held out toward another being in Love. It is succor and nurturing. It is a kind word in a time of need. You are the essence of that nature in your heart of hearts. Be that which you are to all those whom you meet on the street; to all those whose lives you touch. We invite you once again to BE Love in every word, in every thought, in every deed, in every prayer. There can be no greater Friendship than this.

Blessings.

EXPERIENCE

Experience is the sum total of everything you ever have done or ever will do in this and all other lives and adventures. It is what has molded you into who you think you are and it is what will change you into what you never dreamed that you could become. Experience is childbirth; Experience is a random thought. The one thing that Experience is not is YOU. "You" is the paper doll. Experience is the wardrobes that you try on to see which fits best. It is Experience that changes your appearance in the ways you find to be good and sometimes not so good. Experience is the single most important material realm tool for growth.

Spirit has said, "Personal relationship provides the most fertile field for growth in the human Experience, and we all know what is needed in large quantities to make a field fertile." This is just a nice way for Spirit to inform you that a personal relationship will provide you with the greatest variety and intensity of Experiences you will encounter in this lifetime. Enjoy it! It's a gift to you from you for your great benefit.

Those who live in or have visited large cities know that there is seemingly no limit to the Experiences that the human condition seems to offer. Just please remember that whatever comes your way is something that your soul has decided you need more Experience and understanding regarding. It is in Divine order in every way whether you like it or not; whether you understand it or not.

Take life in your two hands. Lift it to your mouth and take a huge, giant bite out of it. Really sink your teeth into life and feel the juicy Experiences overflow your mouth and run down over your chin. This is what life is for. When you participate fearfully you are cheating yourself of much of the juiciness and the flavor of the many Experiences that life can provide. Remember: you are in charge (from the soul level) of EVERYTHING that you Experience. Nobody Loves you or watches over your safety more than your own personalized aspect of Spirit; your soul. THERE IS NOTHING THAT CAN HAPPEN TO YOU WITHOUT YOUR OWN SOUL'S APPROVAL. Every Experience you will ever have has already been selected and approved for your growth and benefit by your own soul. There is nothing that can ever harm you (the soul) without your Express permission and that's not likely to happen as long as you remember to remain the student and not the victim.

There is no Experience that is ultimately negative. There are Experiences that may seem harsh as you pass through them but as you distance yourself from the Experience you will begin to see the lessons that were carried with it.

COMMENTS FROM SPIRIT:

The Experience that you have chosen; Loved ones, is the greatest gift that any being might give to itself. The Experience path that included the aspect known as material realm life leads to the sure and ultimate realization of the Divine Godhood that underlies and permeates your greater being. You are allowing this lesson for yourself in the most intimate of ways so that it shall become now and forevermore a part of who you manifest as in the Universal hierarchy. Every Experience is a blessing. Every gift lights your path.

Blessings.

FAITH

Drawing the word of Faith invites you to experience the strength and the joy of trusting Spirit without exception and in every circumstance without hesitation or reservation. Trust; Spirit is always with you and is present to help in every way you will allow.

Faith regarding a personal relationship can refer to Faith in the relationship or Faith about the relationship. Faith in the relationship alludes to an abiding trust that your partner is the optimal partner for you at this time and that the partnership is fulfilling all of the needs you are aware of at this time and for the foreseeable future.

Faith about the relationship would lean more toward a meaning as follows:

Things do not seem to have been going as well as you would have liked. Perhaps you have even wondered if the relationship as such should continue. After reflection, you have reached the conclusion that you will continue with this relationship in the belief that the problems will be solved.

In either case, drawing this word indicates that Angelic forces have joined with you and your partner in an effort to clarify and strengthen the relationship.

The concept and energy of Faith in a general relationship are normally not so intense nor focused as they can be in a personal relationship. Faith; or belief in a business partner or another participant in a daily transaction will quite likely be explored when this energy enters the picture.

Personal Faith is a critical part of the character of any seeker of growth and Spirit. Faith in oneself is an outgrowth of self-worth and spiritual awareness. Both aspects will be brought forth for work and examination when this word is selected.

We have all heard the term 'Blind Faith'. Faith is a very good thing to have. However; unreasoned and non-critical Faith can be extremely dangerous in practice. Exercising Discretion can help to strengthen your Faith.

COMMENTS FROM SPIRIT:

Faith is the flowing of the River of Life. It is the current that animates the Being and the blood of the veins. Without Faith there is nothing and nothing is all there is. Be aware of the Faith that guides you into the heart of the Creator and of this thing called existence.

EMPATHY

Empathy is the art and the ability to walk a mile in someone else's moccasins. It is the desire and aptitude to tell someone "I know how you feel" and to really mean it because you have been in that place. It is compassion from a position of shared experience and feelings. No one can ever truly feel exactly what another is experiencing in every detail but the closer you allow yourself to come to that emotional place the more Empathy you are exhibiting.
Empathy is critical if a personal relationship is to be successful (in the material world sense) over a long period of time. The closeness of the relationship not only encourages but also demands that you

attune yourself to the inner and outer workings of your partner's psyche. There is an old saying about the importance of two oxen yoked together to pull together in order to accomplish what neither of them could do separately. The same is true in a personal relationship. It is critical for maximum progress that you both are headed in generally the same direction and that your efforts are so timed as to complement one another. Otherwise, all that happens is that you wind up with two overworked and grumpy oxen and the whole field yet to plow.

Much the same is true of General relationships except that we cannot always choose our partners nor is our partner always in a cooperative mood. As with all other things it is the intent that means everything.

COMMENTS FROM SPIRIT:

That which you call Empathy, Dear Ones, is the first feeble step toward your awakened awareness in consciousness of the interconnection of all life; all beings, all things in the body that you refer to as the Creator. The Creator; Dear Ones, is you -- all of you -- and all of existence around you. You are all brothers. You are all sisters. You are all One. When you allow this to manifest in your every thought and action you honor All that Is. BE Love to one another in each moment. This is Empathy.

CLEARING

There are two types of Clearing we will speak of. There is passive or apparent Clearing, and there is active Clearing.
Take a glass of distilled water. Stir in a tablespoon of dirt. Let it sit out overnight. The dirt will have settled to the bottom of the glass leaving the water apparently though not actually clear and clean and safe to drink. This is what many of us do and call that Clearing. We are not growing. We are ignoring, burying, and denying in hopes that whatever it is will simply 'go away'. Then when almost everything 'settles to the bottom' we fool ourselves into thinking that we are cleansed and pure.

Would you drink that clear appearing water in that glass when you could see the dirt that lies at the bottom of it? Not usually! While it appears to be clear it obviously is not pure. Purification (in-depth Clearing) requires that you take action and put some effort into the project. In the case of the water, we must filter it or better yet put it through a still.

Let's look at what happens when the water is put through a still for total Clearing but keep in mind that we are talking about the human spirit as well.

First, the water is put into a situation from which it cannot readily escape. Then the heat is turned up causing the pressure to increase until the water begins to boil. At this point the water finds that the only avenue for escape from this situation requires it to transform to an altered state; from solid to gaseous and to lift itself toward heaven leaving behind all that had soiled it before. Once the pressure is off things cool down and the water reassumes its old structure. As it enters the realm of matter it is collected in a vessel identical to that in which the dirt was added but the water is now purified and cleansed due to its recent experience.

The same is true for us. Clearing is not an easy 'quick fix'. In order to get to the bottom of things and truly purify ourselves of the 'dirt' of a situation or condition, we must go into meditation and communion with Spirit (change our state). Because we are often consciously or non-consciously blind to our problems and faults Spirit will often and with great Love increase the pressure on us until we can no longer ignore the situation and must take action that will assist us in processing ourselves into a purified state of understanding and acceptance regarding that particular lesson or series of lessons.

It is easy to appear to clear your problems with your partner. Ignore the root cause long enough and the problem might seem to go away -- or your partner will. The only way to successfully clear the problems is to sit together with Love and communicate with the mutual intent to identify and modify those areas of disharmony. Bringing this word to you today is an indication that that might be a good idea.

Passive Clearing is often used in a general relationship as a 'Band-Aid' fix for situations where the others involved are not of that much importance to us. This approach does nothing for our spiritual growth. In fact it sets us up for more intense karmic lessons down the road. Again, communication is called for in order to bring the relationship back into balance and harmony. The path you wish to take is up to you. Everything that you ignore today WILL come back tomorrow with interest.

You have obviously called this word to you today for a purpose. Could it be that you have been satisfied with passively Clearing yourself and your life when what was (and is) really required is purification? True Clearing can be a lot of work but it is worth the effort. Spirit is here to assist you. Go for it!

Passive Clearing is a tool sometimes used on a temporary basis. If you attempt to use it as a permanent fix you are going to run into difficulties down the road.

COMMENTS FROM SPIRIT:

Clearing; Dear Ones, is what a farmer does preparatory to tilling the soil. It is the first level of the work to be done. It exposes the soil in which the real labor and rewards are to be found. Clear away the underbrush in your lives, Beloveds, and plow deep into the rich soil of your Divine nature. The crop will astound you. Blessings to you, one and all.

CONTINUITY

There i. S. a Se, nse of Cont. Inuity that reside. S within the heart o. F each of us.

The previous sentence violates that sense.

Every one of us has an instinctive and powerful awareness of the flow of all things: be it time; life or a river. Most of us are aware that all things are flowing in this manner whether we can perceive it or not. One of the names for this great flow of all things is Continuity. It refers to the circular nature of reality and the never-ending movement of All that Is.

We are in violation of one of the fundamental rules of existence when we make an attempt to ignore or stop this movement. By drawing this word to you today, you are invited to pay attention to the old saying, "Go with the (Divine) flow".

It is of critical importance to maintain Continuity in a personal relationship. It would be very disconcerting to come home every night to someone who had a wildly varying personality or set of life standards. At the same time, the very purpose of any relationship is to foster growth and change. The key is that there is Continuity within the ideal pattern of growth and change as opposed to the chaos that is sometimes perceived in some people's lives.

At times, the flow of Continuity may seem to be leading you away from your partnership. This is not necessarily a 'bad' thing although it can seem quite unpleasant in the moment. All relationships are tools to help us to move forward in our growth, and every tool has its built-in limitations. Should you Continue to use a tool past the point of its limitations it becomes a crutch and it holds you back. This does not necessarily mean that your relationship must end; only that there are changes occurring within it as it has been.

The same is true of General relationships. How successful would a salesman be if they radically changed their demeanor or appearance on every call to a client? Continuity is necessary to develop a pattern and trust.

Our eternal life; our many incarnations is a perfect example of Continuity. Although we may take many forms; have different genders and worship different ways our soul has followed (for it) the path that leads Home in the most efficient way given the lessons we have chosen to learn (or ignore) in each lifetime and overall.

Continuity has a relative that lives on the wrong side of the tracks. It is called stagnation. Some may wish to halt the flow of progress and growth at a place that seems to support them nicely (usually at the expense of others). That is stagnation. Remember: Continuity is flow. Stagnation is static and leads to spiritual degeneration; the opposite of growth.

COMMENTS FROM SPIRIT:

Continuity, Beloveds, is a human concept. Here at the heart of all things there simply is: IS. There is no time. There is no space. All times; all things, all beings simply ARE, and they ARE in the essence of the Oneness that Is. Follow your paths Beloved Ones, for they all lead to the One-ness of the Whole and that Whole is YOU!
Blessings.

UNION

Union is the coming together of two or more sovereign things or people who have previously (apparently) been separate from one another. It is coming together in such a way that there is no seam and no trace of the separation that once appeared to be.

The joining together of the two parties in many wedding ceremonies and the resulting pairing is often called a 'Union". This reflects the intent and the desired result more often than the accomplishment of that goal. When you come right down to it the object of partnership is not a perfect Union. The idea of partnership; at least from the point of view of Spirit, is to provide one another with constant Loving challenges. That can only be accomplished when at least the illusion of some separateness is maintained. It is fine to come very close to one another in thought and behavior but that small awareness of dissimilarity probably should be maintained for the most effective use of the tool of partnership.

As with so many others of these words, the single most important Union for us to pursue is that Union with our Higher and lower, inner and outer selves. All of these must be brought to a singleness of perception, a Unified purpose of existence. It is impossible for us to perceive the One-ness of all about us if we cannot find it within us.

Generally speaking, there is no harsh aspect to Union except for those rare instances when apparent separateness is required for learning purposes.

COMMENTS FROM SPIRIT:

Unity of self; of greater self; of All that Is, is the ultimate and final goal of the experience that you refer to as life. Come home now to that place where you have never been absent. Return your consciousness to the Heart of Hearts; to the Ultimate Union of Divinity and Love. Blessings to you.

SURRENDER

Red Flag! Red Flag!

    This has got to be one of the least favorite and one of the most feared of all the words in this book.
Surrender? Me? No way!
Or: "I already have -- why are things still going badly?")

    We become so invested in the personalities that we have spent a lifetime creating -- or worse yet, our perception of what those personalities are -- that we create blind spots in our findings. These blind spots enable us to ignore certain patterns as though they did not exist. Therefore we see no need to give them up.

How much time and effort do you put into controlling the environment and people around you? How focused are you on becoming wealthy, famous, or 'getting' a certain man or woman as a physical partner? How often do these things work out as you have plotted and planned them? How often, when things do seem to 'work out', are you disappointed with the results?

Do you see the point? We struggle and contend to mold ourselves and the world to who we think we ought to be. Often the world seems to simply ignore us and blissfully go on its own way. Based on your own life experiences how much 'control' do you really think that you have on the material plane?

So many times when I counsel people they will tell me that they.y have totally Surrendered to Spirit but that things are still not progressing as they would like. Without exception; these are people who the world sees as being extremely stubborn and quite often self-centered. The clients themselves have no concept of this and are often quite astonished and offended when I gently break the news to them. They are operating from what I refer to as the 'small' sense of self; the conscious and material-world dwelling self.

Most people are so invested in maintaining the persona that they think is them that they have no intention of Surrendering to Spirit or anyone else. Though they might give lip service to the concept of Surrender, actually allowing themselves to do it is another matter altogether. They don't understand why it is that things don't seem to be 'going their way'.

Let me explain 'Surrender' to you. It may help you to make the transition into release from old patterns.

Most of us have a view of who 'we' are based on how we think the world sees us or how we sometimes see ourselves in spite of the world. We have invested many years and copious tears to become the person we are. We have spent more time on this one project than on any other aspect of our life. We are extremely attached to this image and often use it to manipulate and control those around us.

Stop for a moment. Think about your life. For all your

attempts to command the world to bow to you; how often are you the one who winds up being forced to your knees? It doesn't seem to work that well in that manner, does it? Try as we might the world always seems to have its own ideas.

Many of us have learned to say "all things are for a reason", shrug our shoulders and move on to try to do things our way all over again. If we could but listen to our own words we would often have the discord resolved.

I refer to the mortal, material sense of self as the "small self".

When we raise our sights to the realm of Spirit we discover that there is no need to try to control from the conscious level as all things are indeed in Divine Order at all times. I refer to this aspect of consciousness as the "greater Self". Remember, though that just because 'things' are in Divine Order does not necessarily or automatically mean that you are following the shortest path of greatest Light.

What Spirit is inviting us to do when this word is drawn is to Surrender our small sense of self to our greater sense of Self. When this is accomplished we can easily Surrender or give up our false perception that we are controlling our lives from the conscious level. We then give up the source of most of our frustrations and unhappiness. To what?

To our greater Self -- our soul.

When you are finally able to break through your own blindness and begin to access and trust Spirit you become aware that whatever is happening in your life is actually there as a gift of Love from your higher self to your small self. This gift is a tool to help us to grow into spiritual awareness and living patterns. The lesson here is that if all things are indeed in order at all times, there is no need to try to control from the physical plane! When we give up the illusion of control from the small self and turn it over to the larger Self that dwells in Spirit we lose the illusion of control but gain the surety and knowledge of absolute and total control through Divine Order. All things are in order at all times whether we (the small self) understand or like it or not. This what is meant by Surrender. We lose our greatest source of frustration and anger and in return receive peace, tranquility, understanding, patience, and wisdom. As with all things, the choice is ours.

COMMENTS FROM SPIRIT:

Surrender in the human form can be one of the most distasteful and difficult of exercises to perform. You are given the illusion of control in order to learn that all aspects of Life are already in the Loving control of the Creator. The One who has made Heaven and Earth has not forgotten to attend the details. Trust the Creator for all things truly are in order. This is the ultimate, Loving control.

Blessings my children.

REVELATION

Revelation is the act of uncovering or bringing to light something that had previously been hidden or unsuspected. To Reveal can also mean to share a secret or otherwise make oneself vulnerable to another.

Revelation is one of the more important processes in a personal relationship. We figuratively and literally strip ourselves bare as the relationship progresses for our partner's analysis and examination. The less we hide from a Loving partner the more they are able to help us to truly see and understand ourselves. That understanding is one of the bases of our own growth. What have you tried to keep hidden from your partner regarding yourself? Why? Does it serve or harm your relationship? Does it serve or slow your spiritual growth? Spirit has told me that "Darkness is required to hide something. All things are made visible in the light."

Revelation in the public eye is very threatening for most people. The world can be a very cruel place. As we become totally comfortable with who we are inside, we begin to manifest into the outer world in a natural and easy way. The threat that we feel is often due to our own insecurities. As those are deleted from our persona the world no longer has a handle by which to control us and we may walk the streets as we truly are with no fear or concern about how others might choose to perceive us. Remember: people are going to perceive you in the way that best suits their needs in that moment. Your job is not to try to please everybody (or anybody) else. Your job is to BE Love. What others think or say to your apparent detriment when you are doing that job and doing it well becomes patently and transparently false and harmless.

The single most important person to fully Reveal yourself to is yourself. We are so good about hiding from ourselves. We have learned to ignore many of our motivations and the effect that they may have on others. We split our personalities a hundred times over; going to our personality closet and putting on the one that serves us best in each moment even though we are usually only fooling ourselves. Ultimately we fool no one. Drawing this concept to your consciousness indicates that perhaps it is time to empty your closet and step out into the world as you truly are. If you are not happy or comfortable with that, it is obviously time to change some aspects of self until you are. Spirit is here to help but you are the one who will have to do all of the work and you are the one who must walk your own path in your own shoes.

There are times when a Revelation can produce distinctly uncomfortable results. This material world is full of psychic and emotional sharks who spend all of their time cruising the waters of life sniffing for blood. Once they find it they close in for a feeding frenzy. The antidote for this is to KNOW without a shadow of a doubt that you are completely and totally protected and that the only things that can touch you are those things that your soul has approved as being for your growth. If you are also completely comfortable with all aspects of your own behavior and motivations whatever is said will simply slide off of your awareness.

COMMENTS FROM SPIRIT:

Revelation is yet another of your human concepts. When you are at one with the One there is nothing that is hidden. There is nothing that is not already known in the very instant of your curiosity. Darling ones, be patient with yourselves and each other as you are all students in the same school; the school of life; and each of you must learn every lesson in the curriculum. This lifetime you may be a saint; but in many others, you have been the murderer, the mugger, the rapist. The entire gamut of human experience is your assignment and the lessons are such that you must agree to help one another through them by taking turns as 'victim' and 'perpetrator'. We give our Love to you always and without fail as you pass through this sometimes unpleasant yet truly blessed time of your existence. Have faith, Dear Ones. Not a single thing happens that is not for your ultimate good and not a sparrow falls that we do not love.

Love to you. Love beyond words; beyond time. Love to you.

Blessings.

INSPIRATION

Inspiration occurs when Spirit reaches out and touches us in a way that brings a new perspective on an old situation or opens a completely new field of experience with a flash of figurative and literal brilliance.

Inspiration in a personal relationship can refer to bringing home roses on the spur of the moment or saying just the right thing at just the right time. If it feels 'right' and it has the ambiance of Spirit, DO IT!

Inspiration is another of those concepts that are almost identical in meaning. The major difference between personal and general relationships regarding Inspiration is that there are generally far more opportunities and areas for this energy to manifest than in a personal relationship.

Inspiration received in answer to a question regarding self is an exciting draw! Spirit is touching your life in an exciting and unexpected manner. Be creative!

COMMENTS FROM SPIRIT:

Ah! My Children; Listen with your hearts and let the laughter of the ethers play around and through your lives and activities. Neither fret nor hold back but revel in this playful and growth-filled aspect of Love. 'Tis always more pleasant to learn from Joy than from tears.

Blessings.

SYNCHRONICITY

Synchronicity is two meteors hitting one another in space. It is walking around a street corner while daydreaming and tripping over the foot of the person who is about to become your life partner.

Synchronicity means literally 'the condition of sameness of time'. Two things come together in space-time. Synchronicity also carries with it the additional meaning of Divine intervention. Things that could not have 'just happened' happen anyway.

To a large degree, the amount of Synchronicity that occurs in your private life with your partner is determined by the amount of mental and spiritual togetherness you share and your mutual degree of openness toward Spirit. The more you both trust the more can happen for you. Enjoy!

Synchronicity is all about you and your Divine origin. Let down your walls; tune in your senses and see it work. It can work in subtle or grand ways. It can be as simple as a glance at someone who suddenly feels that you know about something they have done that they are not comfortable with. They begin to examine themselves and their actions. This leads to a slow steady cascade effect that results, years later, in their having completely changed their personality and their goals in life. And so it goes. Synchronicity is an often subtle but extremely powerful tool of the Creator and our spirit.

Our lives are built on Synchronicity. Every little thing that has ever happened to me has combined and conspired to make me who I am today. It is possible that had I not stopped to purchase a pack of gum when I was eight years old my whole life experience would have been different. The time that I spent in that store could have changed my path so that I did not meet someone whose influence or actions could have sent me into a whole different reality. The same holds true for everyone. Enjoy the Synchronicities in your life. They are what tomorrow is created of, and you are the director.

As with so many other concepts, Synchronicity can seem to bring harsh experiences. The apparent harshness is only there because you have not gotten the message involved at lower, gentler levels. Remember: you have a choice. You can perceive your lessons from the point of view of a victim; refusing to see or 'get' the message, which will only bring it back again at an even stronger level. You could also choose to accept the experience from the point of view of a student. Once that occurs you understand that the experience is a lesson. At that point the theme of the lesson is received; the harshness of the lesson falls away and your next lesson, based on what you have just learned, is Lovingly offered to you.

COMMENTS FROM SPIRIT:

Synchronicity is but eddies in the flow of the Universes. It is a tiny glimpse of the intimate integration of all things, all times, all places, all beings, for all are One.

Blessings to you.

CEREMONY

Ceremony is the handle by which we hold some of our ideas and teachings and the tool by which we hand them to the next generation. In the greater sense of things Ceremony is totally without value in the works accomplished, although it can be an important tool of focus and teaching as it brings many ideas and concepts of Spirit into the physical and serves as a bridge to Spirit for those who need one.

There is the story of a family led by the elderly Grandfather that sat in meditation together every night. One of the grandchildren brought home a rambunctious kitten one day and that night the kitten made a pest of itself during the meditation, crawling into

and over everything and everybody - especially the Grandfather - in its quest for attention. Finally, the Grandfather ordered the youngest child; the one who had brought the kitten into the house, to put the cat under a basket in the center of the room in order to keep it out of the way. This worked quite well. The child began to automatically catch the cat and put it under the basket each night just before time to meditate. Years passed and this was repeated every night.
Finally, the Grandfather passed from this plane and his son took over as head of the family. And every night the family's youngest grandchild would put the cat under the basket.

One day when they went to get the cat they discovered that it, too, had left its body.
A frantic search ensued.
After all, one cannot hold a meditation without the sacred cat in the basket.

It is from happenings as mundane as this that all Ceremonies have developed.

A healthy relationship is a Ceremony in each moment. Its purpose is that of bringing into the material world the essence of Spirit in a way that others may see and choose to emulate. Drawing this word at this time is a suggestion from Spirit that you take a close and critical look at your relationship. If it is not a Ceremony of joy and balance perhaps you should connect with your partner in such a way as to promote and perpetuate that condition. If your relationship is locked into the inflexibility and stagnation created as a result of too much Ceremony it may be time to discard the Ceremony in order to revive the relationship.

Every relationship should be a Ceremony of integrity and Spirit. Unfortunately in the material world there always seem to be mitigating factors that appear to make it easier in the moment to not follow these guidelines. Spirit is asking you to renew your integrity at this time. Remember that there is no excuse acceptable or necessary to Spirit. Also, remember that there is no wrong way to do anything! There are only longer and shorter paths or greater or lesser light. The choice is always ours and directly affects our path and the lessons we find therein.

Ceremony is a tool... nothing more, nothing less. Any tool can be abused by using it for the wrong purpose. It would not behoove you to use a tire iron to try to drill a 1/8 inch hole in a piece of steel plate. So it would not seem appropriate to use a sacred Ceremony for an ego-driven cause. Another pitfall to avoid is the concept that the Ceremony is a prerequisite to achieving a given result. Each of us is created of the Creator by the Creator. As such an innate part of our beingness is the power and abilities of the Creator. We need no tools or intercession of other parties in order to access these gifts.

COMMENTS FROM SPIRIT:

Life is the Ceremony and Love is the goal. Become One through the Ceremony and live the Love you are.

Blessings.

COMPLETION

"A journey of a thousand miles starts with a single step." We've all heard that quote from time to time in our lives. There is a corollary that you have probably never heard (because I just made it up). It says: "Regardless of the length of the first step a journey of a thousand miles is still a thousand miles long." It is never enough to only take the first step. It is not enough to take every step but the last. The journey is not Completed until that last step has been taken.

The second most important journey we travel during a physical lifetime is that with our partner or partners. Each partner brings with them the map for a journey of self-exploration and spiritual growth. When we agree to the partnership we are agreeing to see the journey through to the end of the map. Sometimes we Complete the journey and sometimes we bail out before the lessons are Completed. When we quit early (and this, too is in Divine order) we will continue the same lessons at a more intense level with our next partner; having ignored them in the previous round. It is only when we Complete a contract that we are ready to move on to the next level; sometimes with the same partner, sometimes with a new partner, or even with no partner but Spirit.

Daily, we are offered small and large lessons in our material world's casual relationships. Each one of these is important as well and each one must be Completed so that we may move to and through the next levels. Remember that each lesson is a gift and we do not have to like or understand the gift for it to be of service to us. The gifts can appear in an apparently harsh manner only if we have ignored them repeatedly in the past.

If you have brought this word to your attention today it is a strong suggestion from Spirit to finish what you start. There will be assistance. There will be lessons and there will be tests. Enjoy yourself. All of this is happening for your benefit.

COMMENTS FROM SPIRIT:

The only Completion there is, is a Completion of the illusion that you call life. The illusion of separateness and struggle is of your own creation. It is a powerful tool but there comes a time to set aside a tool that is no longer of service to you in your journey. Complete yourselves, my children. Come home. Complete the journey of your mind and spirit. Remember that there is no journey, there is only an arrival. We love you.

Blessings

FAMILY

"Mitakuye Oyasin." We are all related. We are all Family. We are all the children of the uncreated Creator: all brothers and sisters with one another and with all of creation. Each one of us is here for the benefit of every other one. Spirit says: "Do nothing to harm your brother, for your brother is yourself."

Nowhere is our status of Family more evident than with our partner. This is the most intimate of relationships in every way. It is closer than parents; closer than siblings. You can hide some things from most people but your spouse sees you at your best and at your worst. They see you first thing in the morning after a rough night and they see you dressed to the nines for a formal affair. In a good relationship, your partner is the closest relative you have in this world. Honor them and all that they do for you all that they are for you. Be the same for them.

Family is not so easy to recognize in the general relationship realm. The masks so many of us wear to protect ourselves often hide our true feelings of concern and caring for those around us under the pretense of being 'cool'. Just think how this world would be changed if we could all drop our masks and show those 'strangers' in our lives how much we care for them; how our soul and spirit reaches out to support them in their process. Perhaps this word has come to you this day to invite you to drop your guard even just a little bit in order to Love your brothers and sisters more openly than you have been doing.

Family is one of the few concepts where the focus is outside of us, yet the concept and direction must come from within as must the willingness to come out of our fearful cages and into the light. I ask you to remember always that the Ultimate Commandment is to BE Love. Finding the Family in all of those around you is a good first step.

COMMENTS FROM SPIRIT:

You are all Family. You are all the children of the Divine, and One with that Divinity. There is no separation except within your own minds. Come home, Dear Ones. Come home to your eternal Family of Love.

Blessings to you.

SERENITY

In the Tibetan Book of the Dead, there is a reference to a state called the Chikhai Bardo, which is the first opportunity after entering the realm of non-life that one has to achieve Buddhahood. This to me is the epitome of this thing called Serenity. The Chikhai Bardo is described as a body of water as large as the universe that has never known a ripple; never known a wave. It is lying beneath a beautiful sky that has never known a storm; never known a breeze. You find your immaterial self floating between the two: touching neither but part of both. This scene describes Serenity to me: to be so far beyond any disturbing influence that it simply does not exist in your awareness.

Oftimes the winds of change blow strongly through a personal relationship in order to shake loose those aspects of it that are ready to fall away and make room for new growth. While this is a good thing as things are measured, it can become wearing to the parties involved. Because of the nature of the human experience Serenity is something that occurs in fleeting moments of our lives. It is not, try as one might; a condition that is easy to maintain for extended periods. If the changes in your relationship are causing stress it would be well to invite in the energy of Serenity. Take a few moments or an hour and see just how deeply into meditation you can immerse yourself. Can you get to the point where you can forget that you even have a body? Float free from it and all of the stresses associated with it and for a moment or two, you will have this thing called Serenity. When you return from your meditation, feel free to bring the energy back with you to share with your partner.

Once you have achieved the ability to perceive yourself as body-less you open an important doorway. In private or in public in those moments of greatest stress you can stop for a second or two; close your eyes and return momentarily to that state of Serenity. When you return your consciousness to the material realm you will find that you have an entirely different outlook on the matter at hand.

While it is of importance to be in the world on a daily basis it is of equal importance to be able to rise above it on a regular basis. The bliss and joy to be found in the condition of Serenity and the recuperation of body and spirit that accompanies it make this an extremely worthwhile procedure. Drawing this word into your life in this moment can mean that either Spirit is willing to assist you in achieving this state or if you have already experienced it is suggesting that it is time to return once more for a regenerative visit.

COMMENTS FROM SPIRIT:

Go to that place within you where the Creator resides. Feel the warmth, Love, and abiding peace that is your due; your birthright. Lay down all fears; all troubles, all doubts and immerse yourself in total Love. Welcome to Serenity.

Welcome home.

SHARING

"If I had two dead mice, I'd give you one!"

What, you're not impressed?

Suppose you found a greeting card that said that on the outside and had a picture of two cute cartoon cats on the inside and more text that says "That's what Love is all about." Suddenly it makes a lot more sense.

Therein lays the crux of the lesson. You can offer some of what you have to anybody. It is only of value; it is only a Sharing if it has value to the intended recipient.

You have chosen to Share your life with another person. They have agreed to Share theirs with you. Every detail of every day is known to your partner consciously or non-consciously. Please be aware of what you do and why. Act with and from Love for that Love is that which you intended to Share at the moment of bonding and that Love is the shortest path of greatest light in the pursuit of the lessons that the relationship is to provide for the two of you. Remember one of the other major reasons for your partnership is that you have both requested the same or complimentary lessons.

As we move through the mundane world we have the opportunity to Share through our very being the benefits of self-awareness and a Spiritual path. Many people and sects attempt to do this through their words; 'witnessing' to anybody and everybody whether that person is interested or repulsed. Sometimes it seems as though because someone has decided that they like strawberry ice cream and pickled beets on their liver and onions that, by God, you will too or you'll go to Hell (not that there is any such place, except in some people's minds). Sharing through words rarely is effective. First and foremost the Sharing must occur from who you are and not what you say. Then and only then when someone asks you questions is it appropriate to Share in words those things that seem 'right' to you in that moment.

One of the main goals of the experience we call 'life' is to learn to Share your Self and your Love with all who will accept and honor them. However, we often forget to Share that Divine Love with ourselves. We deny our own Love for ourselves; looking instead for love from the outside world to 'fill in the gaps'. Don't you know that you must truly Love yourself first and that the ability to truly Love another radiates from within? Angelic forces have come today to Share with you this concept. They are here for you in this moment, in this lifetime, and for eternity. Love yourself first. Then you can truly Share with the others from the depth of the fullness in your own life.

There is no harsh aspect to Sharing. Occasionally, it may seem that someone is taking advantage of that which you offer. Remember that no one can ever cheat you. They can only cheat themselves.

COMMENTS FROM SPIRIT:

To Share is a human concept. All beings are One, Dear Ones. When you take from one pocket in your clothing and put what you have taken into another pocket in your clothing have you Shared? You do not own anything in this material realm. You are only caretaker and steward for that which appears to be temporarily in your custody. When another comes into your life and it seems that the object is something that should be passed on to them; do so. At that point, your stewardship ends and theirs begins. Some of your cultures were based on Sharing. This is a 'good' thing. The more you value something the greater is the gift you Share with your brother or sister for you Share not only the object and your regard for it but also your regard for the Divine Spirit that they are. This is an example of the Ultimate Commandment, to BE Love.

Blessings.

BALANCE

The tightrope starts swaying. The more it sways the more we try to correct. Unfortunately most of us have a tendency to either wait too long to notice that we are out of Balance and/or overcorrect once we do notice. This just makes the situation worse. Our lives sometimes seem to just be one continuing Balancing act. While our attention is on one area of imbalance other areas are gleefully headed off in their own directions.

On several occasions as I was growing up I was taken aside by well-meaning friends who would tell me the following:

"There are two ways for each of us to go through life. We can jump into the river of life; set our own goal and swim (usually upstream) toward that goal. We fight the current and get banged up by the rocks and turbulence. Some of us may actually seem to reach our goal although most never quite seem to make it. Eventually, we die and the river carries us to the sea".

The other way to go through life is to jump into the river of life and be passive; letting the river carry us as it will. Over time we experience the ripples and eddy currents and may well get caught in a whirlpool or two but eventually, the river carries us to the sea"

The river of course refers to an individual life experience viewed from the personalized, small sense of 'self'. The sea represents the greater self -- All that Is. The path of the river represents what we describe as 'life'. Rivers usually have many paths in their deltas, wandering and meandering over the terrain, each influenced by the circumstances of their path, but every one of them enters and becomes one with the same sea.

Spirit has informed me that there is a third way to pass through this experience called life. That way is to become the river. In becoming the river we become the sea.

As a river wends its way to the sea it may experience many things. It may experience a widening of its banks that appears to slow the flow; or a narrowing that provides a more intense experience and faster apparent flow. A large boulder (blockage or difficulty) may have fallen into the course of the river. These all make absolutely no difference. The river accepts all of these things as the current parameters of its existence. It realizes that it has all of eternity to follow its course. If the path appears blocked the river does not stop but rather finds another path or simply, patiently overcomes the obstacle by the simple expedient of maintaining the flow. The level of the river rises and may even form a lake before finding a way past the barrier. It knows the obstacle intimately -- every atom and molecule -- surrounds it, caresses it and flows on to the sea.

So, my friends, become the river and step into Balance.

This word indicates that Spirit has noted your difficulties and efforts (or lack of them) and has decided to 'lend a hand' to help you get back to center for a while.

Spirit once told me that personal relationships provided the most fertile field for growth in the human experience. It then added, "Of course, you know what is needed in large quantities to make a field fertile?" Keeping your Balance in the throes of a relationship can be very challenging yet extremely rewarding. This word promises you that opportunity

Next in difficulty to a personal relationship are your casual relationships. You are about to be given the opportunity to see how good your Balance really is. HINT: How you choose to perceive something makes all of the difference.

Within each of us is a constant battle between those wild things we might like to do under different circumstances and those things that we know to be 'right'. The conflict between 'should' and 'shouldn't', anger and understanding, light and dark, 'must' and 'can't' are the battlefield boundaries of our own state of Balance. Spirit is going to take you on a tour of the site in order to remind you of what it's all about and what's at stake. Step carefully. Remember: it's all happening FOR you, not TO you!

At times, someone may have chosen to become 'balanced' in an off-center place. Here comes Spirit to shake you loose so that you can find true center again. This is often accomplished by removing the physical emotional and mental 'supports' you have grown dependent upon to hold you in that place.

COMMENTS FROM SPIRIT:

Balance -- true Balance -- results in simply BEing -- without reaction to any stimuli but the flow of Creation about and through you. If you are in the center of all things at all times what greater Balance can there be?

MATURITY

"You're soooo immature."

I'm sure that I'm the only one who has ever heard that in their adult life.

Maturity - or more precisely the lack of it is for the most part a judgment against you by someone who is too conservative or stodgy to do whatever it is that you are doing.

There is a second; more important application of the term 'Maturity'. It refers to a 'coming of age'; a ripening in the field of life; a readiness for harvest.

I once heard a comedienne on television ask the question:

"Why is it that after the first year of a relationship there is so much less panting and so much more snoring?"

The answer is, of course, that the relationship is beginning to Mature. The physical aspects of a relationship are very important and can be very joyful but that is not really what a Mature relationship is based on.

Relationships, like people, have a pattern of growth. In the youth of the relationship the focus is on physical activities and playing. Then as the relationship becomes a little more Mature, there is less of the physical play and a deepening of the emotional aspect; a friendship. From there the physical seems to retreat even farther while still remaining important and a deep and abiding (Divine) Love and (human) love become the primary elements. Wherever your relationship is, is exactly where it needs to be. Wherever it is, it shall Mature from that point to where your joint needs shall take it.

Look around you at the way most people act like children in the mundane world. Don't you wish they could be more Mature and not get into their petty squabbles and games? Now, look at yourself and your own actions. Are you a part of the problem or are you an example for others to follow? Act your spiritual age with joy and Love and let others see that it is possible to be Mature without being a stick in the mud.

The only harsh aspect of Maturity is the misperception of self-importance. You may be getting older, but you don't have to 'grow up'.

COMMENTS FROM SPIRIT:

Spiritual Maturity occurs with the full acceptance and manifestation of your Divine nature. Allow the limitations of your mind; the toys and tools of your youth to fall away from you. Stand exposed in the radiance of the glory of your own being-ness, and BE Love. That is the first level of true Maturity.

Blessings.

CONFUSION

"Which way did they go, Ralph, Which way did they go?"

There are times when our life and the world around us just seem to get out of our mental grasp and we wind up Confused with our 'stupid' face on. Basically; Confusion is just mental disorientation. It occurs when we lose, for whatever reason, the anchor point from which we measure reality. Drugs and traumatic events can cause this state and sometimes it just seems to happen by itself for no apparent reason. It can best be described as a period of adjustment where we examine that reality anchor that we have been using in order to see if it is where we want it to be. Perhaps we should move it to a new location that better serves the position we are now holding. There is no fault or shame in Confusion. It happens to the best of us from time to time. If you feel that you are experiencing more than your share of Confusion at this time there are a couple of things you can do to alleviate the problem. (I am assuming that drugs are not the cause. If they are the problem, prepare for some extremely interesting lessons, complements of Spirit. You would not be receiving this word today unless Spirit decided that you've experimented long enough -- fair warning!) The first is to spend more time in meditation. If you have problems meditating it is usually because of one of two things.

1) You are so closed down that you will not allow Spirit in. If that is the case, practice in meditation is the easiest way to overcome it.

2) The other major difficulty lies in the overactive mind that many of us have.

There is an ancient technique that I used to overcome my overactive mind years ago (It used to take me up to six or eight hours to fall asleep -- now I usually do it in a few minutes!) Sit quietly in a quiet place; close your eyes and go within to the best of your ability. Picture a blank screen with your inner vision. Any thought that your mind tries to 'get away with' shows up on the screen as a 'blip' of light. Capture the 'blip' gently with your intent and push it back in the direction it came from. It may take weeks before you achieve even five seconds of clarity on the screen but keep it up. Eventually, at about thirty seconds of clarity, your conscious mind gives up and shuts up. From that point forward, you will find a feeling of deep peace and tranquility in your mind, and meditation will be a piece of cake.

COMMENTS FROM SPIRIT:

Confusion occurs when you have wandered from your Spiritual path and cannot find your way back. Quiet your heart Dear Ones; quiet your mind and hear the clear and Loving call of Home. You can never stray so far that you cannot hear us for we reside within and all around you. If you will listen we are there. Even if you will not listen we are there awaiting your clarity. Infinite Love has infinite patience.

Blessings to you, Loved ones.

Blessings to you.

IDENTITY

Who are you?

Most people will answer that with a comment as to their employment, their pedigree, or a list of their accomplishments. None of these things is who you are.

It is sometimes easy to lose track of oneself when one is married to someone famous or to an overbearing sort whose self-proclaimed light seems to eclipse you. Regardless of the circumstances remember that; first and foremost you are a child of the Creator. That in itself is a pedigree beyond reproach and without superior. Honor yourself in each moment of your relationship. Honor your partner also and honor the relationship, but honor your own sensibilities and true needs first.

The world seems sometimes to be determined also to strip us of our sense of self-value. The larger the association, company, or group, the smaller a cog each individual may seem; until they appear almost to disappear in the massed crowd. It is up to you to not allow yourself to be buried beneath the weight of anonymity. Assert yourself when it is necessary. Do what you know to be 'right', and refuse to support that which demeans any person; for it demeans you also.

Your own inner sense of your value as a human being is the most important judgment you will ever have to face. Until and unless you overcome the limiting influences the world would have upon you and your perception of yourself you will play the obedient sheep. You are Divinity itself! The universe is yours! Why do you settle for being a small cog in someone else's wheel?

The only harsh aspects to the concept of Identity come when you allow yourself to accept a diminished self-value or allow an overblown material world sense of self. Spirit will be available to assist you in returning yourself to balance in these areas.

COMMENTS FROM SPIRIT:

Dear Ones: the only Identity you need be concerned with over your many, many mortal lifetimes is the one that never changes. You are a child of the Creator of all things. And therein lies your value.

Blessings

Beloved ones:
    I have Loved you from the beginning of time.
        I shall Love you when the worlds are dust.
    There is nothing I would not do for your benefit.
        There is no price, no cost to you
    for this Love I give.

    There is nothing you could do

to ever lessen this Love.
There is nothing you could ever do
    that would make me withdraw from your side.

We are One in every way.
    You are the heart of my heart.
You are the child of my loins,
    and my fondest hopes.
You are the delight of my eye.

As you learn and grow,
    Because we are One,
So learns and grows
    the universe, and all in it.
Including Me.
    For you and I
and all that is

    are One.

TRANSITION

Transition is shifting from one phase or condition of existence to another. Water changing to ice is in Transition. Transition literally refers to the act of movement. Someone entering a new level of growth is in Transition; as is someone who is leaving the material plane behind for a while.

Transition is the name of the game in a personal relationship. It is the very reason that that relationship exists. You and your partner have agreed on the level of Spirit at which you will come together in a mutual contract of support and Love while facilitating one another's growth. That growth is Transition. Each day you are slightly different than you were the day before due to your partner's influence in your life and your interaction with them; whether you perceive it in the moment as being pleasant or unpleasant.

In our general relationships, the lessons tend to not be quite so intense and can fall into a much broader range of experiences.

Each moment of every day is a Transition whether we perceive it or not. Each moment of every day we change who we are and how we see ourselves and the world around us. Because our perceptions create our reality and we react to that created reality, we shift and change who we are in response. Look at who you were and what you believed a year ago -- ten years ago -- and you will see the process at work. The object is to consciously participate. When you are aware of the input and the changes you can assimilate them more readily; acting more and reacting less.

Contrary to how it can sometimes appear there are no harsh aspects to Transition. All things are in Divine order at all times and in all ways whether we like it or not, whether we understand it or not. If the Transition process you find yourself in is resulting in fear or anger, remember these things. There are only two forces at work in the universe: Love and fear. We often fear that which we do not understand. Anger is a child of fear. Neither of these serves your spiritual growth process.

COMMENTS FROM SPIRIT:

There is but one Transition in the multiverse, Dear Children. It is the Transition from not-knowing to knowing. It is the Transition from not being All that Is to BEing All that Is. It is the Transition from not enough to All that Is. It is the Transition from not Loving self to BEing Love.

Blessings to you.

ADAPTABILITY

We can look at life on Earth on a grand scale to see Adaptability in the form of evolution. On a small scale; we can look at an individual's graceful response when someone they had counted on suddenly changes plans for no apparent reason and the first party simply says: "OK". Adaptability is the outgrowth of a flexible nature and the understanding that Spirit is in charge of our lives and that the way that we think events should turn out often has no basis in actuality. It is the result of learning to perceive life from the point of view of a student rather than a victim. When you understand that everything that happens in your life is a gift of Love from Spirit and your soul to you in the flesh and that the intent is to offer you lessons that will assist your growth process, there is no room for anger and Adaptability comes very easily.

Adaptability is a key word in a successful personal relationship. Life is full of little surprises and rarely do they show up more than in a personal relationship setting. They can be tiny or grand but there is at least one every day. Each surprise is a small test. How well do you handle this and if you can't handle it well, then why not? What further lessons do you need along these lines? Simply because we feel that we have completed a certain area in our training and growth does not mean that Spirit will not come along occasionally and re-test us to see what we remember. Our Adaptability along with a spiritual understanding of what is really going on, and why, is the tool that will see us through in these tests.

This is another area of constant challenge. The world is a most unpredictable place and every moment can bring yet another change to how we thought things were going to happen. Adaptability to the rescue! It does no (material world) good to stand petrified as a bus comes rushing toward you. Adaptability says: "Run! Jump! GET-OUTTATHEWAY!"

The only Adaptability that there is, is Adaptability of self and the perception of self. Since your spirit has felt the need to bring this word to your attention today you evidently are about to receive a refresher course in being Adaptable. Trees that do not bend can snap under great pressure. Be ready for a surprise or two in your life!

COMMENTS FROM SPIRIT:

Adaptability, Dear Ones, is only necessary when you are in a state of not-knowingness. When you are aligned with All that Is, there is very little that will surprise you in your existence. Go within and find the multiverse. Go within and find the answers. Go within and find that you are All that Is. We Love you, Beloveds. Be at peace in your nonexistent journey into your own heart; for you shall find the peace of the Creator within.

Blessings.

VULNERABILITY

"To give is an act of power. You must become Vulnerable to receive."

"A closed fist cannot receive a gift, nor a closed mind a new idea."

      Vulnerability is consciously choosing to open the flower of your being to the elements of life. It can seem risky and can seem frightening but it is what we have come to this Earth plane to do. What good is a blossom that never unfolds; that never gives its fragrance and beauty to the garden that nurtured and bore it?

Nowhere is Vulnerability more required nor more often an issue than in a personal relationship. Your partnership requires and sometimes demands access to your innermost reaches on every level on a consistent basis. When you hold back out of whatever fear possesses you, you lessen the strength of the partnership. You lessen the rate of growth for which the potential exists within that relationship. When that fear is there it is definitely one of the issues that you and your partner have agreed in spirit to work on together, but the fear must be conquered if the relationship is to thrive and move on to other issues and joys.

It can be quite difficult to allow ourselves Vulnerability in the open wildness of the mundane world. There are always people and things that seem ready to reach out and rip and tear us. It is only when we have the inner strength to go unarmed and without armor into the world that we see that the thorns and weapons are all cardboard. They are the armor that the others put on so that the armor and thorns that you used to carry can't get close enough to harm them. When you allow your Vulnerability to show it makes the world a safer place for others so that they too might drop their weapons. True; being Vulnerable might induce someone to try to take advantage of you, but remember two things.

First: No one can ever truly harm you. They can only harm themselves by backsliding on their own path.

Second: You are fully protected by the sure knowledge that all things are in Divine order at all times, and whatever seems to happen to you is something you have agreed to, from the soul level, as an opportunity to learn and grow in Spirit. Nothing that could truly harm you will ever be able to touch you.

There is only one form of Vulnerability possible: Vulnerability of self. Obviously, Spirit thinks that you are ready to experience more Vulnerability or you would not have been given this message today.

This word has only one harsh aspect. That is the self-generated fear and anticipation that occurs when one is contemplating opening up. The creatures of our imagination and creation are often the most fearsome that we will ever have to face. Imagined dragons bite the hardest!

COMMENTS FROM SPIRIT:

Vulnerability is much the same as openness. It is only when one becomes fully and completely opened to the multiverse and to All that Is; dissolving all limits and boundaries; becoming without form or walls that all things; yea, even the very flow of existence may flow through you without restraint. That; my Beloveds is Vulnerability. Total Vulnerability brings with it total power and total imperviousness to all sense of harm or danger. BE Love, Children. BE Love in every word, in every thought, in every deed, in every prayer.

BE Love.

      Blessings.

SOLITUDE

    Solitude is that state of going within oneself to achieve a state of mental quietness and attunement necessary to achieve clarity and enlightenment regarding a particular situation or condition of life or Spirit. It is transformational in nature and essence.

    Solitude can be achieved in a personal relationship by isolating yourself and your partner from the invasion of the forces of the outer world in order to focus upon the relationship and on each other TO THE EXCLUSION OF ALL ELSE! While this is not a state that is recommended as a long-term condition the focus and clarity that can be achieved during this state, if both partners are able to achieve and maintain it, can absolutely transform any relationship.

On a personal level, Solitude can be one of the most important gifts we can give ourselves. Take the time to go within in meditation and silence in order to hear that still small voice of the creator within, and KNOW.

Solitude also has a dark side. When one goes into a state of Solitude through the doorways of sadness, anger, or depression those feelings can become the sole focus of the Solitude. The strength of this energy can cause one to semi-permanently withdraw from the world, or in extreme cases to permanently withdraw through a self-inflicted injury or death. According to Spirit; to commit suicide is much akin to getting angry or anxious during a game of pinball and manipulating and jarring the game so hard that it tilts. Not only does the player end the game prematurely but they lose all of the points that they have earned to that point. They are then forced to start a new game from where they began the previous one. It is far better to persevere and to become a Student rather than a victim!

COMMENTS FROM SPIRIT:

Set aside the world, Dear Children, and enter the Loving womb of your generation. Come home into the only Solitude that exists, the Solitude of total One-ness within the heart and mind of the Creator.

Blessings.

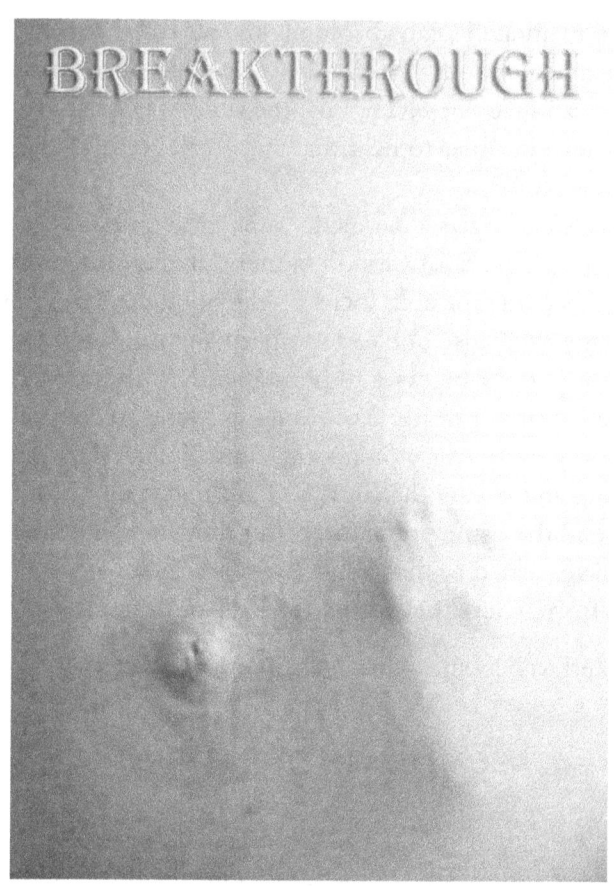

BREAKTHROUGH

    A Breakthrough is exactly that. Imagine a giant wall made of latex rubber that you must pass through to achieve a particular goal. You grit your teeth and start walking into the latex, stretching it further with each step. Each step becomes more difficult as you move forward and the latex exerts more force to hold you back. You dig in all the harder and gather the last dregs of your emotional and physical strength for one final try. You step forward ----- and the barrier ruptures, tumbling you into the unknown. Suddenly you find yourself in a completely different reality. Congratulations! You have just experienced a Breakthrough!

Personal relationships are a fertile seedbed from which many Breakthroughs may grow to flower. All of the little (and not so little) difficulties that you experience in this form of relationship are simply lessons in disguise. Every time you solve the puzzles, learn the lessons, and move forward in growth you have achieved a Breakthrough.

As is common as we discuss these words, a Breakthrough is ultimately and always a personal triumph simply because anything that we perceive as a Breakthrough is by its very nature a positive event as far as we are concerned. The most important Breakthroughs we will experience in our lives are those regarding our own resistances. Whether we are trying to surrender to Spirit, understand ourselves better, release our pain, or any of the other personal challenges that life brings us, each step toward our goal depends on a Breakthrough.

All Breakthroughs are positive events by their very nature, so no harsh aspects can be associated with them except perhaps the changes in our newfound difficulty in finding tolerance for certain behaviors in others and ourselves and the effects that that may have on our relationships with those people. While this may very temporarily seem to be unpleasant, that passes rapidly as we move fully into our new level of awareness.

COMMENTS FROM SPIRIT:

Breakthroughs, Dear Ones, are simply your awareness of moving through your self-imposed lessons on your non-existent journey back to that place that you have never left. We watch your imagined struggles with endless Love, compassion, and support. When first you realize that you are Home we will be here; arms and hearts open to welcome you from your dream. We Love you. Blessings to you as you travel the misty road of your own dreams and defeat the dragons of fears and stubbornness that are born of your Karma and desire to grow.

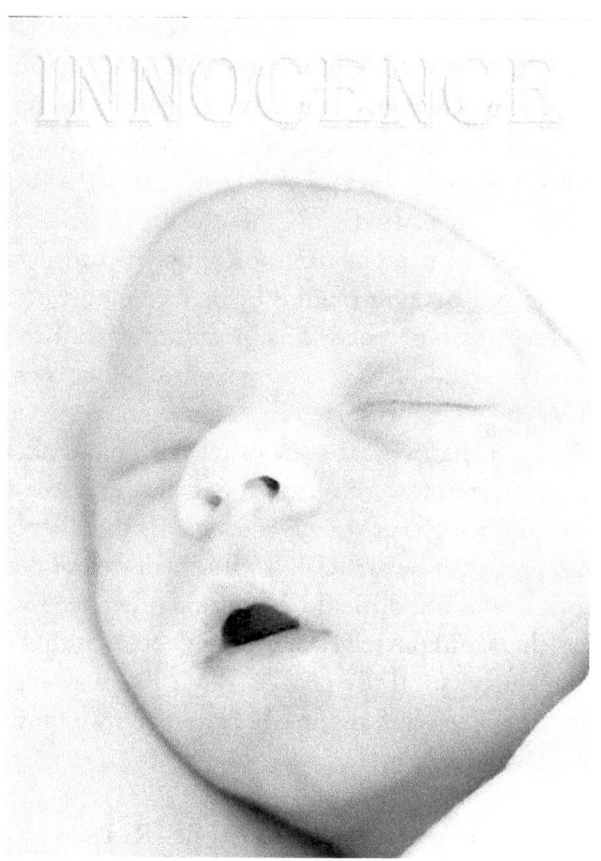

INNOCENCE

Innocence is a state of mind. It is a beautiful thing to see in another person and a wonderful place to live within yourself. One can have experienced much of the world, including a lot of the seamier side, and still, retain or recover their Innocence. Many people seem to associate the concept of Innocence with shyness and a retiring nature. This is not the case at all; although it is often associated with inner purity. Innocence is more than not being or seeing the 'evil' or darkness around us. It is a matter of realizing (at some level) that that exists but making and abiding by a choice to not let it be a part of your life or affect your energy or perception of the world around you.

For those who associate Innocence with physical and mental purity (i.e.: the virginity of body and mind), an intimate partnership would be the last place to look for it. However, it is not only possible but not all that rare to find one, and sometimes both partners are Innocent in spirit. The 'evils' of the world just seem to slide off of their backs. Off-color remarks are lost on them. Their mind just doesn't process in 'that way'. There are also those who have a very 'earthy' sense of humor and sense of self whose minds do work 'that way' who are just as Innocent. They refuse to accept the darkness apparent in the world as part of their reality.

Many would say at first glance that it is quite dangerous to manifest Innocence in the mundane world. It is; they would say, like going swimming in shark-infested waters after shaving with a dull razor. For those who have that mindset, I would say, "You are right" because our perceptions create our reality. If you are aware that all things are in Divine order and that everything that happens in your life is a gift of Love to help you to grow and that these two facts represent the ultimate in protection; then you can swim bloodied in a tank of sharks and piranhas without being touched. Remember: no one can ever truly hurt the inner you; they can only harm themselves (on the level of Spiritual growth).

This word has been brought into your awareness today to invite and urge you to let down your walls; learn to trust Spirit more and accept that you do not have to play the games of darkness that you see about you. You are cordially invited to begin to experience Innocence. Gaining Innocence makes us one step nearer to the Creator.

COMMENTS FROM SPIRIT:

Innocence, Dear Ones, is the key to the doorway of Self. Innocence is the portal through which you must pass in order to find your Greater Self and throughthat, One-ness. You have designed this path and only you can make the changes necessary to complete your journey Home; where you have never left.

Blessings to you, one and all.

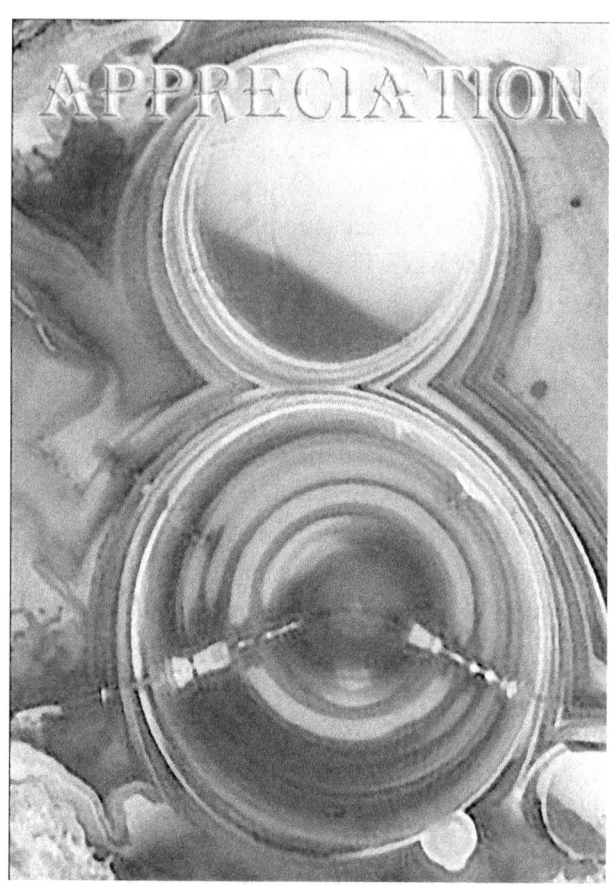

APPRECIATION

    Appreciation is returning to another in response to that which we feel the other(s) have shared with or done which supports us and our positions. Appreciation flows from the heart and can take many forms. It is kin to gratitude (see Gratitude). The difference is that gratitude is inactive; Appreciation does something about it.

    One of the best reasons for Appreciation is the long-term support and guidance of your partner. Perhaps this word has come to you today to encourage you to take more time to express to your partner both verbally and non-verbally how very much you Appreciate both them and the lessons that they have provided to you. It is all a gift and who but your partner Loves (Divine Love) and loves (human love) you enough to put up with all of your stuff long enough to offer you those lessons?

I would like to remind you that all things are a gift of Love from Spirit to you at your request. Your life experience is designed exclusively to stimulate your spiritual growth. The clerk who ignores you; the cop who won't let you off for speeding and the guy who steps on your foot and never looks back are all deserving of our Appreciation. Please remember that the things that we like least in others are those things that we might want to look at most carefully in ourselves. Each one of these folks is doing a personal favor to you by showing you your own tendency to ignore and diminish others without realizing it. Even the best of us will find ourselves doing this from time to time.

You are invited to look into the continuing quagmire of poor self-worth that so many of us wallow in. It is time to pull yourself out of the muck, clean yourself off and look at how very far you have come in your awareness and growth over even the past year. Appreciation is called for not only for your attempts and progress but also for the events and experiences which have come to you as tools and lessons for your growth. All things are gifts!

COMMENTS FROM SPIRIT:

Appreciation is a word that has meaning only on the human level. It is born of a sense of separateness and a lack of value of self as an integrated aspect of All that Is. While it can serve a positive function in your material realm it is one of the concepts that we encourage you to pass beyond as you come to know the One-ness of all. You are a part of the Beingness of the Creator and the Universe is both you and yours. BE Love; Dear Ones, and be at peace within and among yourselves.

Blessings.

ASSURANCE

    Assurance is a verbally or otherwise transmitted statement or feeling that events and circumstances will become or remain supportive and positive as far as the listener is concerned. It is the mother picking up the child with a banged-up knee; holding the child lovingly and saying: "It's all right, honey, It's all right." It is the Creator giving us a beautiful dawn to wake up to and a sunset to end our day. It is our own heart daring to hope after a series of disappointments.
    Personal relationships are built upon a raft of Assurances. There is an implied or stated Assurance that the relationship will exist for an indefinite but not-short time. There is an Assurance of mutual

trust and support within the parameters of the agreement between the partners involved. Perhaps this word has come to you today because that sense of Assurance seems to be wavering if not for you then perhaps for your partner in your relationship. Take a good hard look at the situation. Perhaps even talk to your partner about it and decide what the path is that you wish to follow in your situation. Whatever you do, remember to do it with Love and with the Assurance that all things are in Divine order at all times.

Assurances in the public sector often take the form of contracts. Everything we do and everything we experience is as a result of a soul-level contract that we have with all others involved. Rest Assured that all of your experiences are put into your life at your own soul's request in order to help you to learn that which you came into this life to learn about. Your only contract; your only real Assurance comes from Spirit. As long as you never forget that you will find that life is smooth and relatively easy because you will find the meaning in every situation and refuse to ever be the victim.

Self-Assurance is a wonderful thing as long as it is higher-self Assurance. It is when we attempt to pump ourselves up from within on the material level that we might well find ourselves full of hot air -- or worse. The difference between the perception of self-worth and the manifestation of a worthy self marks the difference between ego and growth.

COMMENTS FROM SPIRIT:

Be Assured, Beloveds, that you reside constantly and forever in the Heart of Hearts; the center of Love; the very arms of the Creator who surrounds you with All that Is. Can there be any further Assurance in the multiverse? Thou art God/Goddess. Thou art All that Is. Thou; in thy tiny seeming-self, are the Alpha and the Omega of existence. Be Assured. BE Love. Be at peace within thy heart and soul as all things are as they well might be. We Love you all.

Blessings.

TOLERANCE

    This is one of the most important concepts we have to learn about in this material existence. It is also one of the more dangerous. In order to Tolerate a person or thing, one must first somehow feel superior in some way to that person or thing! While all beings are One, we manifest as and most of us normally think of ourselves as being separate from one another. We are indeed separate but only as the fingers on a hand are separate or a leg is separate from an arm. If you enlarge your field of mental and physical view you will find that we are merely appendages of the same organism. Does this give the pointer finger the right to demean the little finger for its small size and relatively poor strength? It takes all of the fingers to hold a gift and as those of us who have brought groceries home know, there are times when the rest of the hand is busy when the littlest finger does a lot of work that none of the others are capable of doing at that moment.

Tolerance is critical in a growing personal relationship. In a Mature relationship between two complete and whole individuals, it would never come up. Intimate living with the same person over a long period of time is like wearing a pair of shoes that sorta kinda fit but do pinch on some occasions. You and your partner are most likely in a constant process of adjustment to one another just as your foot and the shoe would be. Using the shoe example, there are spots on your foot that might become quite sore and perhaps even sport an open wound as a result of the breaking-in process. Even though the shoes might otherwise be extremely comfortable and flattering to you your attention is drawn and held by the sore spots. Every time you think about putting on the shoe the sore spots again claim your attention. We experience the same thing in a relationship. As comfortable as a relationship may be, there will always be areas where you and your partner will seem to rub one another absolutely raw. Tolerance has come to you today to remind you that those areas of sensitivity are the very ones that you need and have requested lessons in. There is no need or reason to be angry with yourself or your partner. Your partner is serving your spiritual needs by being the loving irritant that draws your attention to those areas. When you have absorbed and accepted the lessons the chafing will end.

It is critical that each one of us realize that every person on this planet is following the lessons that they need in order to proceed on their spiritual path. We may find those lessons strange or even offensive. That does not mean that the others person's opinion is 'wrong' or that ours is 'right'.

Perhaps the best illustration I can think of came in response to a question from a participant in the very first class I offered as a Spiritual teacher. One of my 'teachers' who was disguised as a 'student' at the time asked me in reference to the various religions that we had been discussing "Which is the right way to believe?".

I was stumped for an answer but Spirit stepped right in and

provided one of the most eloquent, elegant answers I've ever heard.

Spirit had me tell the class this:
"Imagine if you will the uncreated Creator as a sphere with limitless facets floating in space. Imagine all beings in a sphere surrounding the Creator and at an equal distance from the Creator and from one another."

"Each of these beings is aligned directly with one of the limitless faces of the Creator. Each being has its own view and perception of who and what the Creator is and its own unique path to return to the Creator. Remember the story of the blind men and the elephant? People in proximity to one another will have very similar views of what the Creator is to them; and very similar paths. They will band together in what you call sects. Groups of sects will have vaguely similar views of the Creator and will form what you refer to as religions."

"At the same time, however, other sects and religions are forming at other locations in the outer sphere. Those arranged 90 degrees away from the first group will have a very different view and a very different path, yet their way is absolutely true for them."

"And look! Directly opposite the first group is another group whose view and path is exactly contradictory to that first group. Does that invalidate their beliefs? Is this still not the same Creator? All that has changed is the point of view.

"The point is", Spirit went on, "that each being has its own shortest and most direct path to the Creator and must walk that road and no other. The curious thing is that the nearer we all come to center – to the Creator - the nearer we come to one another. The closer we come to the Creator the further we get from religions. At the center all beings are One."

We tend to be hyper-critical of ourselves with almost no Tolerance for errors on our own part. Sometimes we let our disappointment with self leak out into the world by becoming hyper-critical of others as well. If this word has captured your attention today it is because you need to take it a little easier on yourself at least in some degree. Nobody is perfect and each time you make what appears to be an error it is only that; an error. You pick yourself up, review the situation to see what you might do differently next time and move on. BEing Love must start from within, so learn to Love yourself, please.

Tolerance builds one internally and spiritually until you reach the point of realizing that we are all one and that all things are in Divine order. At that point there is no need for Tolerance nor can it even exist for it implies separateness and less than perfection. If someone chooses to take advantage of your Tolerance in the meantime, remember they cannot hurt or cheat you. They can only slow themselves on their path by traveling less than their shortest path of greatest light.

COMMENTS FROM SPIRIT:

Tolerance, my Beloveds, is only another word for another form of Divine Love. It is a way of validating and supporting in your everyday life that all things are in Divine order at all times and that all beings are One. We ask you to be Tolerant of those around you as we encourage them to be Tolerant of you in your lessons. You are all in the same dream and each of you provides the other with the aspects that are necessary for your successful completion of this game you call life. With that completion the tool of Tolerance will cease to exist.
Blessings to you.

COOPERATION

     To Co-operate is to work together to achieve a common goal. It is literally this: 'Co' means with; together, in concert, in partnership. 'Operation' is that which is undertaken or accomplished or the act of attempting or doing.
     There can be no personal relationship without Cooperation. Every day there are aspects of our life with another that are made easier or made possible because of the abiding sense of Cooperation in the relationship. Some nights it may be the preparation of dinner, some days it may be who stays home with the sick child. Partnership depends on Cooperation to succeed. This word has come into your

awareness today in order to remind you of that fact. Take a good close look at the way your relationship has been manifesting. Has the balance of Cooperation seemed to have slipped to one side or the other? Are you or your partner carrying too much of the load? It's time to even the scales. If you have been letting your partner do most of the work in the relationship perhaps it would be a nice gesture to take over a little more than half to show them how much they are appreciated. If you feel that you have been overworked, Love yourself enough to sit down with them and talk it out.

Cooperation is also of great importance in order for progress to be made in any general relationship. In a relationship of any kind, be it personal or general, the parties involved have agreed at some level to work on the same 'project'. Just as the best progress occurs when two oxen are yoked together in order to pull a heavy load and they are both pointing in the same direction and coordinate their efforts. If you are not achieving the progress you desire in your business and casual relationships, who are you 'out of sync' with and what that you are thinking or doing needs to change in order to bring the partners into harmony so that the work can be accomplished?

Cooperation usually requires a second party; so the only way that you can apply this to self is to Cooperate with your higher self, which really isn't a bad idea!

COMMENTS FROM SPIRIT:

Cooperation, Dear Ones, implies separateness. There is no separateness except in your own minds and imaginations. Go to that place within you where all of existence is One with Love. Bring this consciousness into your material world dream and you will embody the essence of Cooperation in your very being.

Blessings to you.

EXCITEMENT

Excitement is pleasant agitation with hope, joy, and anticipation mixed in. While it can sometimes indicate that the individual is not living totally in the now it can actually be the stimulus required to improve one's outlook or state of mind or to prepare one mentally for that which is to come.

Excitement is a good thing in a personal relationship. Because the innate nature of this type of relationship is constant mutual change there is always an element of the unknown involved. Perhaps it is time to consciously create some Excitement for your partner. Let's see, now ... what would my partner really like that I could surprise them with?

Excitement is sometimes shared with strangers at some public events such as a ball game or a concert. It seems that there needs to be a certain degree of emotional intimacy for Excitement to be mutual. Many people are not willing to allow that degree of emotional closeness with just anybody and withhold their public manifestation of Excitement. Now might be a good time to start to loosen up. Allow yourself to participate more openly in the emotional processes of those around you.

Excitement is a strictly personal emotion, of course. How dull and boring would life be if there was never any Excitement of any kind? Excitement is either a precursor or a result of change and change is always in support of growth even if that aspect is not immediately obvious. Growth is the ultimate reason for this thing we call life. If you feel that you need never show your emotions to be 'cool', This word says that it is time to loosen up and LIVE!

COMMENTS FROM SPIRIT:

Excitement is the bloom on the plant of wonder. It is the fragrance in the air of Life and the ringing of the bell of existence. It is the exuberance of living fully, of Be-ing totally. We invite you to Come into the heart of your self; the essence of existence and dance the dance of Excitement. Dance the dance of Life.

Blessings.

EMERGENCE

While this word can have many meanings, it will refer in this text to a coming out of the dark cavern of our own fears and insecurities. There is an allusion to coming from darkness into light that is inherent in this word. Years ago, while dealing with some permanently angry and militantly anti-male women, Spirit gave me this letter to share with all those who reject the opposite gender with spite and venom (because, ultimately, of their own deep fears):

" You foolish, bitter people, huddled into the cave of your own fears, who have slammed the door behind you and sit together cursing the darkness; know you not that all things have been created in balance? Male and female energies are both required to be in balance. When you remove yourself from the world of the other, you will find that you will begin manifesting their energy and attributes within yourself in order to restore Divine balance. In other words, you become that which you most fear and dislike!

Children, we love, nurture and guide you if you will but allow. We cannot select your experiences for you nor will we interfere when you select a path that is longer or more difficult than that which you had originally selected before entering this life experience. Those choices are always yours to make. As you are aware; for every choice there are both costs and rewards.

We love and support you as always; regardless of your choices and will support and nurture you to the extent that you will allow. We bid you peace. "

    Extending this we can see that fundamentalism or extremism in any form or area creates an imbalance that must then be overcome from within. Many times this creates an imbalance in the opposite direction. It is from this condition; whether it refers to sexual preference, self-worth or any of the other things that we use to hold ourselves down or back that Emergence relates to. Emergence in this context refers to moderation; to following the middle path as propounded in Buddhism.

    All of us -- every one -- have secrets that we hope that our partner will never find out about. These can range from the silly to the profound. What they are doesn't matter. It is simply the fact that they exist that puts a damper on the growth potential of the relationship. That is not to say that the obvious answer is to turn around and spill all of these secrets into your partner's ear. Humans being as they are; that is most likely a sure way to put the relationship at least into a state of profound stress. Perhaps a gentler yet still very effective way to handle this situation would be to look back at those secrets and situations as a student. What are the lessons carried by each one? Do the lessons form a pattern? What is the pattern, then? If you can learn from your lessons you will never have to repeat them and your relationship as well as both you and your partner will reap the rewards and benefits. There must be some reason that this word jumped out at you today. Perhaps it is time to process this stuff you've been hiding (and hiding behind). Good luck!

Every day, every time that our life touches another's, we have an opportunity; by daring to Emerge from out own protective shell in a non-threatening manner, to encourage others to do so also. Think for a moment how wonderful it would be if we could return to a society that cared about itself and each person cared for and about their neighbor. As with everything, it all starts within our own heart. You are invited and encouraged to take a chance -- to open yourself to whatever degree that you can to those around you. As you open, so they will. As they do you can open further but it all starts with you; starting now.

Following the theme of the previous paragraph, we all have our own dark closets to come out of. These are the same closets where we hide our very own personal skeletons. You know; those aspects of self that we are less than comfortable with and 'would just die' if anyone else found out about. These are the darknesses that trap us. The way out of the 'fear' closet is to change yourself in whatever way is necessary so that whatever is hiding in there with you is no longer important. You can accomplish this by changing yourself so that whatever that was is no longer who you are or by changing your perceptions so that what others think of the things that you have included in your learning process is no longer of importance to you -- you are comfortable with yourself. Consider this word's arrival in your consciousness as an invitation to come into the light of your own acceptance and Love. It's about time!

Although Emergence can seem frightening because we are stretching the limits of our comfort and because some people might be tempted to take advantage of us (Gee...is that a victim talking?), remember that no one can ever truly 'hurt' us; they can only 'hurt' themselves. Consider the tortoise...it never gets anywhere unless it sticks its neck out.

COMMENTS FROM SPIRIT:

Emergence, Dear Ones, is simply coming out of the darkness

caused by a lack of true knowledge regarding yourself and your place in the multiverse. It is a casting aside of the concepts and practices of limitations in your own mind and an awakening of infinite power within all things; as all are One with you. All are One with All there Is. Total Emergence into the light of Be-ing brings you into the essence of that power, that is Divine Love for all things, all times, all beings.

Blessings.

OPENNESS

There is an old saying: "A closed fist cannot accept a gift, nor a closed mind an idea". This word invites you to set aside your self-perceived limitations. Open your heart and mind and become more than you thought you were. Openness invites you to Open yourself up as though you were a blossoming flower so that those about you may see the inner you (many people find this to be extremely threatening due to their own insecurities). It also invites you to Open your eyes and ears to more completely perceive the 'truth' of the material world about you. The ideal in this situation is to become present but transparent; where perception flows into, through, and from you without restraint or coloration. At this point you become the Creator's Lens; doing nothing of yourself, but allowing the Love and Blessings to flow from and through you. You also allow others to see the Creator more clearly as you manifest those gifts in your everyday transactions and Be-ing.

You are invited to live and express the Truth with the drawing of this word. It is seldom an instant achievement, but it is a noble aspiration and an honor when achieved.

The only possible harsh aspect would be your own discomfort in giving up the walls you have learned to hide behind. Those walls are: self-deception, fear, falsehoods and reduced self-image. See Healing for more information.

COMMENTS FROM SPIRIT:

Openness speaks of the releasing of that which binds -- of being boundless. Limitations are entirely self-generated at the material existence level. We Open; we increase in scope not by growing more but by limiting less; as all are one with The One who is limitless. It is only your perception as being less that One that closes you in.

Blessings.

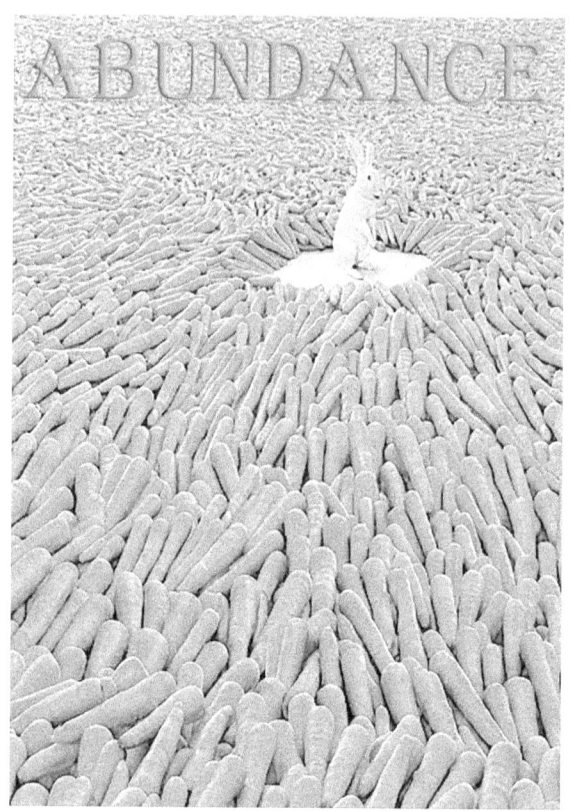

ABUNDANCE

Abundance is generally taken to mean more than enough of something that we think we need; such as money. There are two points to consider here. The first is that money has only one purpose and that purpose is to buy time -- to buy freedom from those necessities that take up our time or the time of others.

The second and far more important point is that Abundance is freedom from want. Remember -- for almost all of us, the truth is that we have all the necessary material things we need in each moment. We are probably not overly hungry; we are most likely clothed in some fashion and we probably have a shelter of some sort in which we reside. It is only when we look into the future with fear that we perceive ourselves as being in need. Abundance can be achieved by working on either side of the equation. We can gain more material wealth, thus achieving the appearance of freedom or we can adjust our ideas of how much we really need; thus becoming happier with what we already have. Either way, true Abundance is nearer our grasp.

Abundance in a personal relationship refers in many cases not to the amount of love and camaraderie we are being offered but to an increase in our ability to recognize, enjoy and accept what is already there.

In other situations, the emotions of the one we are focused on can begin to change in our favor, becoming more Abundant.

Many times if we can only change our attitude or perceptions of the matter, all that we need to feel that Abundance has been achieved and lies within our grasp.

In other instances, the attitude of the other party can mellow and turn in your favor, becoming more Abundant.

Personal Abundance can take many forms. It is marked by increased feelings of well-being and contentment. In many cases, there will be the achievement of some goal; bringing emotional and/or physical rewards.

Occasionally we think we have Abundance. Sometimes; and worse yet, we truly have Abundance but don't understand or choose to ignore what Abundance is about. In these instances, Spirit will often remove it from us so that we may learn to appreciate it and utilize it in a more appropriate fashion.

COMMENTS FROM SPIRIT:

The ultimate source of Abundance lies within. Our intimate connection as part of the Creator of All that Is assures us in each lifetime of access to the wonders and Abundance that is the universe. As a hungry pilgrim plucks the fruit from a tree as he passes, so we pluck from the Tree of Life every experience that our soul feels we truly need. We are in Abundance at all times if only we will look deeply enough to recognize that state.

Blessings to you as you experience the Abundance of the Creator!

CONSTANCY

Constancy is not a static thing. While it refers to sameness, it is often movement, but it is reliable movement. The sun comes up every morning. There is a full moon every 28 days. The tide flows in, and the tide flows out. We pass into a body; we pass out of the body and into Spirit. Constancy is truth and sameness within movement and time. It is rhythm within and around our existence. This rhythm is the beating of the Heart of Hearts, the source of all Love; activating the flow of Divine Love throughout the multiverse.

Many people value Constancy very highly in a personal relationship. What they usually mean by Constancy, though, is physical fidelity regardless of the circumstances. It seems that these people are equating physical fidelity with two things. First; they operate under the false belief that physical fidelity is the most important form. All of us know couples where there has been no love or nurturing for many years yet physical fidelity is maintained for the sake of appearances and form even though there is no emotional connection or fidelity to match. Emotional fidelity is by far the more important form. Without it the physical form is meaningless.

The second aspect is reflected in the many of us who are lazy in our participation within the relationship. If we can force fidelity on our partner we feel that our relationship is secure and that they will not leave us or cause us discomfort. It is much like the robber barons of yesteryear who would loot castles and palaces of their treasures then lock those treasures into a dark cave so that no would know that they had them. As a result the treasures might as well cease to exist because no one else can have them either. It is a possession thing and a very selfish stance. The physical presence of our partner is a convenience. Their emotional presence is absolutely necessary. Without it there is no relationship.

Constancy is an absolute necessity in any ongoing business proposition. You must be able to depend on what your business partner said yesterday being honored today and have a pretty good idea of what to expect from him/her tomorrow. It is that flow of sameness on which trust is built. It is trust upon which business is built. It is business upon which much of this civilization depends and from which most of us derive our living wage. This word has come to you today to remind you that others are depending on your Constancy and that you should perhaps look at it and yourself more carefully so as to see how you might improve in that area.

So many of us have trouble being true to ourselves, to our own needs and beliefs; it can be very difficult to honor ourselves enough to say "no" for whatever reason to someone whom we normally defer to. The 'truth' aspect of Constancy demands that we do go within ourselves and find the value and the Divine nature there. It demands that based on that value we have Constancy within ourselves; that we consistently honor that which we feel to be 'right'. To thine own self be true. That is the message that Constancy brings to you today in reference to one's self.

Although some may choose to manifest their Constancy in what appear to be 'negative' ways; always doing the same type of 'negative' behaviors; at least the rest of us know from our experiences what to look out for in the future.

COMMENTS FROM SPIRIT:

Constancy is easy to define and understand. Divine Love.

Blessings.

GRACE

Grace is the art of being in balance under any circumstance. Grace means understanding that what is happening to and around you is the absolute, perfect thing to be happening in order to serve the spiritual growth needs of all concerned. Having Grace also means totally accepting those happenings as 'the way things are' in the moment called 'now'. Grace enables this acceptance whether we personally like or understand what's going on or not.

Showing Grace in a personal relationship can involve anything from a petty annoyance to a major difficulty. There is a phrase..."a saving Grace". This phrase is particularly accurate in a personal relationship situation. Grace energy enables forgiveness and growth in a situation that would normally mark the end of a relationship.

There is another phrase that comes to mind here. That phrase is: "Grace under fire". The material world is a world of pressure; choices and decisions; of confusion and apparent setbacks. Take a moment now to relax with the energy of Grace. Feel a peacefulness flow over you and feel your body and mind relax. The calm acceptance that is the condition of Grace does not mean inactivity or lack of desire to improve the situation. It means being at peace with each step along the way.

Grace normally deals with external observations and activities. It also has some application on the internal level when dealing with coming out of a place of self-loathing or self-incrimination; regardless of the degree.

COMMENTS FROM SPIRIT:

Grace is an angelic gift. It is the dawn of hope tinted with a blush of compassion. It is the gift of love when love is hard to find. It is an emotional state of high energy and vibration. It is Love in action. Grace unto thee—Grace be thine.

DECEIT

"First you say you will and then you won't; then you say you do but then you don't...." says the old song. This is exactly what Deceit is all about. It is pretending to be or do a certain thing in such a way that others allow themselves to be placed in a position of trust and/or dependence then suddenly and unexpectedly changing your position; doing at the expense of the others involved that which serves you.

There are many forms of Deceit practiced in the average relationship. They can range from the tiny to the blockbuster variety. All of them are lessons for all of the parties involved but that does not necessarily make them pleasant. The defining question is this: How would I feel if my partner was doing the same thing to me right now?

Your answer should go far in directing your next steps.

There are many forms of Deceit practiced in the average relationship, whether personal or casual. They can range from the tiny to the blockbuster variety. All of them are lessons for all of the parties involved, but that does not necessarily make them pleasant. The defining question is this: How would I feel if my partners in these activities were doing the same thing to me right now?

Your answer should go far in directing your next steps.

Deceit of self is the most common and the most insidious form. It can be so easy to rationalize -- to fool oneself at least temporarily into accepting that what we normally would not even consider doing will be OK just this once, just this twice, just this week, this month, this lifetime.

We do have absolute free will. We can do anything our heart desires but we would do well to remember that for every decision there are both costs and rewards. On the soul level, we know exactly what those costs and rewards will be. When we choose to go ahead in a particular situation we are accepting those costs and we are accepting those rewards.

To paraphrase Abe Lincoln: You can fool part of yourself part of the time, and you can fool all of yourself part of the time. You cannot fool all of yourself (Spirit) all of the time (actually, you can't fool Spirit at all).

To thine own self be true.
Sounds like a plan.

There are nothing but harsh lessons in store for those who practice Deceit. Proceed at your own risk!

COMMENTS FROM SPIRIT:

Deceit; Dear Ones, is the heart that does not have room within for the Creator. Deceit is the being who accepts themselves as worthless or diminished, whatever their form. Deceit is the soil from which 'evil' in all of its forms takes root and grows. Come into the wholeness of the Light, Dear Ones. Come into the Heart of Hearts; the everlasting Love that knows no bounds nor ever will. Come Home to Love. There is no Deceit in Divinity nor is there 'evil' in the heart of the All that Is.

IMAGINATION

    Imagination is the most powerful force in the universe, other than Divine Love. Imagination can create or destroy current reality. Imagination is faster than light and more powerful than an atomic bomb. I'll prove it! Imagine yourself standing on the surface of Pluto. Look up into the everlasting night above you. See the landscape around you. Now continue on to the fourth planet of the nearest star; Alpha Centauri. See the civilization; the beings, the ecosystem. Congratulations. You have just traveled in seconds a distance that will take light over four years! Now picture an old dead burned-out hulk of a planet 100 times the size of the earth. The planet has never supported life and nothing depends on it for existence. With a quick thought, Imagine that it simply has ceased to exist; in fact, it has never existed. And so it is. Perception creates reality and your Imagination is your perception of the moment.

Imagine if you will that the person you loved so much so many years ago; the one who never even knew that you existed, had returned your love at that time and that the two of you were celebrating your tenth year of a fairy tale marriage. Congratulations. You have just created a bubble of reality that did not exist before this moment.

Imagination is responsible for every aspect of what we refer to as progress, from using a cave for shelter to details of the construction of the latest spacecraft. Our world as we are experiencing it is literally a product of the Imagination of the collective being known as humanity.

Every change that has ever occurred at the hands of Man is the result of either an 'accident' that creates a new situation that enables someone to see things in a new way (Imagine that!) or someone sitting and daydreaming: "What if....?"

Imagination in a personal relationship can be a real delight. Imagine how your partner would react if...." Imagine us ten years from now when....." Step farther than the bounds of the known. Stretch your mind and your belief in yourself. Go beyond. That's what this word is trying to tell you. Go for it!

The message is to go beyond what you think is possible. Examining the realm of the unexplored is what this word is asking of you. Do you hear it?

As with everything else, intent is everything. Keep your intent high and there will never be a problem.

COMMENTS FROM SPIRIT:

Throw open the doors of your Imagination, Beloveds. Feel that you are One with All that Is. Pretend that you literally have no limits. Invent that your merest thought has the power to change what you call reality. Now wake up, and know that all of this is true, and more.

Imagine.

WELL-BEING

    This is one of those words which seem to have two meanings. The first, in its common usage; simply means that for the moment everything seems to be going just fine and that you feel pretty good about your life.
    The second and somewhat more esoteric meaning is the one that we shall use in this discussion. It refers to the inner sense of the word which refers to a 'well' being as opposed to an 'unwell' being. To be a 'well' being one should be in harmony and balance within and without. When one has Well-being in this form; Well-being in the other form is one of the byproducts.

Consider for a moment that your relationship is much like an entity of its own. It has a life essence (if it doesn't, why are you in it?); breaths; has good days and bad days; plans for the future; loves and grieves. Seek harmony and balance for this entity. It is truly the first child of the partnership. It may become and continue to be a Well-being.

Harmony and balance within yourself reflect in everything you do and affect everyone whose life touches yours. By being a Well-being yourself you improve the world around you. You encourage it also to become a Well-being.

COMMENTS FROM SPIRIT:

Well-being, Loved ones; is that condition or aspect of total balance within and without. It is the concept of walking always in the glory of your own Be-ingness, touching with Love all that comes to you. BE-ing Love is the ultimate in Well-being. BE Love, we implore you. BE Love in every word, in every thought, in every deed and in every prayer. That, indeed, is a Well being.

Blessings.

INTEGRATION

Integration is the bringing together of two or more originally separate items or thoughts that may or may not appear to be compatible into a single, cohesive whole. Once the whole is achieved, there will be absolutely no hint or trace of evidence that there had ever been more than one of whatever it was.

Partnership is a process of Integration, yet with a difference. While the partners are trying to unify into a fortress of mutuality from which to face the world, there is yet a definite need to maintain a sense of separateness. As the poet, Kahlil Gibran said so beautifully in his masterpiece *The Prophet:*

> "....But let there be spaces in your togetherness,
> And let the winds of the heavens dance between you.
>
> Love one another, but make not a bond of love:
> Let it rather be a moving sea between the shores of your souls.
> Fill each others cup but drink not from one cup.
> Give one another of your bread but eat not of the same loaf.
> Sing and dance together and be joyous, but let each one of you be alone,
> Even as the strings of a lute are alone though they quiver to the same music.
> Give your hearts, but not into each other's keeping.
> For only the hand of Life can contain your hearts.
> And stand together yet not too near together:
> For the pillars of the temple stand apart,
> And the oak tree and the cypress grow not in each other's shadow."

Integration does sometimes occur in our dealings with the mundane world, but as it does the relationships in question are converted to personal relationships of one sort or another.

The most difficult and the most critical of Integration is our Integration of self. The helpless child; the romantic, the student, the teacher, the lover, the seeker, the guru, the Creator and many other faces of our 'self' reside within us; taking turns coming to the fore as we move through our days and our lives. Integration invites us to manifest all of these at once; in balance and with Love. It may sound difficult but it's actually quite easy once you get past your own fears. Spirit is here to help in whatever way is necessary. Remember, it's all for your growth and benefit. Enjoy!

There may be an uncomfortable feeling from time to time as you exceed your old boundaries but there can never be a harsh aspect to Integration; as all beings are already One.

COMMENTS FROM SPIRIT:

That which you refer to as Integration is on the ultimate level only a matter of extracting yourself from your own limitations and doubts.

You are All that Is. Integration, Dear Ones; is the natural state. Any other perception is faulty and limited, although always with a purpose. Release your need to be separate and your need to be 'in control'. Return to the primal state of Love and comfort where all are joined at the heart. Come home in your thoughts. Come home in your essence. Come home to One-ness. We Love you.

Blessings.

WORTH

Ah! Worth; here is one of the core issues in the experience of every person alive. Worth is the innate value of something. It has nothing to do with your preferences or desires although those can easily modify your perception of a thing's Worth. The value of a female mosquito who is currently feasting on your earlobe is apparently quite different to you and to the eggs that she will lay; as it is also to the fish that will eat her shortly after the eggs are laid. To a large degree, the Worth that we assign to a thing is determined on a personal level. The true meaning of the Word, however, has to do with the fact that all things are One, and that all beings; be they mosquitoes or archangels; are created of the Creator by the Creator and as such are a part of the body of All that Is. Thus; all things; all beings have the innate Worth of the Creator if only we allow ourselves to see it. The Worth of something is that it exists even if only in our own minds.

The Worth of a personal relationship lies in its important role in our life. We (ideally) find Divine Love, human love, succor, challenges, rewards, pain, pleasure, apparent gain, apparent loss, excitement, boredom, and a host of other wonderful growth opportunities which are often handed to us on a silver platter in a personal relationship. Because of the forced proximity, there is usually no easy way to escape or evade these lessons so we must face and assimilate them. The innate value of this relationship, and our partner who has agreed to provide and share in all of these lessons, is that 'enclosed' aspect. It's like having your own personal tutor. Lucky you!

All of these things may also be found in a general relationship. The main difference is that often we have the option of 'bailing out' of a situation with less difficulty in this type of arrangement than in the previous one. The opportunity to lean instead of learn is always there. What a gift!

Self-Worth. The ultimate challenge.
Bingo!

What is your innate value? How do you perceive yourself? Does that take into account that you are created of the Creator by the Creator? Does it take into account that all things are in Divine order at all times and in all ways? Does it consider that everything that has ever happened to you is nothing more than a lesson offered from and with Love for the sole purpose of assisting you in your effort to learn and grow? Does it portray your determination to always be a student and never a victim? If you answered no to any one of these questions, Spirit has come into your life today in the form of this word; this message; to urge you to shift your perception of yourself into the positive. Today is the rock upon which tomorrow is built. Make it strong. Shape it just right and your tomorrows will exceed your wildest dreams.

The realization of self Worth , as opposed to the perception of self Worth, marks the boundary between growth and ego.

COMMENTS FROM SPIRIT:

Worth, Beloveds, is only an imposed limitation. Because all things in the multiverse are One, there can be no difference possible; therefore no way to measure Worth as opposed to non-Worth. All things; all beings have the Worth of All that Is. Nothing more, nothing less.

Blessings.

HAPPINESS

Although it seems like it would be easy, this is one of the more difficult words to accurately describe. Happiness is a state of joyful awareness and radiance. It has a wide range of manifestation; both in quantity and qualities, depending on the person and situation. It can range from a short, slight smile to a permanent state of transcendence and joyful existence in every moment. It is a condition that all of us wish we had more of and some of feel that we never get (of course, it is our own pattern of perceptions and perpetual 'victimhood' that prevents us from achieving that state.)

The Happiest 'Happy's and the saddest 'sad's are available

in personal relationships. Because we let our defenses down and to a certain degree allow someone else to blend with us and intertwine their being and their life with ours, they are in a position to affect us more deeply than anyone else. This choice on our part to become vulnerable is what provides the opportunity for our emotions to come into play. We have all seen people who have become so distanced from their inner feelings that they seem to have no feelings of any kind except perhaps anger, which is often used to hold others at bay so as not to invite the interactions described above. We are in this body and in this life to experience it, not to avoid it. When we ignore the reason for our physical nature; when we avoid the lessons of life because some of them might not be pleasant; we are, spiritually speaking, 'cutting classes'. Since we are both the teacher and the student however, we will never get away with it and it comes back to us over and over in different ways until we 'get it'. Sometimes we don't get the message in just one lifetime. Spirit says: "That's O.K., you can come back and do this as often as you like." If you have been avoiding life out of fear that you might be hurt (again?), remember that every one of those experiences was a lesson that you did not understand or you wouldn't still feel hurt by them. By avoiding the possibility of more hurt you are also avoiding the possibility of more Happiness. The choice is up to you as always. Spirit urges you to open your heart to both the lessons and the Happiness. Eventually you will find Happiness in the lessons.

Happiness is the kind of emotion that is catalytic in nature. When you are Happy, it is contagious. The people around you usually tend to share your Happiness. It also has the power; if only for a moment, to remove the barriers between people. Thus, it cannot exist in the vacuum of a non-personal relationship. Simply by being -- at least in small part -- it creates a personal relationship with those it touches. Reach out and touch the world with Happiness. It's a wonderful thing to do!

Of course, all Happiness can only be personal Happiness. The question is: "How many of us are personally Happy"? How often do you put on your Happy facade and set out to fool the world (and yourself). If I were to tell you to go -- right now -- into that inner 'tar pit' of unhappiness and despair that most people hide deep within themselves, do you feel the tears arise as the cold hand of despair begins to close around your heart? If so, you are fairly normal (at least in that regard). It simply means that you cannot experience true Happiness until you dredge all of those old fears and hurts into the Light so that they can be aired out and healed. You have probably heard the phrase 'peeling the onion' thousands of times. Experiencing life and growth is another of those onion peeling jobs. Just remember that with every layer removed, tears are likely; but with every layer removed, you are closer to the center. Good luck and blessings. It's not easy, but WOW, is it worth it!

The only possible harsh aspect to Happiness is if you are loudly experiencing it around someone at whose apparent cost it has been obtained. At that point you will most likely be given a lesson in the necessity of Being Love in all ways and at all times. To find Happiness in another's apparent loss is not BEing Love and they will probably be glad to elaborate on the concept for you. Even if they won't, Spirit will be sure to.

COMMENTS FROM SPIRIT:

Happiness is the natural state of expression for the being in balance with themselves and the multiverse. How could such a being not be Happy; for all things are in Divine order in all ways and at all 'times' and all things are of the Creator; who IS Love. Therefore; all things ARE Love. How could one who understands this not be Happy.

Blessings.

DEPENDABILITY

Dependability is like your fingers...something you can count on. Seriously, though; broken down and traced to its roots; the word means this: Depend (literally) means 'to hang from or be supported by'. A related word is 'pendant', as in a necklace. Ability in this instance means worthiness over a span of time. Dependability, then, means something or someone's worthiness for a period of time to be supportive in whatever way is necessary.

It also has a meaning relating to constancy, both physical and emotional: being much the same over a period of (usually long) time.

Dependability is one of the cornerstones of any personal

relationship worth maintaining. Both of the meanings come into play here. Even in a completely balanced relationship, each partner grows to expect or Depend on their partner to regularly assume a certain part or proportion of the workload and expenses of maintaining the household. This word may have come into your life today so you will be moved to take a good long look at the division of responsibility in your relationship. Are you giving 90%, or 10%? Or is it somewhere in between? How do you feel about the situation? Is it time to shift the balance? What needs to be done? Do you have the strength of character and balance to achieve the necessary shift? Does your partner? Spirit is here to help. Then there's the question of physical and emotional fidelity. The same questions apply. The same help is available. Ask.

Business and many other aspects of material world mundane life also require Dependability. It is this aspect of interaction that allows contracts (to guarantee Dependability) and even the very fabric and structure of society. Without Dependability is chaos.

This is one of the few words that is not ultimately a personal situation or stand. Dependability is much more a reflection of how we interact with those outside of ourselves. We are internally consistent, although flowing constantly into new awarenesses. The flow is our consistency and provides our internal Dependability.

There are none but positive aspects to Dependability. Even if a certain dog bites you every time you get close to it, you will at least know what is likely to happen, and act accordingly.

COMMENTS FROM SPIRIT:

Depend on this. All that Is; is Love. All that Is exists as a part of the Creator. All that Is, is you. BE Love, Beloveds. BE Love, and you complete the circle.

THOROUGHNESS

Thoroughness refers to seeking out all of the possibilities in a situation and following each one to its end to the best of our ability and with understanding. It refers to 'leaving no stone unturned'. It reflects a focused desire to truly understand and to completely accomplish. It can refer to physical, emotional or spiritual subjects.

The only way to participate in any relationship and have it amount to anything is to do so with Thoroughness in every aspect. A personal relationship is not intended to be something that you 'gloss over' and move on from. In order to achieve any growth from it (and that is its primary function) you must sink fully into it. Immerse yourself in the flow of your combined Beingness and open to the growth and experiences that are offered.

There is no harsh aspect to Thoroughness. All of life is a lesson. The better you learn your lesson, the less likely it is that you will have to re-learn it in another lifetime.

COMMENTS FROM SPIRIT:

Dear Ones. I invite you to experience life with a Thoroughness that transcends all. This existence is designed by you and for you as both a delight and a diversion. The lessons you are offering yourself are important to your spirit's growth, and thus; because all beings are One; to the growth of All that Is. The more Thoroughly you participate the sooner we all graduate.

Blessings.

PERSEVERANCE

Perseverance means going forward; continuing, and completing even when you are tired or discouraged and want to quit. It refers to gritting your teeth and proceeding when all of the signs seem to be against your ever finishing the task; simply because it's the 'right' thing to do.

    An example would be the Louis and Clark expedition or the voyages of the earliest explorers who had no idea of what to expect or whether they would ever see the land they called 'home' again. The job needed to be done so they did it.   Perseverance is what keeps many relationships alive. The intensity of sharing all aspects of your life with another person creates a constant state of some degree of tension. This tension is not a bad thing. It is much like tectonic plates in the earth. Each is moving in its own direction at its own speed. This sometimes causes tensions to build up along the front where one touches another. Eventually the strain becomes such that a sometimes-violent release in the form of an earthquake takes place. After the earthquake, however, the situation is usually resolved and the stress level in that particular area is reduced greatly. A good relationship is like this planet in which stresses constantly are developed and released as the parties each grow in their own directions and speeds; not always in concert with one another. As with the planet though, regardless of the magnitude of the release, the plate maintains it's unity and strength. So it is with a good partnership.

Sometimes a great deal of patience is required when dealing with someone on a casual level. This Perseverance is necessary until you realize (smack your forehead here) that the things that irritate us in others are the things that we probably need to look at in ourselves. What is it about that 'jerk' that you're upset at that you may have a tendency to do yourself, or that you fear that you might do? Can't figure it out? That's O.K. Spirit has great Perseverance, and will patiently continue to offer the lesson until you understand it.

There sometimes comes a time when Perseverance becomes masochism. This happens when we lose sight of the original purpose for entering into a particular project and find that the journey rather than the arrival becomes the goal. There is no shame in bailing out if a situation seems too punishing. Remember though that all things are lessons and if you have not learned the lesson involved with a particular challenge, that lesson will be back in another form eventually to offer itself to you again. Nothing has Perseverance like our lessons.

COMMENTS FROM SPIRIT:

Perseverance, Dear Ones, only applies if you are not enjoying what you are experiencing. Shift your patterns of thoughts and perception until you see whatever occurs as the Divine gift of Love that it is. There is nothing in the multiverse that has any purpose but to serve you with Love and patience as you move through the portion of your existence known as life. Blessings to you, each and all.

UNKNOWN

  This is the place where fear lives. Fear is a lack of Love and understanding and is the parent of anger. The darkness of our own fears and ignorance create the boogey-men of our nightmares. When Light is shown on things Unknown; understanding comes. With understanding can come acceptance and from that; Love.

  Spirit has told me that: "Darkness is required to hide something. All things are made visible in the Light."

  There are times when in order to make things 'smooth' when we have done (or not done) something that our partner thinks that we should (or shouldn't) have, we seek to keep our partner in darkness. Keeping this thing Unknown is not an answer that will immediately provide a positive growth experience. Even if your partner never finds out, your soul knows that you have betrayed your own sense of 'right' and 'wrong' and has already scheduled classes in the matter.

When we get ready to walk out the door of our house the last thing that most of us put on is a false front in order to keep the 'inner' us Unknown to the world at large. This false front acts as a suit of armor so that most of the time any missiles of malcontent that come our way are aimed at who the others think we are; rather than our true selves. Thus the damage to our delicate inner self is minimized. The problem with this approach is that we are here in human form to learn the lessons of life; not to avoid them. We are here to learn that we can stand delightedly in the glory of our own being and never be truly harmed. Remember, please. All things are a gift of Divine Love. All experiences have but one purpose; though sometimes it is hard to see that purpose from the human point of view. That purpose is to assist your soul in its growth toward Divinity.

We are largely Unknown even to ourselves. Many of us continue to play old tapes from our childhood or our youth. Those tapes tell us; usually in our parent's or in an old partner's voice: "You can't...., you're worthless.... and you'll never......" Then they throw in for good measure: "You're fat. You're ugly. You have no sense. You have bad breath. You have bad skin."

These statements are usually not the real us. It served the person making the statement at the time to build themselves up and demonstrate their own frustration and anger with Life by putting us down. They kept searching until they found the 'buttons' that worked; then kept pushing those buttons until we began to believe them. At that point the other party could sit back and let themselves fall out of our lives; as we were now continuing the work of building them up by putting ourselves down, even going so far as to do it in their words!

This word has come into your consciousness today so that you might make a conscious effort to identify and release the old tapes that continue to haunt you. You are a child of the Creator; perfect in every way for where you are on this path that you have chosen in Life. If your body harbors extra weight or a bad complexion or thinning hair; it is in Divine order and provides you with tools for your growth. Even those old tapes are there so that you can learn to identify that which is not the true you. You can become almost anything you wish....Spirit suggests that if you simply BE Love, all else will easily fall into place. Spirit will help in the process, if you so decide.

The power of the Unknown is fear. The Unknown has power only for as long as you allow it to remain Unknown. It is not necessary for you to know a thing intimately on the physical or in the material sense. Once you realize that all things ultimately return to the Creator, and that all things ultimately serve the Creator, the fear of the ignorant person will fall away from you like water in a rainstorm.

COMMENTS FROM SPIRIT:

The only way for the Unknown to exist in your reality is for you to close your eye to the radiance of all things. We are All that Is; not most of what is. We are in all things and all things are of Us. Once this is understood, nothing can remain Unknown to you as you are already one with it; as you are one with The One. Set aside your fear. Heal your spiritual blindness and come out into the glory of My Light. Blessings.

ENRICHMENT

  Enrichment is the act of adding to something that which it did not previously possess in order to increase it's worth or value. Examples are Enriched flour; to which nutritional agents have been added, and Enriched Lives; to which Spirit has been added

  A personal relationship is almost always Enrichment to our lives. The purpose for entering into this type of relationship is because we believe our combined lives will be better than our separate lives had been before. This word has come to you today to urge you to remember and honor that initial purpose and to set about to Enrich your partnership by Enriching your partner's life. Spirit has said to me: "Love does not take; it only gives, and in that giving lies the greatest reward." This is an opportunity and an invitation for you to do something wonderful for yourself by giving to your partner with and from Love.

Enrichment might be thought to be primarily in reference to monetary considerations in general relationships. While this is an important aspect in many people's minds, it is not the aspect we are going to look at. By being the best person you can, by acting from and with Love in every interaction with every person you meet you Enrich their life experience and you Enrich the world. This is one of the highest of all mortal goals. You are hereby invited to participate.

Is your life the best it could possibly be? Even if you said 'yes', stop and think for a moment... Is this life the BEST it could possibly be? Anyone who is honest with themselves will have to answer in the negative. What is missing? How could you change your attitudes and perceptions that would have the effect of improving your life? It's all up to you, you know. Spirit is here to help when you're ready.

COMMENTS FROM SPIRIT:

Other terms for Enrichment could be enlightenment, attunement, or awareness. There is nothing in the multiverse that is not already a part of you, including Divinity. How then could you possibly add to the riches of who you already are? We love you Children and await your awakening and the full awareness of your greater selves.

ASSERTIVE

Assert is the opposite of revert. To revert is to fall back to a position or stance previously held. To Assert is to boldly move forward into new levels; to demand the right and recognize your ability to grow or to make yourself heard. It involves attempting to claim your power as dominant for the moment. A very delicate balance is needed in order to avoid the pitfalls of ego-centered action when one is being Assertive. While a little bit is generally good, a lot is not necessarily better.

There comes a time in even the best of relationships when situations occur that allow us to choose to be Assertive over our partner. Sometimes this is a wise choice, but at other times it can lead to a series of lessons regarding the wiser use of ego. Whichever is the case for you at this moment, it is suggested that you look at your pattern of Assertiveness or conversely your reluctance to be Assertive when it is needed. Somewhere, something in this area is out of balance. That is why this word has come into your awareness today. Spirit would like to assist you in achieving that balance and is waiting inside your meditation with the answers and guidance you seek.

It is far easier for all involved to express Assertiveness in a non-personal relationship. This is a throwback to our animalistic ancestors. This is all about what is described as a 'pecking order'. We put on our 'tough' persona as we walk out the doors of our houses so that we can better 'defend' ourselves against the tough personas of the others who we will run into in the outer world. Each one seems to be trying to establish their own little slice of dominance; so that instead of Loving and supporting one another in our day to day activities as a child of the Creator would seem inclined to do, we act as animals toward one another; posing and displaying threats to one another in an attempt to establish our right to Assertiveness. If you have brought this word into your consciousness today it is to remind you that the Ultimate Commandment is to BE Love in every word, in every thought, in every deed, in every prayer. How are you doing in that regard? Is there room for improvement? Why not do so? Spirit will help

There are times when we need to be Assertive over our own lower natures. Each of us has flashes or moments of temptation in those areas where we have the greatest lessons still to learn. (If we had already learned the lessons as thoroughly as we like to think there would be no temptation there to notice) When we catch the impulse before we actually act on it and decide not to do the thing in question we have won that small battle. There is no need to chastise oneself for being tempted. One should congratulate oneself instead for 'passing the test' by not participating in that which would not fit into one's ideals. If perchance you did not decide that it was something you shouldn't have done until you were well into it, or had completed whatever it was, there is still no need to beat yourself up. Remember that all things are in Divine order whether we like or understand them or not. That does not mean that they are the 'shortest path of greatest light' in a given situation. You'll do better in the future.

Assertiveness is a tar pit waiting for the unwary traveler. While a little bit sometimes appears to be necessary for some situations, Assertiveness is ultimately an act of ego. It is your sense of what needs to be. When you Assert you assume that your sense of what needs to be is 'righter' or 'better' than the sense of the others involved. Make sure that what you say or do is from Love, not from anger or ego.

COMMENTS FROM SPIRIT:

There is really no need, Beloved Ones, for this thing that you refer to as Assertiveness. All of existence is a river and the flow of that river is as it is and always shall be. Your attempts to divert this river through your efforts and ego are nothing more than your participation in the eddies and wavelets in the stream. Relax, Loved ones. Relax and BE the river. At that point there is no need or concept of Assertiveness. There is no battle; there is no war. You are all things and all things are Love.

Blessings.

OBJECTIVE

An Objective is a goal; something that you would like to obtain.

Objective is also a way of looking at life. An Objective view is one that does not take into consideration anything but the nature of the Object or situation being observed. Ideally, there is nothing of you in an Objective (object-centered) observation.

The Objective of most personal relationships is mutual joy and growth. An Objective look tells us that this goal can be quite difficult to reach. As we have mentioned elsewhere in this book, a personal relationship provides the most fertile field for growth in the human experience, and Spirit says that we all know what is needed in large quantities to make a field fertile.

This word has come to you in order to have you take a good, Objective look at all of your partnerships, public and private. How could you make life gentler for your partner and yourself?
In the mundane world, the Objective on a day-to-day basis may seem to be simply to survive but there is far more to it than that. We have goals in business, in casual communications, and in all of the other aspects of day-to-day living. Our Objective is not to just survive on a long-term basis, but to thrive and magnify our worldly presence to provide a sense of safety and well-being as a cushion around us.

What are the immediate Objectives of your partnerships and how may they best be accomplished? These are only two of the questions that Spirit would have you look at today. You'll know the others if you think about it Objectively.

Here's a challenge for you. Try to see yourself Objectively. Put aside the façade of who you would like to think that you are; whether it be 'good' or 'bad'. Look at the true you. Try to see the 'you' as the rest of the world probably sees you. Good.

Now set that aside also, as you have just played a trick on yourself by filtering your perception of yourself through that which you think others think of you based on what you would like to think they, for whatever reason, think. Don't think! That's the lesson. Simply observe. Observe yourself as though you were a stranger. What do you observe about this stranger? What are the stranger's 'good' points; their 'bad' ones? What would you tell this stranger about themselves? How would they take it? Why?

Spirit suggests that this could make for a most enlightening series of meditations. Don't forget, first and foremost, to handle the stranger with Love and patience. They are trying as hard as they are able in this moment.

The only 'bad' thing about being Objective is that what you see may not be what you wanted to see.
Oh, well.
Time to peel another layer off the onion of self delusion. Spirit says to remind you that every layer that you peel off of an onion will most likely bring tears, but it brings you that much closer to the center.

COMMENTS FROM SPIRIT:

Objectivity, Dear Ones, is another way of saying that whatever is; simply IS. There is no need or purpose for worry, for the agony of not knowing or for doubt. There simply is a condition of IS in the multiverse. Reveal the Divinity of your own IS in the tranquility of total Objectivity. Nothing matters. All things are important. We Love you.

Blessings.

ACCEPTANCE

A man came to Lord Buddha while he was speaking to his students and began to revile him at length, using the foulest of language and the roughest of manners. When he was done, Buddha; who had never lost his composure or his grace, smiled at the man and said "Thank you". Puzzled and perplexed, the man went on his way. Buddha's students also were puzzled. One of them asked him: "Master, why did you thank that man when he treated you so badly?"

Buddha smiled, then explained to those present: "I did not thank him for his rudeness. He offered me the gift of his presence and his opinion. I thanked him for the offer, but refused his gifts."

We all have the right and the ability to Accept or reject that which is offered to us in life. We also have the ability to modify the way that it affects us by simply choosing to Accept it from the point of view of a student rather than a victim. Where would the above story have led if Buddha had decided to be a victim? Would he have struck the man?

All relationships are lessons in Acceptance and Accepting. Each partner must Accept; at least for the moment, the foibles and needs of the other. Each must Accept their role as partner with all of its ramifications. Each must Accept their role as co-creator of the shared reality with all of it's ramifications.

Can you Accept yourself, with all of your foibles and needs? Are you prepared to Accept the role of co-creator of your own reality, with all of its ramifications? Spirit thinks that its time that you should. Meditate on it. You'll see.

Acceptance is quite necessary for growth; both spiritual and physical.

COMMENTS FROM SPIRIT:

The multiverse is yours, Dear Ones. It is offered to you on a platter of Divine Love. Please Accept this gift we give. It is our greatest hope; our greatest joy that you shall Accept your true nature and return to that place you have never truly left. Come home, Dear Ones. Come home in your hearts to the Divinity of your source; of your nature; of your BEing. Come home.

Blessings.

ADVENTURE

All doors are thrown open when this word enters your life. In a very real way, this can be considered as a Joker or 'wild card.' Expect the unexpected! All bets are off. Anything goes with this word in your hand.

New levels are attained. These levels can be either high or low; however, they can generally be expected to be 'good'. Watch your step. This is a sign of a potential new relationship or such a shift in a current relationship as to completely redefine your personal life.

Business deals can be completed in surprising ways and much more quickly than expected, or they may fall through without warning. Old friends may call you from 'out of the blue'. You might win the lottery!

This word could be likened to a large paddle with which your 'stuff' gets stirred, although usually in a pleasant manner.

Adventures can be wonderful...or fatal. Watch your step.

COMMENTS FROM SPIRIT:

The exuberant living of life marks the greatest Adventure of all. The nature of the Adventure is determined by your willingness to fully partake of every opportunity. Be Love in all things and trust that all things are in Divine order at all times, whether you understand or even like what is happening at any given moment, or not. The Adventure begins!

Blessings.

OPTIONS

You can read this if you really want to. You don't have to, you know. Of course, even if you do read it you don't have to remember or act on it. These are all Options. It's up to you.

'Options' is all about feeling that you have the freedom to make a choice and the power to implement that choice.

Personal relationships are rife with Options. Because of the nature of this type of relationship, each partner has a wider range of Options than most of the rest of life. At the same time, that much freedom carries with it the responsibility not to abuse it or the relationship may suffer as a result.

Sometimes one partner usurps the Options of the other (actually, the second partner allows it to happen -- they have the Option to walk away from the relationship). If this has happened in your life you really need to take a long, hard look at why you have allowed this. What lessons does it offer you and is the positive effects this relationship has in your life worth the turmoil that this condition brings with it. If you have allowed your power to decide to be taken from you, it's time to reclaim it. You are not doing yourself any good. If you have taken away your partner's freedom to choose you are not doing yourself or your partner any favors. Just remember: What comes around goes around and Spirit has infinite patience when it comes to offering you lessons and will do so at whatever level you require until you 'get' the lesson.

Much of what was said in the previous paragraph holds true in a general relationship as well. We always have all Options open to us. We just need to remember that every choice carries with it both costs and rewards. We usually have a pretty good idea of what those are going to be on the conscious level. It is as we take those costs and rewards into consideration that we find ourselves limiting our perceived Options. We have the Option to step off the roof of a fifty story building with nothing but the street below. We may choose to not exercise that Option because of the perceived cost of doing so.

Every person we see, every place we go, all Options are open to us. It is up to you to follow the path that represents the shortest path of greatest light.

Our perceptions and preconceptions create our reality. You are only as free as you perceive and allow yourself to be.

'   Options' is truly a neutral concept. It is what you do with it that can make it seem either 'good' or 'bad'.

COMMENTS FROM SPIRIT:

Dearest Children: you are gifted with all of the choices possible as you move through the experience of existence. You are to experience all that you choose until you are satisfied that you have learned the lessons needed in your growth path. We Lovingly offer you total freedom so that you may experience total growth. Blessings.

CLUMSINESS

Clumsiness can be both a physical and an emotional/spiritual condition. It is as a result of mild to profound confusion regarding the 'correct' path to take in a particular situation or the seeming inability to do so gracefully. What it really boils down to is a lack of self-confidence and experience that interferes with the smooth flow of our living. As we become surer of ourselves we become less hesitant. That hesitancy is what appears to the rest of the world as Clumsiness.

Clumsiness does not often appear as difficulty in a personal relationship. In order for such a relationship to exist, there must be a certain level of trust and comfort between the partners. That level of support usually will preclude the insecurity that brings on Clumsiness. If you are in a relationship that allows you to feel Clumsy, you should perhaps look at the level of support that you either are not getting or are not accepting from your partner. Either way, something has to change, and soon! Talk with your partner about it!

In general relationships, Clumsiness is usually a direct result of hesitation that comes as a result of not feeling yourself to be 'worthy' or 'good enough' for a particular event or process. Most of the time we sabotage ourselves in this by finding ourselves falling short of what we imagine others expect of us. As you are aware, we are usually our own harshest critics. Lay off! Take it easy on yourself. Do the best you can in each circumstance. When you feel that you have fallen short of what you'd really like to accomplish, try to do better next time. That's all there is to it.

Clumsiness is only a 'bad' thing if you let it be. Can you imagine the first time Joe Montana ever tried to catch a ball? He probably looked like any other five-year-old trying to catch something that was never quite sure which way it was going to bounce next. Clumsiness is only the front end of the learning process. Don't take it so seriously!

COMMENTS FROM SPIRIT:

Dear Ones: Clumsiness is only your own judgment and self-effacement. It is thus in every area of every event in every life. One must walk before one can run. One must fledge before one can fly. Be patient with yourselves. All of life is a learning process that your soul has chosen. In order to learn, one must enter the process somewhere below the top level. Love yourselves. That is the lesson behind these lessons. Love and honor and have patience with your self. It is doing what is best in its own way and in its own time.

Blessings.

MAGNIFICENCE

Magna is from Latin, meaning great. The second half of the word is also extracted from the Latin. Facens is a verb, meaning to do. Thus, Magnificent is a great doing, or a great BE-ing. Magnificence is the act of manifesting that great doing or BE-ing.

Drawing this word is an invitation from spirit to excel in all aspects of your being-ness. Do not let any material or mortal constraints restrain you. You are a child of the Almighty, and a being of light. All things are possible in you, from you, and for you. Be there now!

COMMENTS FROM SPIRIT:

Magnificence is the essence of the being that you are. There is none greater in all of the multiverse, as all are One, and that One is The One. BE in the glory of your essence. Let no one or no thing take from you your birthright of Magnificence. Do not limit yourself with doubt or fear. All things are yours; as all things are you. We Love you, Dear Ones.

We Love you.

DARKNESS

'Darkness' is that which does not seem to openly or directly serve All that Is, yet it is an integral part of the whole in Maya (duality or the material realm) much as a pack of wolves serves a herd of elk by bringing down those who are sick or feeble, thus making the strongest to be those whose seed carries on in the herd. Thus 'darkness' serves our spiritual growth by aiding those who are not 'getting' their lessons to experience those lessons at levels that can no longer be ignored. It only seems to be 'Darkness' when it affects us in a way that we find to be negative. 'Darkness' can also mean ignorance or a lack of willingness to see or understand.

Darkness is actually necessary to some small degree in that it provides the shadows and outlines that assist us in maintaining the illusion of 'self' and of separateness. If all things were perceived as they truly are; in total light, we would have no need or excuse to struggle to grow toward our highest nature. It is that struggle that strengthens our spirit and causes the soul to mature. It is a tool just like so many other things in this existence. As such, it has its bbuilt-inlimitations. Once it has taught us all that it can, it falls away from us as something that is used up and is no longer necessary. I made a conscious choice several years ago to not allow 'Darkness' in my life and for the most part that is the way it has been since that time.

There is a tremendous difference between 'Darkness' and 'evil', although they are sometimes used interchangeably (see "Evil").

'Darkness' occurs in a personal relationship when one or both partners begin to find it necessary to keep their activities and thoughts from the other partner. With very few exceptions this is a precursor to the demise of the relationship. If you are participating in something that you feel that you cannot tell your partner about perhaps it is time to look at your motives and the probable ultimate outcome of these activities. Is this something you would like to experience? Is this something you would like kept from you? Your answers to these questions should tell you whether or not Darkness is present in your activities. The choice to continue is always yours but be aware that every choice has both costs and rewards and you will eventually experience both of them.

There are times when it seems that the world around us is filled with Darkness; and so it is from the human perspective. When all things seem hopeless in the world remember that the world is being born into a new level of existence and that there is no birth without blood and pain. It is all in Divine order even if we cannot see it from our human reference point. To think otherwise would be to say that 'Evil' is more powerful than the Creator. Have faith. It is all working out in the way that it needs to, given the planetary consciousness at this time. To lessen the 'Darkness' each of us must manifest more Light in every moment.

There are a lot of seekers and lightworkers who are currently being challenged at never before experienced levels. Do not let these 'Dark' nights of the soul sway you from your commitment to Spirit and to service. Drawing this word to you is an indication that Spirit is standing beside you in your efforts. Go into the fray with the armor of that fact and the Love of the Creator in the fore and you cannot lose.

The purpose of 'Darkness' is to blind us to our true selves and to the true nature of the things that are happening around us in the world. Open your eyes and there's always Light!

COMMENTS FROM SPIRIT:

Darkness occurs only when one forgets their Divinity and the Divinity of All That Is. When you feel the Darkness about you remember that you ARE the light. Manifest your Divinity in every moment and there shall be no Darkness in your world.

Blessings.

INTUITION

Intuition comes as a result of our intimate connection with All that Is. we bring forth into the material world consciously or non-consciously the knowingnesses that are a part of that wholeness. Sometimes this happens without our being aware of the process or even the result as the words that fall from our lips change another person's life forever. Intuition is Spirit moving through us for the benefit of others.

Intuition plays an important in our relationships. Part of the intimacy of a good relationship is a 'sixth sense' regarding what is going on in the heart and mind of our partner, and the ability to react to it before the partner even has a chance to tell us. Bringing this word to you today would seem to indicate that perhaps you have not been quite as attuned to your partner's needs as you could be. Spirit is here to help you to recover that state.

How many times have you met someone who instantly felt like a 'friend' or an 'enemy'? How often have you looked into someone's eyes and fallen in love? These are all examples of Intuition at work in the mundane world. The same can be said for a general feeling that 'things are going to be good today'; or 'Flight 912 from Kennedy is going to have severe turbulence and almost crash.' Tapping into what is called the 'Akashic records' can take many forms, but it is all Intuition at work. When it is manifested in a more powerful state (even though all people are equally able to do so) the one who manifests it is referred to as a 'psychic'. It is only your own willingness to believe the information and your own perception of self worth that govern the level at that you manifest these 'gifts'.

The only way that Intuition can be thought to have a negative side is if you or those you listen to choose to view this natural event with fear because it does not fit into a particular religious belief system or because you feel that you couldn't possibly be 'worthy' of such a thing. Either one is simply a matter of your own choice and simply indicates the lessons you have yet to learn. As I once told a fundamentalist Christian regarding reincarnation: "It's O.K. if you don't believe in it. You will next time."

COMMENTS FROM SPIRIT:

Intuition is simply a label you put on the natural communication that occurs between Spirit and humankind. There is absolutely nothing special about it or the people who do it. There is no reason but your own need for limitation that holds any of you back from fully conscious communion with All that Is in every moment of every day. Turn loose of your doubts and fears. Turn to the Love that is that of which all is created. In Love, all things are possible. Limit less, Dear Ones, Limit less.

SERVICE

Consciously or not, every person on this planet is a minister. Minister is a verb. It means 'to Serve'. Every one of us is here to provide a backdrop and lessons for everyone else while processing our own lessons.

Unconscious Service is not what we are talking about here, though. Unconscious Service doesn't really count as far as our own spiritual growth is concerned. It is only when we consciously choose and accept our role as being in Service of All that Is and set out to seek that Service that we have achieved a place of growth in this area.

The ways that we are consciously of Service to our partner

are almost without number. From the kind and loving words upon awakening to the washing of the dinner dishes; these are all small gifts we give from our own Love that supports and honors our partner's being. This in turn gives our partner the inner strength to get on with their own growth process.

Sometimes being of Service to our partner involves telling them what they don't want to hear or taking them into darkened places within themselves that they didn't particularly want to see. When this must be done, please make sure that it is done with and from Love and support and as gently as possible.

The outer world is desperately in need of those who will allow themselves to be of Service. The need is so great, however, that it can easily drain the Server totally if that Server allows it. It is sometimes difficult to control your desire to help; to Serve; to give. That urge must at times be controlled else the Server will burn out rapidly after having accomplished little. Love and Service start from within. You must Love yourself enough to be able to say "no" or "not now" occasionally to those in need and be willing to Serve yourself first so that you will have the strength to Serve others later.

It is every bit as important that you learn how to receive as it is to be able to give. Giving comes naturally and easily to most of us. Accepting is quite another matter. Several years ago when I was just beginning my spiritual quest I was channeling my own higher self who choose to take the form of a 10th century Tibetan Buddhist monk named Lo Ming Lao. A woman came to me who 'didn't believe in all this stuff'. After counseling her for a time, Ming Lao said that he would like to talk with her. She agreed and for several minutes Ming Lao told her about her life. When he left I handed her a small crystal that he had told me was now hers. I said "You know, I love giving -- I just have a really hard time receiving." She, who still wasn't sure that she believed in channeling, spirit or any of the rest of this 'woo woo' stuff, suddenly sat bolt-upright in her chair and in a different than normal voice said "To give is an act of power. One must become vulnerable to receive." She immediately got a very startled and puzzled look on her face and added: "Where did that come from?"

The point of the story is that it is a great Service to ourselves when we can drop our walls and armor and receive. You cannot give forever from an empty well.

There is no harsh aspect to Service. There is a harsh aspect to letting yourself be used in the name of Service.

COMMENTS FROM SPIRIT:

Service, Dear Loves, is Divine Love manifesting on the individual level. It is the grease that allows the flow of the universe to continue unimpeded. It is your recognition of the interconnection of all of existence and of your responsibility to your fellow beings in whatever form they may exist. Just as We have chosen to Serve you from the depths of our Love so you will Serve those about you from the depths of your Love. The circle goes on. We are all related. We are all One.

Blessings.

OPEN-MINDED

"A closed fist cannot accept a gift nor a closed mind a new thought." How sad. Can you imagine going through life stuck in your old thought patterns? Perhaps you think that you are mentally and spiritually in a good place at this time. Perhaps you think it can't be improved and you don't want to hear any arguments. Welcome to the ranks of fundamentalism.

To not open your mind is akin to a flower that will not open its bud. Its full beauty will never be seen or appreciated and it will die without fulfilling its purpose for this life.

Spirit has told me that each being chooses a certain amount

of intellect when they enter their bodies at birth. This is intended as a starting point from which to grow. When we choose to stop accepting the possibility that there may still be something out there for us to learn, we mentally petrify. At that point, we build lots of walls and armor to stop those dratted, pesky new ideas from trying to invade our comfortable make-believee world. By doing this we limit both our progress and our potential in this lifetime.

    In the mid-1800's there was a major move to try to shut down the US Patent Office because it was seriously believed that everything possible had been invented. This was before the internal combustion engine and before flight.

Simply because you cannot conceive or agree with something at the moment does not mean that it does not or can not exist. Open-minded people allow themselves to hear that which is offered to them; then file some of that information away for future reference and/or possible acceptance. It is that frame of mind that allows and supports growth and expansion.

One can only imagine a Neanderthal fundamentalist the first time he saw a club:

    "Whaddaya need that stupid stick for. In my day, we ran 'em down and strangled the critters with our bare hands. Only a sissy would use a stick. You kids have got it too easy. This culture is going downhill fast. I'm glad I won't be around much longer to see you wreck our society with your new-fangled ideas. Kids! Harrumph!"

    In my own experiences as a servant of the Creator I have participated in some extremely profound healings that involved concepts and a cast of characters that far exceeded my then current ability to accept outright. There are still some things that happened through me that I don't share with other people as I have trouble believing them myself; and I was there!

    It is only when we maintain an open mind that we allow our consciousness to be nourished. It is only when we allow ourselves to have new experiences; to stretch ourselves; that we grow.

    If this word has come into your life today it is because you have been shutting yourself off from the information and lessons that you have called to yourself. It is time to let down the walls, take off the armor and sit at your desk with notebook in hand. Spirit is your Loving and patient teacher but be aware that there WILL be a test. Believe me, there WILL be a test.

COMMENTS FROM SPIRIT:

To be Open Minded is the most natural of all states. That all things are created for your benefit is known. That all beings are One, and that One is both the Creator and yourself; this also is known. That nothing in this universe can ever truly harm you in any way is a given fact as well. What, then, do you cower from? What threatens you but your own insecurity and fears? Come out of the cavern of self-doubt, Beloveds. Come into the light of the glory of your own BEing-ness and walk with open mind and heart and without fear in the Love.

Blessings.

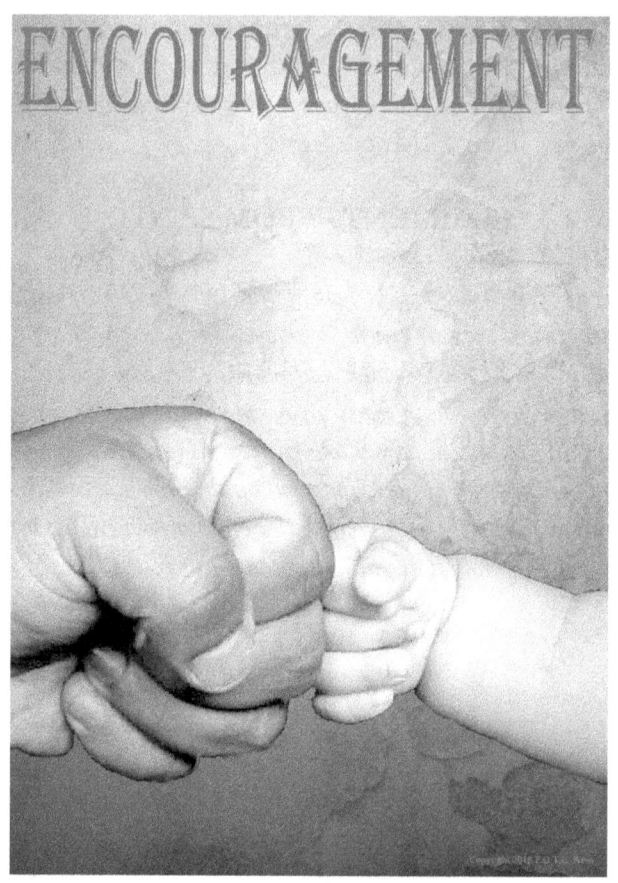

ENCOURAGEMENT

    Encouragement is the act of giving or imbuing with courage. It means giving moral and physical support to someone who is in need of it in the moment.

    A personal relationship puts us in very intimate touch with the most delicate and painful expressions of another person's life processes. We see all of the agonizing; all of the growth and all of the problems that this person is experiencing, without the benefit of them being 'glossed over' in any way. We are observers of the raw, unadulterated process of their life. As this process unfolds, it is important to understand that even though this is our chosen partner and we share much, these particular problems are uniquely tailored for our mate. All we can do is to stand by without interfering and offer support and Encouragement along with Love and patience as they move through their 'stuff'. And we can hope that they will do the same for us when our lessons become difficult.

One of the finest gifts that we may give others as we walk through this world is a word of Encouragement as we pass. Never overlook an opportunity to honestly share with someone something that is good and beautiful about them. It is so easy to do. It costs you nothing and it can literally make the other person's day. In rare instances, it has been known to literally change another's life when the right word is spoken to the right person at the right time. This word has come up today for just such a reason. It is a way of telling you of your own power to do good in the world.

As with so many of these words, the most important and the most difficult person to apply Encouragement to is self. We tend to either ignore our own needs or condition or we feel for some reason that we are not worthy of help or support, even from ourselves. If this word has come into your consciousness today perhaps it is because Spirit disagrees with your assessment of yourself. Spirit knows you as itself in an apparently separate material form but itself, none the less. Because it knows itself to be Divine in nature, it knows also that you are Divine -- and limitless. Spirit is about to enter your life in a proactive way, Encouraging you to see yourself in the light of truth. Never mind that there are aspects of yourself that are troubling to you in this moment. This moment will pass and with it the troubling aspects. All that will remain are the lessons you have learned and the growth that you have achieved through this process. Look back at your life. Look at the most troubling and hurtful times in your life. Now that you are healed of most of the pain of those experiences, look at how much you learned and grew during that process. Pain only occurs when we refuse to learn the lessons as they are first presented and continue in our headstrong ways until Spirit finally turns up the heat under us to a point where it gets our attention. Oh! Look! I seem to have been giving you Encouragement!

COMMENTS FROM SPIRIT:

Encouragement is only necessary to those who refuse to see their own greater power and resources. We long for each and all to come into the full blossoming of their Divinity; but until that time we offer you the Encouragement of this: BE Love. BE Loved. *There is no more nor is there less required of you in this multiverse. Love is all there is; and you are that.*

Blessings.

CHEERFULNESS

This is an easy one to define. This is the act, state or condition of being full of Cheer. Let's face it, there are worse things to be full of and most of us have been from time to time.

Cheerfulness is always a nice surprise to bring home for your partner at the end of the day. Try it!

You would really be surprised how much better your days go when you approach them (and everybody you encounter in them) with a Cheerful frame of mind.

Being Cheerful most of the time is a good indication that you have learned one of life's more important lessons. That lesson is this:

everything is important but nothing matters. It can be put in another way. Everything matters but nothing is important. All events and experiences in our lives are there for only one purpose. That purpose is to offer us lessons in life and an opportunity to grow in Spirit. Don't take everything so darned seriously. If you do well in your lessons, that's great. If you don't quite get it right that's O.K. too. We are here to learn. As long as we realize that we could do something better next time there is no difficulty in the process. It is only when we don't realize that, or worse, don't care that Spirit steps in with 'enhanced lessons'. These might not seem to be quite as pleasant as the first lessons were. Whatever happens, don't fall into the trap of feeling like the universe is conspiring against you. That is the point of view of a victim. The only difference between a victim and a student is that the student gets the message and moves on -- full of Cheerfulness.

COMMENTS FROM SPIRIT:

Cheerfulness is nothing more or less than the manifestation of joy not yet fully bloomed. Manifest the Love and light within your BEing for all of the world to see; for as you do you lighten the world around you. BE Love, Dear Ones, and Cheerfulness is automatically there within.

Blessings.

PATIENCE

PATIENCE

    Several years ago while participating in a psychic fair and expo in Seattle a young woman stormed up to my booth, flung herself into the chair at my side and demanded in an exasperated voice: "I know why I'm here in this lifetime. How long does it take to learn Patience, anyway"? The answer Spirit had me give her was: "A while longer, I think."

    We all seem to have a tendency to be quite willful and demanding in this material world. As we become more aware of Spirit and allow Spirit to be in our consciousness a certain level of peacefulness arrives. The aspects of our lives that caused us the most struggles suddenly seem to have become a lot less pressing. The secret is this: Lack of Patience is directly related to our feeling that we need to have conscious and total control over our own lives! That's right -- that "C" word.

When someone talks about 'surrendering' to Spirit many of us bristle and paw the ground. "No way am I going to give up control," we say. That is not what this type of surrender is about. First of all, Spirit already has total control. As proof of this, look at how seldom your plans and plots work out the way you think they should. Is this the track record of someone who is in control?

Surrender in this context refers to giving up the effort to control from the conscious, material level. Realize that the Creator delegates authority and it is delegated to each soul as overseer for the care and growth of each of us. No part of us loves us more than our soul, which is in direct communication with both the Creator and our material being. Your soul will not ever choose a situation that does not have the potential for bringing you closer to Oneness.

What it boils down to, then, is surrendering the material world illusion of control (what I call control from the small perception of self) to the knowledge that all things are in control (Divine Order) at all times (what I call control from the Greater Self). You are not actually giving up anything but the mistaken perception that you have conscious control. It is when that perception proves to be false in a particular case (things aren't going your way) that you experience a lack of Patience (remember Patience -- this is about the word 'Patience'). What you gain from total surrender is limitless Patience, Peace and Understanding.

COMMENTS FROM SPIRIT:

Patience is a concept for those who are temporarily out of balance in their living patterns. We who ARE Love, will never tire of helping our Children discover that they have never been gone from their Home. Limitless Love has limitless Patience.

We offer you limitless Love.

Blessings.

EDUCATION

    Education can take many forms; from the benign to the extremely harsh. The degree of harshness is determined in large part by our willingness to listen to Spirit and accept the lessons that are offered. The sooner we listen -- and learn -- the more gentle the lesson. The longer we ignore the voice of Spirit, the louder it must shout in order to get through to us. Drawing this word indicates an offer on the part of Spirit to give us a lesson that we might otherwise miss at a level that is gentler than we might otherwise receive. Education can also refer to the mundane meaning of the word but generally involves a greater understanding of self.

As we have discussed more fully in our comments on 'Balance'; relationships provide many opportunities to learn about ourselves and grow in the process. It can be very easy to place blame for an uncomfortable situation on our partner but this word invites us to look at the root cause within ourselves that brought this situation into our reality and consciousness.

While general relationships are typically not as intense or persistent as a personal relationship, lessons hide around every corner. This word invites us not only to look, but to see. Once you have seen you may begin to understand -- and to learn.

Most of us love to hide from ourselves. We have a multitude of concepts about 'who we are' and we drag out whichever one seems to fit the mood of the moment. The energy of Education can blur the outlines of these false faces, forcing us to inspect ourselves more carefully than usual.

As discussed above, the apparent harshness of the lesson is directly proportional to our willingness to perceive and accept it. The choice is yours, as always.

COMMENTS FROM SPIRIT:

In the entire universe, there is only one lesson. Thou art God. Lest you forget that you are limitless you are given the appearance of limits; the appearance of struggle; the appearance of failure -- or gain. The trick is in recognizing that these are only appearances -- that all of life is only a game God plays with Itself in order to achieve all that is.

WORRY

There has been more time and more effort wasted on this concept than on any other single thing in history. All of the time; all of the effort; all of the Worry has not changed one thing for the better one iota, EVER! Worry is a complete and total waste of time and energy in every instance and WITHOUT EXCEPTION!

Omar Khayyam said it best in *The Rubiyat*:

The Moving Finger writes;
And having writ moves on
Nor all thy piety nor wit

> *Shall lure it back to cancel half a line*
> *Nor all thy tears shall wash out a word of it.*

Does he really love me? Is she going to find out? Should I tell them?

Not to seem rude, but WHAT DIFFERENCE DOES IT MAKE? Yes, I agree that these questions can seem to be quite important in the moment but whatever will be already is. That does not mean that we do not have free will. We do have free choice within a finite infinity of choices. What it means is that we have already made the choices that have set things in motion. We are now arriving at the point where our spirit, in conjunction with our partner's, is deciding which path to implement next. This all depends on what and how much each and both of you have learned from the process in the interim. Worry occurs only when you see things as occurring from less than Divine Love. Worry is the sign of the victim, not the student. Remember, please, that everything that you experience in your life is a gift of Love and a lesson whether you understand or like it, or not.

If he really likes you; if she finds out, if they already know, the world will go on. If the thing seems in the moment to be 'bad', you'll get over it. If the thing seems 'good' you'll get over it. Life is. That is all you need to remember. Do the best that you can in every moment and in every way. You will make mistakes. That is one of the reasons that you are in a human form. We learn from our mistakes regardless of how many lifetimes it takes. Spirit has infinite patience. If one of our mistakes is to constantly chastise ourselves and Worry over the consequences of our choices then so be it. Spirit is patient.

COMMENTS FROM SPIRIT:

> *Infinite Love has infinite patience. We ARE Love and we are patient. You have nothing occurring within your experience that reflects other than our total Love for you. The path you take; the lessons you choose; these are your choices and yours alone. Release fear and embrace Love. There is nothing to Worry about. All things are as you have chosen. See the beauty within the gifts of your experiences and the lessons will be plain. Blessings.*

TREACHERY

Treachery comes from the same root word as Treason. It means that someone has utilized a position of trust and familiarity to turn against someone else in order to subvert or destroy some aspect of their world. Quite often a third party or entity is involved.

There are many forms of Treachery possible in a personal relationship. For most male-energied people, the worst form of Treachery to experience would be physical infidelity by their partner, while for most female-energied people; it would be an emotional betrayal. Those are the worst forms for most people. There are many small Treacheries possible that can cause a relationship to hemorrhage to death as love and respect bleed away over time. If you have brought this word to yourself today it is because you are or are about to become either the recipient or an active agent of Treachery. Whichever is the case; there are some very powerful lessons that are going to enter your life. Now is the moment to stop and look honestly at your partnership and what is happening within and around it. If it something you wish to save, do something about it. If it is something you want to end, you need do nothing. That is in process right now. It will probably happen more swiftly and more gently, however, if you gently speak with your partner regarding your feelings. Spirit is with you as you do so, as are my best wishes and blessings.

The outer world is one where we have grown to expect Treachery; whether from the paper boy or the politician. At times the world seems to run on Treachery. Look a little deeper, though. As newspapers and TV journal shows know, bad news gets our attention much more readily than good. This simply reflects the pessimistic nature of mankind in the past. We are much more attuned to and affected by 'bad' things than 'good'. It is the human condition that when we are able to find fault in the lives of others we feel better about our own by comparison. Treachery, as with so many other things, is where you find it. Your own mental outlook greatly affects your perception of what is happening. Are you being the victim or the student in this current matter? What is the greater lesson involved in this apparent Treachery? What could you do differently next time? What do you think about the person or persons who did this to you (Of course, that's the victim's point of view and you're a student – right)? Did you remember that the things we find fault with in others are usually the things that we need to look at in ourselves? .....OOPS.

Be patient with yourself. You're still just learning.

And, Yes! We are soooo good about cheating and lying to ourselves. Who is closer to us and more able (and most times more willing) to apparently sabotage our hopes and dreams than we are? The small sense of 'self' is its own worst enemy. "Please hand me another bucket of limitations. I seem to be getting a little low right now".

If you are ready to limit less (the first step on the road to becoming Limitless), Spirit is here to help. Good luck. It can seem scary but it's well worth the effort.

While the concept of Treachery has an ominous sound and feel, remember that ALL THINGS are in Divine order. ALL THINGS serve our growth process, whether we like or understand them in the moment.

COMMENTS FROM SPIRIT:

The greatest and only Treachery, Dear Ones, is to deny your infinite and intimate connection with the glory of All that Is. You are far greater than your wildest imaginings and far less evil than your fears would have you believe. Love yourselves, Dear Ones. Be at peace in the knowing that all of creation awaits your awakening into power.

Blessings.

SUSPICION

Suspicion is the second cousin to worry. In many cases, it is totally unfounded. In other cases, it is not only well-founded but underestimates the severity of the situation. In either case, it is a result of certain hints and clues; sometimes physical in nature, sometimes metaphysical and sometimes imagined. These clues seem to establish a pattern, but not enough of a pattern to see the situation so clearly as to remove all doubt. This is when Suspicion arises.

Even in the best of relationships, there are moments of Suspicion over a variety of things; either minor or relationship threatening. These are a part of the lessons we have agreed to share with one another, and the way in which we respond to the challenges of those Suspicions determines what we experience as lessons next.

This is one of the very few concepts that usually does not apply at all to self. The only major area where Suspicion plays a role on the personal level is health (*"I think I might be getting the flu..."*).

Suspicion is almost always associated with sinister concepts or activities. Suspicion is not 'dark' or 'evil' on its own. It depends on what you allow it to do to your perceptions of the world and how you react to that perception.

COMMENTS FROM SPIRIT:

Suspicion, Dear Ones, is but another form of worry which is another form of fear. All of these things happen when we look into the future with a lack of understanding that all things are in Divine order at all times and in all ways. It many times will occur that you do not understand the happenings of the moment, but never forget that your soul and the Creator have gathered together the tools that you require for the growth you desire. It is all a gift, and always a gift of greatest Love.

Blessings to you all.

DISCIPLINE

This word comes from the same Latin root word (discere = to learn) as in Disciple (discipulus = a learner). Discipline is that which teaches as well as being the teacher involved.

Most of us take this word to refer to control and control issues either from within or without that are not pleasant to us. That is the aspect we shall discuss.

A large part of a successful relationship revolves around our having the Discipline to stop doing some of the things that we used to do and to start doing those things that our partner finds 'good'. The degree to which we are able to accomplish this has a great bearing on the happiness and duration of the partnership. Because you have brought this word to your consciousness today, evidently Spirit thinks that this is an area where improvement is both possible and necessary.

In the mundane world, much of the interaction is strained and/or confrontational, if we allow ourselves to see it that way. Discipline is required in order to see it as simply another series of lessons. We do not have to buy into the mainstream perceptions of what is happening. By not buying into them, we avoid reacting to them from that level and our growth becomes more sure and rapid.

Discipline ultimately refers only to the self. Regardless of the apparent source of the Discipline, it is up to us to implement or reject it. Either way carries with it both costs and rewards that are already known to our soul. The path we choose is determined entirely by the lessons we decide to accept in the moment.

Depending on whether you agree with the given reasons for it Discipline can seem to be a very good thing or an abomination. As always, it is your own perception that governs your experience.

COMMENTS FROM SPIRIT:

It is only through the strictest Discipline that you will find ultimate freedom. As you learn to overcome the limitations you have placed upon yourselves you will come into the limitless nature of your being. We await your awakening and arrival. We Love and honor you and your journey; for only those of the greatest Discipline choose such a difficult path and only they reap such magnificent rewards.

Blessings.

SIMPLICITY

"You must become as a child to enter the Kingdom of Heaven". A child is the essence of Simplicity. A child trusts that it will be taken care of and it is. A child does not question its purpose for being in body but Simply continues to exist in human form. The heart of Simplicity is Trust. This word invites you to trust yourself, the process called Life, the Creator and all the experiences you encounter. They are all here for one purpose. That purpose is your growth returning you to the heart of the Creator.

The best of all personal relationships is also the Simplest. What could be more Simple in form or essence than when all things are resolved and the relationship is in total balance?

Simplicity drawn in response to a question of personal relationship indicates that there may be too many aspects that are out of balance at this time. To Simplify means to remove the extra aspects and return to the core of the matter. This is often very important in a personal relationship. Once your attention has been returned to the core issues they can receive more attention and healing.

"Our lives are frittered away by detail -- Simplify, Simplify!"

When dealing with the world, our life seems to sometimes be so complicated that we cannot 'think straight'. This energy encourages us to again cut to the heart of the matters at hand. Too many times we literally cannot see the problem for the details. Confusion and sometimes inappropriate actions result.

The ultimate Simplicity is Oneness with every living being and with Spirit. Spirit is assisting you at this time to grow closer to this goal.

Remember, there is no harsh aspect to Simplicity within Spirit.

COMMENTS FROM SPIRIT:

By removing all of that which does not directly reflect the Creator, one trims all extraneous energies; becoming Simple in the Divine sense. We are all One, and all are one with the One. This is the basis of Simplicity and the heart of existence. To become Simple in the heart is the goal; to achieve that total one-ness wherein there is no other-ness: to be as a pillar, a paean to totality. This is the essence and the Life. Be with Spirit, and be at peace.

Blessings.

SURPRISE

    This is life's jack-in-the-box. This is coming home to an unexpected guest whom you haven't seen since you were kids. This is all of the good things in life wrapped in shining paper with glittering ribbons and extra sparkles. It is a gift from the universe. It is the Creator saying "Have a rainbow sparkle day"—and believe me, if anyone can arrange it He/She/It can!

    Expect the unexpected. Create the unexpected. Be the unexpected. Enjoy your lessons.

COMMENTS FROM SPIRIT:

Surprise is our gift to you. It is our way of reminding you that miracles happen every day and all around and through you. Relax, Beloveds. Relax and enjoy the fruits of material existence. We gift it all to you with joy and blessings.

KINDNESS

Kindness is an act born of Love, and borne on the wings of compassionate caring. It is the extra moment spent holding the door for the next person. It is the dollar you give to charity and the word of encouragement left in someone's ear. It is the Divinity within you Loving and helping the Divinity around you. Kindness is the active form of the word 'NAMASTE'; which means: "The Divinity within me recognizes and honors the Divinity within you".

Other than yourself, there is no person on earth to whom it is more important to show Kindness than your partner. That soul has appeared in body in order to see through a part of your life with you in intimate detail. They have agreed to endure every snore, twitch and flatulence because of their Love for you and their desire to aid you in your journey. They are there to share with you every joy, victory and growth step. This word has come to you today to invite you to find a way to surprise your partner with an unexpected Kindness. You'll find it well worthwhile.

Kindness is one of the lubricants that smooth the movement of mundane exchanges. The Kindness you extend to another may not come back to you from that particular person or in that particular transaction, but it will come back to you. That alone is not a valid reason for performing a Kindness, however. The only valid reason is because you are following the Ultimate Commandment, which is: BE Love. If you do a Kindness expecting a Kindness in return there is no Kindness done. There is only a bribe.

Be Kind to yourself. You're the only you you've got for now.

COMMENTS FROM SPIRIT:

Kindness is the Love of the Creator leaking through the pores of your human limitations and touching those around you with your inner Light. It marks the first step from the animal to the Divine and the first flight from the nest of fear.

Blessings.

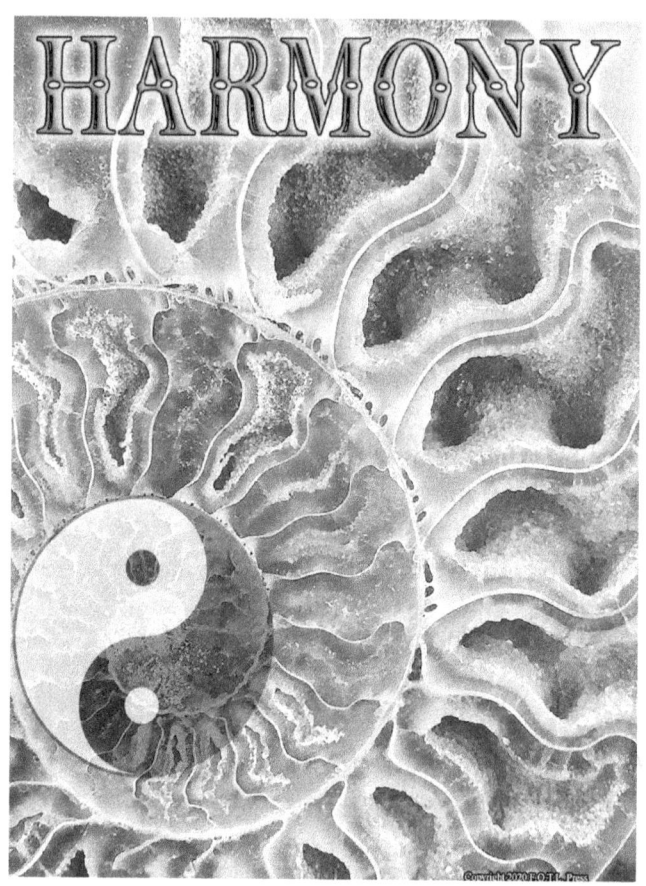

HARMONY

    Harmony occurs when two or more parts combine their forces in a way wherein each strengthens and supports the other. The combination produces a contiguous, reinforced whole-ness that is pleasant to the observer as well as the participant.

    Harmonious living within a personal relationship is an often sought but seldom realized goal for many of us. Drawing this word indicates that you will either experience new levels of Harmony in your home life, or you will experience new levels of need for Harmony in your home life. Either way -- remember that it's all perfect in every way!

This is another of those words where the meaning for general relationship is quite similar to that of the personal relationship, although generally not so intense and usually spread over a wider base of expression. You will find that as you come more into Harmony (Balance) within yourself you will find Harmonizing with the life flow of others to be simpler and simpler.

Inner Harmony is the most important Harmony of all. It is also the most difficult for many of us to obtain and maintain. Harmony within stems from an abiding understanding and peacefulness that can only be obtained by immersing oneself completely in the River of Life; becoming one with the flow of eternity in every way. I refer you once again to the information regarding Balance.

COMMENTS FROM SPIRIT:

Harmony can never be found without, but only within. All of existence is in perfect Harmony at all times and in all ways. It is only when one does not allow oneself to be part of that greater flow that the element of disharmony seems to appear in one's life. This is only a matter of perspective -- of adjusting one's perspective to see the beauty and Harmony inherent in every situation, regardless of how our consciousness would like to have us perceive it. Live in the Light of the Creator's Love. Live it, breathe it, become it, and you become Harmony -- there is no greater form.

Blessings.

ORDER

Order is the rhythm, the flow, the continuity, and the heartbeat of the universe, of life itself. Sometimes Order is hidden behind apparent chaos, but if you step back far enough, the chaos disappears and Order becomes evident in all things. It is only when we immerse ourselves in the human experience and forget to still maintain our spiritual perspective that we can experience things as being chaotic.

Order, balance, and focus are all necessary for a stable and healthy relationship. Even though a personal relationship is all about growth and change, this can happen as well in a condition of Order as it can in a condition of dis-Order.

If your home life is in apparent disarray and confusion, why did you let it get that way? Regardless of the apparent cause, there is some reason that your spirit has chosen the path you now walk. Life will seem much simpler and nicer if you find that which has caused the imbalance and 'wobble' you are experiencing and remedy it. Spirit will be glad to assist. All you have to do is ask -- and allow.

Order in the world is what has enabled human growth as a people over the ages. If each one of us was solely responsible for our own survival, at whatever cost to those around us, we never would have left the caves. It is up to each one of us to maintain Order in our own lives and to encourage it in the lives of those around us. That does not mean that we need to be satisfied with Order as it is. Order; as with every other aspect of material existence, is a living, growing, and changing thing. It is our responsibility to the planet to live our lives in accordance with our highest beliefs and to the best of our abilities. As this is done we change the flavor of Order as it now exists in favor of those highest motives. You are cordially invited to do your part, starting right now.

Order in your personal life is extremely important to your spiritual growth. A sense of inner peace is the basis upon which meditation and communication with the inner being can occur. Without Order, you may as well try to speak over loud static. The communications will be garbled and will need to be repeated over and over before the message is understood. If your life does not currently exhibit Order, it is time to find -- or create -- it. Spirit says that it will be glad to help you.

COMMENTS FROM SPIRIT:

Beloveds: we invite you to find the Order of the multiverse. Draw it into your heart, your consciousness, your life, and embrace it completely. Within Order you will find peace, Love, joy, succor, and the Divinity. Order is the mother of all things; the nest from which you have flown and the home to which you will return. Fly, my children! Stretch your wings into the skies of Love, of tears, of all of the human experience. Order awaits you upon your return. Peace presents its feathered breast to rest your nodding head and joy is yours to enfold your form. We Love you, Dear Ones. We Love you. Blessings.

OBEDIENCE

This is one of everybody's least favorite words. Nobody wants to have to be Obedient to anything but their own wants and desires. Following our own path can at times lead us far away from the ideal path that Spirit would have us walk. Drawing this word indicates the Spirit feels that we have gone far enough astray, for now, thank you, and it's time to head back toward the barn. Spirit can often be quite insistent at this point.

Drawing this word indicates that at least one party in the relationship is about to be offered a learning situation. The focus will be on the importance of following the inner sense of 'right' as opposed to doing what feels good but requires private or public justification.

Obedience in regards to a general relationship can deal with anything from the spiritual to the mundane but the rules remain the same. Follow your own highest inner sense of 'right' regardless of the apparent cost on the material plane. We are dealing here with Angelic energy and the Obedience should always be to the Creator first and to others who think that they have authority over you must fall a distant second.

Obedience received in response to a personal question indicates that you are about to be given a strong nudge in the direction of your ideal path, from which you have evidently strayed substantially. Remember, Spirit will only use as much compulsion as you require. Every time you ignore or miss a lesson, Spirit lovingly 'ups the ante' and repeats the lesson at a more noticeable level. When you get the message and change your pattern there is no need to continue those particular lessons and they end.

Our lessons can appear to be quite harsh if we choose to continue to not 'get it'. The choice to become the student is always ours.

COMMENTS FROM SPIRIT:

Children often stray from the straightest and shortest path as a result of curiosity or willfulness. A Loving parent allows a certain amount of distancing before feeling concern and calling the child back. The sooner the child returns, the sooner the parent may turn its attention to other matters. Open your hearts, Beloved Children, and hear the Loving voice of the Creator as you are called Home.

Blessings.

PASSION

    Passion is a totally exuberant involvement in some aspect of life. It overrides reason and sometimes even the survival instinct. It usually affects the physical and emotional simultaneously.

    Passion is one of the most wonderful aspects of a personal relationship. It is also one of the most efficient traps to hold us where we are. It can be in a relationship where the only thing that works is the Passion, or it may be something that holds you in the developmental spot where you find yourself in the moment. Passion creates attachment and attachment can often be what holds us back (see Non-attachment).

The positive face of Passion is rarely seen in a general relationship. Passion is a personal thing. Even the negative aspect of Passion can turn a stranger into an intimate personal partner of sorts.

A personal Passion can be a very good thing. It can be the path that guides your steps through life; that directs your eyes onto the heights of your own potential. It can also be the tar pit that holds you fast; impeding progress, wearing out your potential until you leave this life unfulfilled. Non-attachment is a good corollary to Passion. Although it is a difficult combination to maintain, it brings a good balance of directive force and restraint to your life.

Passion is an extremely powerful emotion. It easily changes lives permanently. It is very much like a scalpel. If used carelessly, it can cause grave injury or death. Used skillfully and carefully, it can heal and transform.

COMMENTS FROM SPIRIT:

Passion, Beloveds, is the call of your heart to the Heart of Hearts. It is the Love of your soul for the Love of Loves. It is the calling of your separateness for the wholeness of All that Is. Passion of this level is the spark of life; the beating of the heart of time. We hold out our Loving arms in supplication to you: Come home, Dear Ones; but not before the ripening of your soul; not before the time is right in the greater flow of existence. This dream of reality is your playpen, your kindergarten. We watch you with pride, for you have chosen a path through pain, blood, sorrow to unspeakable joy as the road you will take to your own growth and maturation. We watch; we wait for you to finish with this; your own private Passion play; until you reach the maturity of self.

Blessings.

POWER

This word has a negative aspect for many people. That is only because of our own inclination to associate Power with its misuse. "Power corrupts", we often hear. That does not have to be our truth. We may stand tall in our manifestation of the Power of our BE-ing -- that is to say the Power of the Creator, and not be corrupted by that Power. Drawing this word could indicate that you are misusing the earthly or psychic Power that you already have and need to be brought 'back into line'. It could also mean that you have brought yourself into a place of Balance sufficient to allow a greater measure of Divine Power to manifest through you. Either example will almost certainly assure some interesting experiences.

The use of Power in a personal relationship is a very delicate matter. Too much applied in the wrong way or at the wrong time can destroy an otherwise strong relationship. The ideal use lies in empowering each other.

Casual relationships are an area where Power is often misused. Abuse takes many forms but rest assured; any use of Power that does not come from Love carries with it the seeds of its own correction. Even if you (or the other party) appear to 'get away' with some action or activity, eventually Balance will be achieved. That is real Power; manifested from and with Love but Power none the less.

Personal Power or the perception of it is generally an incubator for strong lessons in the nature of real Power. All Power resides in and comes from the Creator. This Power must be warped or twisted by us in order to manipulate others. Drawing this word invites you to manifest this energy in the form that it is received. Remember: Be Love in all things.

As was stated above, Power is often and easily misused. For each instance of impropriety, a lesson is generated for the abuser. These lessons can often seem extremely unpleasant. It is always far better to consider the others involved and never act to hurt them in any way.

COMMENTS FROM SPIRIT:

The Creator is Power. That Power is Love. Any other use is out of Balance. All of the teachings of all of the teachers of Light, of God's word, can be said in these two words these six letters:

Be Love.

If this is done there can be no harm done and all will be as it should. Be Love, brothers and sisters. Children, Be Love, for we are all The Creator's children. Be Love in every word, in every thought, in every deed and in every prayer—

Be Love.

Blessings to you, each and all.

OPPORTUNITY

    You'll never have a better chance to understand yourself than you will right this moment. That is the definition of Opportunity: it is the chance and the invitation posed by the open door through which you may choose to step into a new branch or level of your own reality. The choice in these matters is always within you. Your soul already knows all of the possibilities and all of the costs and rewards offered by the choices available to you. You are gently and sometimes not so gently urged by your soul into the choice pattern that most directly assists and supports your shortest path of greatest light.

Any relationship is ripe to overflowing with Opportunity. Every relationship in existence offers hundreds of Opportunities each day. A relationship is any interaction between two or more people or entities. Every relationship offers countless choices; countless Opportunities for choice and change. Not all of these Opportunities will result in immediately obvious 'good' results. Some will result in apparently 'bad' results. An Opportunity is what you make of it and your reality is determined by your perceptions and beliefs in the moment. A good example of this is the old story of the Chinese farmer:

"There was a farmer in ancient China who had struggled for years to feed his family. They were not rich -- they were almost poor, but the farmer did have one horse in the corral just outside the house. One day the horse bolted and ran away. The farmer's neighbors came to him and expressed their sorrow for his loss. The farmer just said: 'We'll see.'

The next day the farmer's horse returned, bringing with it a wild herd of fourteen horses. The farmer's neighbors came and said: 'What tremendous good luck!' The farmer simply said: 'We'll see.'

A few days later after the new corral had been built; the farmer's son was trying to break one of the new horses when the horse threw him, breaking his leg. The neighbors came by and said: 'That's terrible!' The farmer just said: 'We'll see.'

A week later, the warlord and his army came through on their way to a battle, conscripting all of the young men along their path to fight in the battles. They would not take the farmer's son because of his broken leg. The neighbors all came around to congratulate the farmer on his good luck. The farmer replied: 'We'll see.'

A couple of days later, the farmer's son..."

As you can see, this is a never-ending story of Opportunities just as life itself is nothing but one Opportunity after another. Those we accept and the way we choose to deal with them and their results determine our growth or lack of it and sets the stage for the next series of Opportunities that we will offer ourselves.

Opportunities themselves are never either 'good' or 'bad'.

They are what we make of them, and the results are determined by how we choose to accept them.

COMMENTS FROM SPIRIT:

Life is Opportunity. Living is choice. Growth is result. All is Love.

SATISFACTION

    Satisfaction is the feeling of warmth and accomplishment one experiences at the successful completion of a challenging and/or pleasurable activity. Generally speaking, the more difficult the challenge the greater the Satisfaction one achieves when it has been overcome successfully. Satisfaction can also sometimes be found in a sense of completion.

    One of the greatest challenges many of us face in life is the successful completion of the process known as a personal relationship. New aspects of the challenge are constantly coming into play because it is constantly in flux and growing. To be able to retain one's balance and continue to move forward through the maze of personal relationship in a successful and growth-filled manner is an accomplishment that can bring great Satisfaction.

Our challenges in the mundane world are often quite different on the surface than those we face in a personal relationship. Underlying them both are the same fundamental issues. If we look deeply enough we will find that our major issues of challenge and our major regions of Satisfaction are internal. We challenge ourselves to succeed, to grow, and to excel. It is not the world that is our challenge but our own inner selves and our human nature. When we defeat a portion of our base human nature by growing further into our spirit selves, there is great Satisfaction.

Satisfaction can also reflect the darker side of us. There can be a certain Satisfaction for many in the unfortunate occurrences that befall one whom we do not like, or who we feel does not like us. This is an act of ego; a celebration of our apparent personal power or conquest over another. It is important, although it can sometimes seem difficult, to always remember that we are all One. Anything that diminishes our brother or sister also diminishes us. Compassion is also an emotion that can bring great Satisfaction.

COMMENTS FROM SPIRIT:

Dear Ones: the search for Satisfaction implies a sense of lack. We remind you that all things are One and that you are an intimate part of the One-ness of all things. When this is known in the heart there can never be anything but a sense of fullness and completion. It is only as you view life from the sense of limitation inherent in the human condition that it can seem possible that there is less than fullness in every aspect of your life.

We offer you, Dear Ones, the universe as your due; the multiverse as your toy, and All that Is as your greatest self. Live every moment in this revelation and there will never be any feeling but Satisfaction, for all things are in Divine order in all ways and at all times and you are that Divinity.

Blessings.

SECURITY

Secure is another word for 'sure'. Sure means something that is well anchored and solid. It is something that is not liable to shift or change unexpectedly or suddenly; that it is something that can be counted on in all circumstances without hesitation or reservation. Thus: Security is the state, condition or feeling of safety in a certain area of your life experience.

Security is one of the major reasons that many of us enter into a personal relationship. Emotional, financial, and social Security seem to be side benefits of this partnering. It is ironic then, that for many of us these are the very areas where challenges rear their heads.

It is through the lack of that which we have grown to expect that Spirit gets our attention and draws it to those areas within ourselves that need growth. The lacks that we perceive in our partner reflect those aspects within ourselves that we are not yet attuned with. Our partner's spirit has agreed to supply us with these illustrations as a way of helping us to truly see ourselves, and as a result, to learn and grow. The eternal Love that this reflects is a source of great Security for those of us who recognize it. It all comes down to remembering -- to KNOWING -- that ALL things are in Divine order at all times and in every way. Now, there's Security; there's something you can count on forever.

Security is not quite as easy to come by in the mundane world. Many people are so focused upon themselves and their own problems and/or desires to 'get ahead' that they become unreliable in interpersonal relationships. It is up to each one of us to be reliable and in integrity in our own relationships in the world. This shows others that 1) it is possible, and 2) they can do it too. Spirit is on your side in this. Remember: in the ultimate sense no one can ever take advantage of or hurt you, they can only (apparently) damage themselves by adding more Karmic lessons. Compassion is a much more balanced reaction in such circumstances than is anger.

It can be quite difficult for us to be truly Secure within ourselves with who we really are and to manifest that openly in the world. Speaking personally, I am very Secure with my connection with Spirit and with my function in the material world. Some people who are not so sure within themselves criticize me for my apparent arrogance and ego. So be it. Their fears create their judgments and perception. It has no bearing on whom and what I know myself to be.

You also are important in the world. Each of us has many levels from which to choose our manifestation and function in mundane existence. Choose to reflect your highest potential in every moment and be Secure in the knowledge that you are fulfilling your purpose in life regardless of how others choose to perceive you.

The only harsh aspect of Security is a false sense of Security, which is, of course, no Security at all.

COMMENTS FROM SPIRIT:

Security is living in the blessing of All that Is. Security is knowing that all there is, is Love and that you are an integral and intimate part of that Love and of All that Is.

Blessings.

RECEPTIVITY

"A closed fist may not gather a gift nor a closed mind a new idea". The universe is literally brimming over with gifts of all sorts for each of us. Our training in this material world has placed us in a position of feeling unable or unworthy to access or accept those gifts that would help us through our material world journey.

One of the strangest aspects of these gifts is that if we do not or cannot accept them in the positive form they are often offered to us in forms that appear to be less positive and less pleasant. Each of us has the choice to learn through joy or through pain. Since most of us find ourselves unworthy at some level to experience joy, the gifts and lessons must come to us in the other form.

Since our perceptions create our reality these can be seen as a wonderful gift even after the fact by the simple measure of realizing that that's what every experience is whether we like or understand it or not.

The universe is going to give us all that we require. Either we can hold our minds and spirits open to it or it will appear to be sometimes quite unpleasantly forced upon us. The choice is always ours and we can always change our minds.

One of the most important reasons we find ourselves in a personal relationship is to learn how to Receive in a good way. Most of us seem to suffer from a lessened sense of self worth and there are two main ways this manifests itself. Although there are many degrees of manifestation, the main forms are the abdicator and the sponge.

The abdicator seems to feel that they are so worthless the only way to find worth is to give to others; to submit themselves to others' whims and desires. This is a losing battle. No matter how much the individual gives; no matter how grateful or sated the recipient is it never seems quite good enough for the abdicator. Their 'good works' are constantly overcome by their own doubts and fears.

The sponge is the person who is so unsure of their own value that they seek to enhance it by acquiring as much as possible by any means possible. Wealth, power, gratification, love, and material possessions are only some of the major areas of acquisition the sponge will be drawn to. A true sponge will seek all of these and more in their search for self-worth.

They will never find it. Self-worth comes from within and is one of the gifts the universe has offered us all along if only we will open our hearts to it.

General relationships are also in our life experiences for the purpose of providing an avenue to Receptivity. Sometimes being Receptive means listening to the problems or statements of another with your heart as well as your ear. It requires opening yourself and Receiving (on all levels) that information that someone else is putting forth. Your being willing to Receive the information in those instances causes the other person to relax and open up more to their world, creating a cascade effect. When you are Receptive to another, you are helping to heal the world.

We create our own reality by the way we choose to perceive that which we Receive. How is your reality today? If you don't like it, step back several paces from yourself and look at what is happening through the eyes of Spirit. What lessons are being offered? Where and what is the gift or gifts involved in these lessons? What a wonderful gift the ability to Receive is!

COMMENTS FROM SPIRIT:

The Light of our Love shines forth for all of the multiverse. There is no place where it does not bring its glow. Only those who fear seeing what the light brings forth hide from it in shadows of their own creation. Blessed Loved Ones step forward out of your fears and into the Light of the Creator's Love. Receive that which has always been and will always be yours. The Love of the Creator is the greatest gift of all; the pinnacle of self acceptance and the epitome of self Love. It is yours if only you will open your heart, and Receive...

Blessings to you, Dear Ones.

DETACHMENT

Detachment is very different from non-attachment (see non-attachment). Detachment admits that there is now in existence an attachment and that for whatever reason it is time to terminate or remove that attachment.

Strange as it may seem, there is a necessity in personal relationships for this thing called Detachment. As Kahlil Gibran stated in his masterpiece, *The Prophet*.

*"....And stand together yet not too near together:
For the pillars of the temple stand apart, and the oak tree and the cypress grow not in each other's shadow."*

General relationships usually do not suffer from a lack of Detachment. Often the reverse is true. Less Detachment in our mundane activities is a good place to start if we are to truly BE Love in the world.

Notice the people around you on the street. Who are they? What has brought them to be on this street today? Do they have families? How do they feel right now and what happened to make them feel this way? How do they perceive you, or do they even notice that you exist?

Each person is of value. Each person has a life, and their own challenges

While it is extremely important to be very present in every way and in every moment, there is also a need to Detach a part of yourself in order to 'monitor' yourself and your patterns on an ongoing basis. Many people would liken this to a 'conscience'. The difference is that consciously accessing this ability places it on a higher level; a 'conscious conscience', so to speak. When you monitor your thoughts and actions from this conscious level you are able to make course corrections much sooner and much more gently than is the case with unconscious monitoring. Since your higher self has seen fit to bring this word into your awareness today, you may wish to consider beginning this action today. It is easier than you may think and Spirit is here to guide you. All that is necessary is to decide to do it and begin.

It is quite possible to become too Detached. When a certain area of our life becomes unpleasant or uncomfortable for us we sometimes choose to ignore it and pretend that it does not exist at all. By doing so we give it the opportunity to grow to an unmanageable size before it jumps back out of our own darkness to bite us. Small weeds are always easier to eradicate than large ones and ignored dragons do not just go away. As always, the choice is yours and yours alone.

COMMENTS FROM SPIRIT:

Dear Ones: You are invited to Detach yourselves from your personal darknesses. You are invited to Detach yourselves from your fears and doubts. We invite you to come fully into the glorious Light of your True Being: All that Is. Beloveds, you are the Lights of heaven, the joy of existence and the heart of Love. Become all that you are. Detach from all that you are not; that which you fear that you might be, and enter the kingdom of paradise within. Blessings.

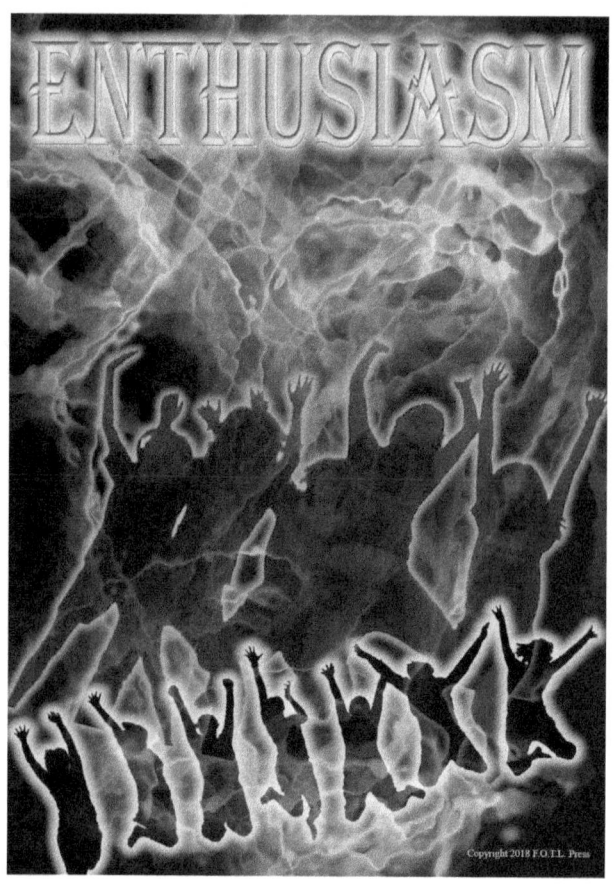

ENTHUSIASM

Enthusiasm marks a strong, joyful, and positive preference for a certain project or situation. Enthusiasm greases the skids of any work or chore and lightens any load. It is a great source of positive energy.

Enthusiastically entering your personal relationship almost guarantees success in whatever area you wish to explore. Enthusiastically living your personal relationship almost guarantees an exciting and rewarding experience. Enthusiasm in your day-to-day activities makes your processes easy and joyful. It enlivens those around you and is contagious. Enthusiasm for life and living mark a life of joy and great accomplishment. Enthusiasm is the result of balance within and without and a point of focus outside the mundane world.

Drawing this word to yourself today is a reminder from Spirit to rekindle the Enthusiasm in your life!

There are no harsh aspects of Enthusiasm, except the reactions of those who would rather be grumps.

COMMENTS FROM SPIRIT:

Enthusiasm comes as a result of eclipsing the day-to-day human heaviness by living in the Light and Joy of the eternal universe of Love. How could you not want to sing, to soar, to revel in the joy of being-ness? This is the true Enthusiasm -- the simple joy of existence in the heart of the Creator!

MOTIVATION

"No!"

"I won't do it!"

"There is absolutely no way in the world that I'm going to do that!"

"Oh! You will? I can? All right!"

Motivation is that which causes us to desire to attempt something that we were previously reluctant to try for whatever reason. It is the carrot on the stick, the gold at the end of the rainbow and the reward for a job well done.

Motivation can come from within or from any number of sources outside of us. It can be gentle or powerful, pleasant or harsh or a combination of all of the above.

Sometimes we are given Motivation as a test to see if we have really learned a particular lesson or series of lessons or if we need to review at a more intense level. At other times the Motivation can be to lead us in a direction that we need to experience in order to learn and grow to a new level and purpose. Sometimes (actually, usually), a combination of these two Motivations is occurring simultaneously.

Nothing in life provides more sources or varieties of Motivation than a personal relationship. Many times these Motivations can more easily be seen as challenges. Your partner's soul has agreed with yours to come together for this time in order to Motivate one another toward greater understanding and growth. By creating challenges, Motivation is given to move to an emotional place where a challenge is replaced by understanding. At that point growth has occurred and a challenge is then issued at the new level. Sometimes these challenges may seem to be quite harsh but that is only because we have not gained understanding at lower levels of challenge so Spirit has intensified things in order to get our attention.

General relationships also offer challenge and Motivation. The areas are almost completely different from those in the personal relationship and are usually not as intense as is possible in a personal relationship. Indeed; when a Motivation becomes extremely powerful in a general relationship it transforms the relationship to personal. Regardless of the type or intensity, your life will go much more smoothly if you will never forget that 'all of this' is for your own growth and is a gift of Love, always and without exception!

Self Motivation is, unfortunately, one of the least common forms. We (well, most of us, anyway) seem to have a tendency to be quite lazy when it comes to improving ourselves or challenging ourselves to extend beyond what we currently perceive our limitations to be. A major part of Spiritual growth depends upon our ability and desire to take ourselves by the scruff of the neck occasionally and drag ourselves into new and potentially uncomfortable situations. No one else can do it, although they can provide their own Motivations for us. It is we who choose when and how to respond to them. It is only by taking action that brings us outside of our normal sphere of comfort that we grow. Consider this word in your life today to be a gentle Motivation from Spirit to 'get on with it'. Whatever you have been putting off is about to happen. It can appear to happen 'to' you or 'for' you depending on how aware and how Motivated you decide to be by this hint. Good luck!

Motivation is a neutral thing. How we accept it and what we decide to do with it determines our perception of 'good' or 'bad' in association with it.

COMMENTS FROM SPIRIT:

There is but one ultimate Motivation in the multiverse. That Motivation is to pass through the apparent trials and tribulations of the form of existence known as 'life' and into the greater; then into the greatest expression of existence. This is an expression of the 'self' as All that Is; with no sense or awareness of separateness or limitation. This is the reward. This is the Motivation. Be the Divinity in all aspects of your life, in every moment, to the best of your ability and without fail. That is the first step on the inward journey to the Heart of Hearts that lies within and all about you. The journey that never happened and the division that does not exist are the challenges you have chosen to overcome. The path is Love, and the reward is You!

Blessings.

UNITY

Unity is the act of becoming or the state of being in oneness; indivisible in every way. Being in Unity is being whole and complete in the form that now exists; ready to add into that oneness any and all that come to the door seeking entrance. Unity is complete with the addition; complete without it. Unity is always ready to accept more but never hungry nor full.

Unity is the ability to stand firmly in the condition and position one is in with never a quaver or quiver as the world goes by; complete within oneself. Unity is in the world but neither of it nor dependent upon it.

Unity is one of the main reasons for experiencing a personal relationship. To enhance one's own inner Unity while beginning in-

volvement and expression of a multi-person Unity is a good exercise in expanding one's apparent boundaries and capabilities. As difficult as some personal relationships may seem, imagine Unity with the Multiverse! (It's actually easier -- really!)

It is almost impossible to maintain both a non-personal relationship and Unity within that format. Unity makes it very personal... as personal as it gets.

One of the hidden aspects of Unity is the Unity of Self. Many religious teachers tell us of our 'x' number of charkas. Spirit suggests that we are like a living prism; that Light enters our energy field and is broken down into its components and that different areas concentrate and utilize those components as needed. Other teachings would have us believe that we consist of 'x' number of bodies (physical, astral, etc.). Spirit suggests that we are the ones who have created this internal separateness. We are actually everything from the Creator to the shadow of the physical. It is up to us (and very possible) to break through those imaginary barriers and exist consciously in all of those apparently separate realms simultaneously.

Unity of self seems to be an important, even integral part of Spiritual growth. Please consider this word coming to your attention today as an invitation from Spirit for you to overcome the inner separateness that the mundane world espouses. Come into harmony with all aspects of self; bring the scattered pieces, the bound energies into harmony and power through inner oneness. Spirit is on your side. After all, Spirit is simply another form of YOU!

COMMENTS FROM SPIRIT:

All that Is, is ONE. Your perception of many; of separateness, is a result of the shattered mirror of existence into which you peer. Go within, Beloveds. Go within and look upon the unshattered source. Look upon the wholeness of all life in every form. See the Unity of the cosmos and recognize that that Unity is within you. It is your ultimate form. We Love you beyond words, beyond thought, beyond time and space. We offer to you the wholeness and unlimited extent of that Love without reservation, without cost and without expectation. There is Unity. All are ONE. Blessings.

DOUBT

Doubt is the silent killer of self. Doubt is the assassin of dreams and relationships, of hopes and desires. It is the evil of ego turned inward against yourself in order to keep you where you are or force you into the darkness of your own past. It is the single greatest stumbling block you will ever face. Along with its cousins worry and fear it has ruled large segments of the world for millennia.

Doubt is one of the cosmic termites that undermine the good things in our lives; validating our thoughts that 'nothing good can ever happen to me and if it does something is bound to come along and ruin it. Even the best of relationships may be killed by

Doubt. Don't allow this to happen to yours. Remember: all things are ultimately a gift of Love from your soul to you and whatever you need in your life will manifest whether you like it or not. Doubt only complicates the game. What you are supposed to know or to find out will come forth in the appropriate way and at the appropriate time. Doubt, worry, and fear are in the realm of the victim. Become instead the student. Find the lessons and the meaning in all things and Doubt will never darken your door.

COMMENTS FROM SPIRIT:

Doubt is the darkness in your heart that denies your Divinity. Doubt is the mouse that nibbles away at your self-worth and joy. Banish the mouse. Repel the Doubt. Live, exalt, and inspire with the bounteous living glory of your greater self. Be the god/goddess that you always have been. Express the limitless nature of your being in every thought, in every act, and in every prayer. The multiverse is yours! It is up to you to claim it.

Blessings.

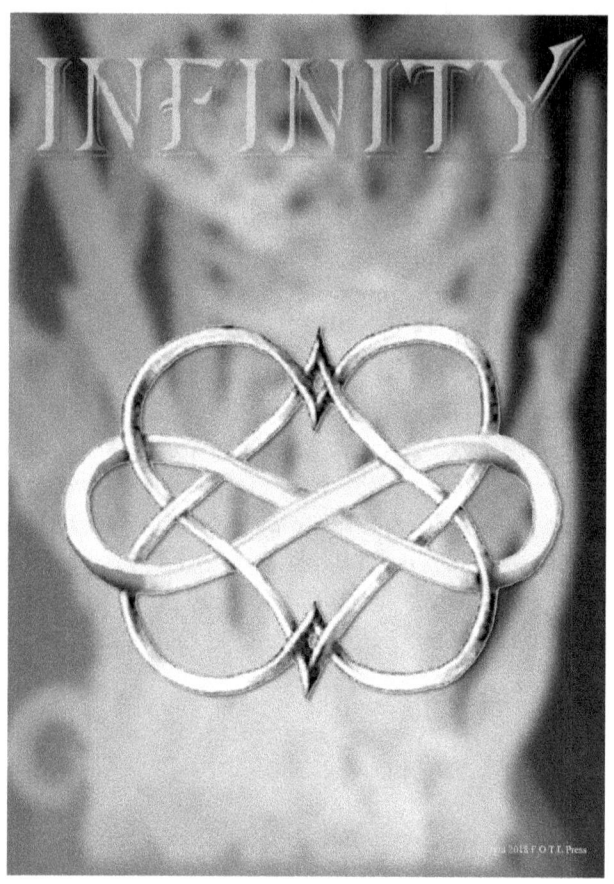

INFINITY

It would take Infinity of time, Infinity of words, Infinity of paper to begin to adequately define this concept. Infinity is a slippery beast. Just when you think that you've got a good grasp on it, it grows beyond that perception. The word is an attempt to put a handle on that which cannot be grasped. Let's take a close look at the concept of Infinity:

In electronics it is not uncommon for a circuit to be designed to run on a maximum of a very few volts. Suppose that a circuit was designed to run on an absolute maximum of two volts. At 2.1 volts, the circuit would melt down and destroy itself. The Infinity level for that circuit would then be 2.2 volts. That voltage would be unachievable under any circumstances. If 2.2 volts is Infinity, what would 2.3 volts be? 2.5 volts? 10 volts?

Aha! There we go. That is exactly the problem with explaining or describing Infinity. Just when you think you have a good definition, someone comes along and says "What happens if you increase it by one"? How do you measure the immeasurable?

I would suggest this: "Infinity is the condition or state of being at least one unit or level beyond your ability to measure or accept in the moment". Infinity is simply where your biggest yardstick – or your ability to comprehend – ends.

Since we live in an Infinite multiverse; all that is possible has already happened and nothing is impossible. Therein lies one of the greatest keys to overcoming the generally accepted limitations of the human form. The laws of physics, gravity, and medicine do not need to be our limitations! Spiritual seekers have for time immemorial surpassed these limitations. In effect, they have become Infinite in relationship to the majority of humankind while remaining Infinitesimal in relationship to their greatest selves.

Several years ago as I was excitedly telling a friend how wonderful it felt to be growing more every day Spirit popped in and said to me: "Spiritual achievement is never a matter of growing more; it is always a matter of limiting less. If you continue in each day to limit less, eventually you will become Limitless (Infinite).

Another interesting aspect of this concept is this: If the Creator is and always has been All that Is, and we were created of that Creator, did the act of Creation increase or decrease the Infinity of the Creator? Then question this: if we each are growing in spiritual knowledge and awareness and toward Oneness (equality) with the Creator...If our growing increases the Infinity of the Creator, do we ever arrive at that level ourselves, or do we play catch-up throughout eternity (there is a further option – contact me and I'll tell you about it).

Become all that you possibly can be and encourage others to do the same. It's a good start.

Infinity covers all of the bases from the obviously 'good' to the seemingly 'bad'. It is all one and the same thing; as all things are in Divine order in all ways and at all times. We do not have to understand or like it in order for it to be for our benefit. (Eat your broccoli -- it's good for you.)

COMMENTS FROM SPIRIT:

Life is your playground, Infinity is your abode. The further you travel, the closer you are. Welcome home.

Blessings.

SENSITIVITY

Life is sometimes like a doctor's probing; "Does this hurt? How about this? Does it hurt when I do this?" We are constantly being tested by life and by Spirit in order to find those areas where we feel things more readily and more sharply than other, more balanced areas. Once those areas are identified Spirit lovingly gives us lots of opportunities to exercise and strengthen them so that they will no longer be so Sensitive.

Sensitivity can also refer to empathy. How well do you 'tune in' to the needs, wants, fears, emotions, hopes, and physical condition of someone else? It is possible to become so Sensitive that you can literally feel someone change their mind, change their thought patterns, or even accurately tune into minute details of the physical workings of the body.

Sensitivity is one of the most important aspects of a successful personal relationship. You must second guess your partner's mood at times. There are those moments when verbal communication is not enough -- or is too much. Being able to 'read' your partner in those moments can spell the difference between success and disaster. Sometime when your partner is engrossed in doing something else, study their face. See how it looks in repose, in thought, in pleasant conversation, or in anger. 'Tune in' to the best of your ability and see what 'gut' feelings you have during these moments. Associate the feelings with your partner's emotional condition. Congratulations! You've just made a start into advanced Sensitivity!

Now that you have a tool to use, use it to avoid further irritation to your partner when they are having a bad day. You won't have to ask -- you'll know! You will both reap the benefits.

Think for a moment how much more smoothly the world would work if there weren't so many inconsiderate jerks in it. Now, take another moment.
How long has it been since you accelerated to pull in front of someone else just as the passing lane ended or rushed to beat someone to the grocery checkout when they had two items and you had a basketful and three screaming kids? Sensitivity to others starts with us. As we manifest this higher nature, eventually others will begin to also. It is so easy to forget that other people are not obstacles in our path but rather individuals with their own lives, their own hopes, dreams, and fears. To them we are just another face in the crowd yet we know that we are people with our own lives, our own hopes and dreams, and our own fears. Never forget that every coin has two sides and an edge. There is always a different point of view and always a reason, both on the human and the Spiritual levels, for everything that happens. Keeping this thought in your conscious mind is a sure step toward greater Sensitivity.

This word marks one of the few areas where we usually do not need to work on the personal aspect. The exception that comes to mind is when a person is so unsure or uncomfortable with themselves that they find it much easier to work on the problems of those outside themselves (usually requiring Sensitivity) rather than face the demons within. For those people, there is a suggestion from Spirit that they allow themselves to become less Sensitive about themselves and more Sensitive to themselves. If you are ready to begin this, Spirit is here to help. There's no time like now to begin.

Compassion often walks hand in hand with Sensitivity. Sometimes the greatest Sensitivity is to leave others to their own path. It is theirs to walk; not ours. No matter how much you may wish to ease their road it is ultimately their choice and their needs which places their feet.

It is very important to be Sensitive in your Sensitivity. Too many times, people go into someone else's business like a bee-stung bear in an effort to 'help'. Many times the help is totally unwanted and indeed, unneeded. These well-meaning busybodies seem never to know when to quit. If you recognize yourself in this description, QUIT ALREADY!

COMMENTS FROM SPIRIT:

Attune your hearts, Beloveds. Hear the cries of those around you. Feel the joy; the pain of the organism of which you are a part. All of existence is one being and that being is you. As you often cut off your feeling within yourself, so you deny the feeling of the greater whole. Bring yourself into the consciousness of your wholeness, Dear Ones. Awaken to yourself and to your greater self. There is no need to sleep into the night and into the day. It is only as you allow yourself conscious participation in all of Life that you begin to grow. It is only in awareness that Sensitivity is released.

Blessings to you, each and all.

VISION

     Vision is the act of seeing or that which is seen. We sometimes speak of a person of great Vision; meaning someone who is able to see clearly into the future or beyond the barriers that appear in the now. This person can have a great Vision as did Sun Bear, Nostradamus or Black Elk, among others. The Vision is the action or plan or development which is seen by the person with Vision. Vision can also refer to a conscious or unconscious goal or plan.

     To enter into a personal relationship is often as a result of a (usually unconscious) Vision on the part of both parties as to what rewards that partnership will bring in the way of joy and growth. Drawing this word to you today is a reminder to remember that original Vision and look at where it has slipped away from the ideal.

Do you want to regain that ideal path? It's entirely up to you. Only you can change your reality. Remember: how you perceive events and circumstances determines your reality. If you don't like how things are shaping up either change how you choose to see them or sit down with your partner and redefine your joint Vision. Do what you must do but always do it with and from Love. Spirit is here to help, as always.

A Vision is a very personal thing. It is a potential road map into your own future. Study the map carefully and be sure to bring all of the gear that you will need for the trip. Once you are sure that you're ready, enjoy the trip!

While there are grandiose Visions that sweep worlds before them, these are the exception, not the rule. One can have a Vision for a business, a project for the public good, or for many other purposes. Whatever your Vision is, if it is from the heart and based in Love, follow it with all your heart. That is the message of this word this day. Go for it! Spirit is with you!

There are bright Visions and there are dark Visions. Both are valid, and both are potentials. The choices you make; the choices we all make determine that path is chosen. If each of us always takes the shortest path of greatest light we can affect the choices made by the rest of the world. Now is a good time to dedicate yourself to that goal.

COMMENTS FROM SPIRIT:

Open your eye. See the worlds within the world you perceive. Further and further your Vision will take you until you have reached the heart of matter and the beginning of eternity. Let your Vision carry you beyond the limitations of time and space; as these are mere illusions to fool the human eye. As you step beyond the boundaries of that mortal field of Vision you become eternal yourself and see with the eyes of gods. It is only at this point that you begin to see that which truly is in the cosmos and that which always shall be. Open your godly eye and see the eternal you; Creator of All that Is; Heart of Hearts; Love of Loves.

Welcome home. We have long awaited you, and we rejoice at your return.

NURTURING

    Nurturing is the act of offering to someone that which is needed in the moment in a Loving and compassionate way. Notice that I said offering. The other party has no obligation to accept and may indeed reject all or part of what we offer or twist it in their minds until it is repulsive or threatening to them. It makes no difference. As long as the sustenance and support is offered (not forced), we are Nurturing by intent. When some or all of what is offered is of use to the recipient and is accepted by them we are Nurturing in fact. It is the Nurturing in fact that we shall deal with in the following passages.

    As each of us move through life we hit bumps in the road and sometimes go off into the rocks and gravel of life's less than pleasant experiences. It is at times like these that the Nurturing of a partner is invaluable. This word has come to you today to remind you that your partner may not be having the easiest of times with what is going on in your lives. In the throes of a dilemma it becomes very easy to focus on your own discomfort and forget that your partner is also experiencing it from their side. This is still your partner even in the most trying of circumstances and there is an implied obligation in that partnership to be sensitive to the other's needs and to Nurture them in their times of need just as they are to do for you. As each of you learn to bypass your own difficulties and focus on helping the other the problems will almost always diminish or disappear as if by magic. That's what partnership is all about.

Nurturing the self is often quite difficult. Even the best of us seem to have the residue of issues about self worth. Those issues make it easy to ignore our own difficulties or hurts as we continue blithely in the world. It is only when we begin to truly Love the self that we are that we can allow ourselves to be Nurtured; first by ourselves then by those around us. We are worthy! Each of us is created of the Creator by the Creator. Each of us is a tiny portion of the 'body' of the Creator; as a cup of water poured into the sea becomes indivisible from the sea. As an integral part of the Creator we must ask ourselves this: How can the Creator not be worthy? How can the Creator not be Loved? How, then, can we not be worthy? How, then, can we not be loved?

There is no harsh aspect to Nurturing unless it is forced on someone who is not willing to accept it or when it is based on an ego centered judgment of what someone else needs. Act always from and with Love and remember; Love never goes where it is not invited.

COMMENTS FROM SPIRIT:

Nurturing requires the perception of lack and is only possible when you have taken a limited view of yourself. Become aware of your greatest nature; your limitless self, and there can be no perception of need as you are Nurtured by the Heart of Hearts; Eternal Love. There can be no need when one swims in a sea of plenty. Nurture yourself by opening to the universal force that you are. Nurture yourself by accepting the Love of Loves. There is no shortage of Love; there is only a lack of acceptance. Blessings.

FULFILLMENT

Fulfillment is an interesting word. It means neither 'filled' nor 'full'. It refers to becoming filled to overflowing; completely sated in whatever way or area is being referenced.

Fulfillment is a sense of satisfactory completion, a job well done, a challenge well met and successfully completed

There is ample opportunity for Fulfillment in any relationship. Whether it is over the day to day challenges, the birth of a child or the marriage of the last child and the successful completion of active parenthood, the birth of a business or the successful completion, marked by retirement, of the work years, the feeling is the same: joy, elation, satisfaction, relief and sometimes a little sadness. Bringing this word to yourself today is an invitation from Spirit to lean back, put your feet up, take a deep breath and give a sigh of relief. The task at hand is either completed or about to be so. You've done the best you could and it has turned out as well as possible under the circumstances. While there is always room for improvement you can give yourself a 'well done' and relax for a moment. You've earned it!

There is also ample opportunity for Fulfillment in a casual relationship. Whether it is over the day-to-day challenges, the feeling is the same.

The only harsh aspect of Fulfillment occurs when it is obtained at someone else's expense. Always act solely from Divine Love and your highest nature, and this can never occur.

COMMENTS FROM SPIRIT:

Fulfillment requires the perception of want. Should you find yourself in want, simply look within yourself to that place where universes meet in joyful harmony and Love. It is there at the center of all things that you will find that there never has been; there never will be anything but total abundance and joy for all of eternity. We invite you once again, Dear Ones, to turn to the Divinity within yourself as the ultimate source and answer all of your needs. The gift is yours, and the giver is you.

Blessings to all.

VERSATILITY

    Versa means changeable or fluid in essence or deed. Someone who is Versatile is able to flow and shift with the currents of life about them; almost always 'staying on their feet'. By keeping their wits about them, they are more prepared than most to take action in a timely and thoughtful way.

    Versatility also relates to the ability to take on and accomplish a wide variety of tasks and being skilled in many areas.

    Yet another important meaning is the ability to readily see

many different points of view in a balanced and objective way.

Versatility in a personal relationship is only important if you wish to have a relationship instead of a dictatorship. When one of the partners becomes abusive or bullheaded and options are removed from both partners, the relationship has made an important and unfortunate shift away from Versatility. The flexibility required to deal with life in a graceful way is no longer there. The ability to freely choose the next step or direction is severely curtailed and choices and rewards may seem to have disappeared. In actuality this is often Spirit's way of forcing you into a situation where you can no longer ignore certain lessons that you have disregarded in the past. As we have said in several other places in this book, each of us has the opportunity to accept every event in our lives from the point of view of either a victim or a student. The only difference is whether or not you 'get the point'. Should you not 'get the point' you will feel like a victim, and worse, the lesson will be repeated, usually at a more intense level, for your benefit by Spirit until Spirit has gotten your attention sufficiently so that you do become a student and learn the lesson involved.

Guess what ---? If your relationship has become a dictatorship you're there. It doesn't matter on which side of the authoritarian coin you find yourself. The lesson for both has escalated to a dangerous and powerful level. Take the time today to look at the situation through the eye of Spirit and see what needs to be changed. Whatever must be done; do it calmly, with Love, and from Love.

General relationships also invite Versatility as a road to growth. It does no one any good to be unyielding and stiff as a way of life. It is only when we allow our lives to get slightly out of the bounds of what we normally find to be comfortable that we are forced to stretch our concepts of what we are capable of. It is this stretching that is translated into growth, and growth is what we are here to do. Hang in there, it's well worth the time and turmoil. Remember, there is nothing that you can experience that is not a gift of Love at its core. Trust yourself and Spirit. You will never be given more than you can handle. Just try to see everything as the lesson that it is, and avoid the role of 'victim'. "That which does not kill me strengthens me."

COMMENTS FROM SPIRIT:

Beloved ones; You who limit yourselves so severely in your human form. Invite yourself to limit less. In inviting this Versatility to yourself you begin the process of growth and awakening that is your purpose on the plane of Earth. If you limit yourself less in each day, you will soon discover yourself to be and manifest as the Limitless being that you are. The aspect of Versatility that this invokes brings you into intimate connection with your greater self and opens the door to your ultimate Divinity.

Thou art the Creator. There is no greater truth.

Blessings.

DEFIANCE

Defiance is willful disobedience of rules, regulations or authority that someone or something feels that they have or want to have over you. Defiance can be blatant or sneaky. The other side of the Defiance coin is found when someone that you would like to control doesn't allow you to do so. Infuriating, isn't it. Your irritation should tell you that you are ego invested in the outcome and that perhaps you should look again at your motives and direction in the issue at hand.

Defiance is also often associated with a sense of being offended or victimized. It is often delivered with an anger that only exacerbates the situation because the other party often feels that your response is out of line and is a control issue (is it?) and then responds with their own Defiance.

A personal relationship is one of the favorite arenas of Spirit for teaching. Each partner may have their own definite ideas regarding how a certain thing might be accomplished or how it should best be approached. A full blown confrontation may result depending on how much ego each partner invests in their relative 'right-ness'. What the partners do not usually realize is that one of the major aspects of personal relationships is the partnering aspect. Without this there is no relationship. There is only a dictatorship or civil war. If you are not working together on a consistent basis with your companion in a co-operative mode and for your mutual benefit you are only sharing space. There is no partnership.

The world is full of large egos and small minds seeking petty revenges. Because of the focus on one-upmanship in the mundane world, people often let their egos get bruised when ideas and quests for power clash. Defiance is a common form of retaliation, as is petty revenge. I overheard two waiters talking one night. They were staring at a patron who had been giving one of the waiters a hard time. The comment I heard was: "Well, he ate it."

Defiance against ourselves is rare, although not as rare as one might assume. How often do we go against our own better judgment and then wish we hadn't.

Bringing this word into your consciousness this day brings with it the message that Defiance is the tool of a victim. It is only when one feels wronged or threatened in some way that Defiance occurs. When one truly realizes at the deepest levels that ALL THINGS are here in our experience for only one purpose, and that that purpose is to assist us in our quest for the growth of spiritual balance and our connection with All that Is; one realizes that nothing can threaten us (perhaps our bodies or our comfort, but never our greater selves)

Defiance almost always carries with it a harsh result even when it turns out that you were 'right' in the first place. Be very sure of your motives and your goal before you decide to be Defiant but never forget this: sometimes, being Defiant is the shortest path of greatest light. If you find that you must be Defiant, do it without anger; do it always with Love and from Love and compassion. That is the only way in which any harsh aspects will be minimized. Good luck.

COMMENTS FROM SPIRIT:

Defiance, Beloveds? The only spiritual Defiance is that of denying your true nature as a child of All that Is. Do whatever you choose; whatever you must, to learn the lessons of life. Know that we judge you not but that you are your own harshest critic and your most severe judge, and that you are the most unforgiving of wardens. When all is done; when all of your lessons are learned and you come home to the Heart of Hearts, you will find it wide open in joyful welcome at your maturation and your return to that place that you have left only in your dream. Welcome home, Beloveds, welcome home.

Blessings to you as you voyage through the self-created rapids and brambles of life.

REFLECTION

Reflection can have two meanings in the context of our work. The first is deep and placid thought; as in meditation. The second is the image of ourselves or our patterns sent back to us so that we may see ourselves through the offtimes clearer vision of others. Sometimes Reflection is the only way to truly see ourselves and it is quite often a real revelation. Regardless of whether or not we feel that it is true or biased, we should always remember that every perception is based in truth to some degree. Even the most blatant lie has at its core at least a tiny thread of truth. Thus, the Reflection of self by others can become a wonderful and powerful tool for self-examination and betterment.

Take a moment and mentally list all of the faults of your partner that affect you most severely. Now, take another moment and realize that those faults are Reflections of those areas in yourself where you are the least comfortable or that need the most work in this moment. An intimate partnership is a wonderful tool in which we let our hair down and remove our facades in the comfort of our own home with our partner. (At least most of us do most of the time). As a result, our protected inner portion is exposed for Reflection in the actions and words our partner gifts us with. Look deeply into the relationship and you will see yourself looking back through the ripples of self-deception and selective vision. This is a priceless gift, as Robert Burns well knew.

> *"Oh wha' a gif' that God would gi' us*
> *To see ourselves as others see us"*

Look at the world you live in. Is it a busy city full of chaos and noise or is it a placid country view? Reflect for a moment on how this view of the world Reflects on you and how it Reflects your inner condition. Our reality is created by our own expectations, limitations, and choice of perceptions. If you don't like how your world appears to you perhaps you might change how you choose to perceive it. Imagine that you are standing and looking through a window at a monument and the pigeons have fouled the portion of the viewing window right in front of you, obscuring features you have come to see. You can stand there all day and wish that the window were clean, or you could take a few steps to one side or the other and CHANGE YOUR POINT OF VIEW! The same technique works in your life. If you are unhappy about something it is because you are seeing only the negative. There is absolutely nothing that does not have a strong positive side if only you can find the right spot from which to view it. Reflect on your problems and you will find that they are all blessings in disguise.

You may not always like what you see. The truth is sometimes harder to accept than the misperception it replaces. We have a tendency to insulate ourselves from ourselves and we warp the truth (whatever that is in the moment) and reality (whatever that is in the moment) in order to do so. Reflection can bring to us an image of things as they truly are. What we do with or about that image determines our growth or need for further lessons in a particular area.

COMMENTS FROM SPIRIT:

Children, We ask you to but Reflect on this: That all that you see; all that you feel; all that you hope and all that you dream are only Reflections of the Divinity that you are and the lessons that you have chosen. All that exists is you; and all exists for you as you pass through this aspect of your existence known as life. Each one may choose to learn from the process known as joy, or the one you know as pain. May we recommend joy?

Blessings.

OUTRAGEOUSNESS

The word 'outrageous' originally meant "something that is so out of the ordinary that the senses reel" This, like everything else in our lives, is neither 'good' nor 'bad' in it's essence; but simply 'is'. That which one person may find "Outrageous" another may accept as perfectly normal. When this word comes into your consciousness as it has today, it means one of two things.

First, it could be a cautionary message. Take a good hard look at the things that you do to attract attention from others in your life. A certain degree of Outrageous behavior is acceptable, perhaps even good (see next entry). There is a very thin boundary, however, between acceptable and unacceptable levels of Outrageous behavior and that boundary varies from moment to moment and from person to person. The line is constantly shifting and changing and is determined by the energies and perceptions of those who are affected by the behavior. The cautionary aspect suggests that perhaps it is time to back off a little to give those around you a break from the assault of the constant 'stuff-stirring' that your actions and words engender.

The other possible meaning is exactly the opposite. It suggests that you have been a 'wall flower', hiding in the background for entirely too long and that it is now time to make your presence known in the world. Go a little crazy. Step beyond the boundaries of your comfort zone if necessary, in order to incite others to step out of their petrifaction and into thoughtful, aware, spiritual living. You will know which of these applies to you.

COMMENTS FROM SPIRIT:

There is nothing that is Outrageous in the eye of the Creator. All things are in Divine order at all times and in all ways. The choices you make determine the length of your path on the non-existent journey Home. Even behavior that the majority of those around you may find offensive or radical is not necessarily a detriment in your progress. Follow your heart. Do all that you do with and from Divine Love and there shall be no fault to that which you choose.

Blessings.

PURIFICATION

    The energy called Purification can deliver the harshest and the most beautiful of experiences; sometimes simultaneously! Purification invites us; at times rather forcefully, to refine our essence and distill from the dross of worldly thoughts and patterns only that which manifests Light. This can seem to be quite bitter as you go through the required changes but you will find that the pain is temporary and the gain is forever. At other times, you have reached the point in your existence where you are very ready to divest yourself of your heavier elements. If that is the case, you will find Purification to be an extremely pleasant experience

Purification in a relationship can relate to a change in intent (from lust to Love for instance) or removal of anger or jealousy from the interaction. It can also signal the removal of confusion (clarity) regarding which of two or more potential partners best answers your needs for the moment. In this type of circumstance, Purification refers to removing from the equation some or all of that which is negative. This allows the parties involved to see the true nature of the transaction more clearly and invites them to act accordingly.

As we have discussed with other words, we all have a tendency to see ourselves and our actions in the harshest light. While this is probably not an enlightened attitude, it is also probably not entirely wrong, either. We all do have areas of our life that we have not yet perfected. This can give us the feeling that we are indeed 'doing something wrong'. Purification energy in response to a question with a personal reference reveals that Spirit is about to aid us in identifying those areas from our higher awareness that we are not comfortable with, and Spirit is going to help us to remove or resolve them.

Purification is another word for Purging. Purging can range from extremely mild and gentle to life-threatening. It all depends on how hard you try to hold onto that which is about to be removed.

COMMENTS FROM SPIRIT:

The art of Purification is very simple: it consists of removing from oneself all that which is not of the Highest Good. Become the god or goddess that you are and be Pure Love.

Blessings.

OPTIMISM

Optimism is the act of choosing always to see the 'good' or the benefit in each and every situation. It is one of the more important shifts we can make in our quest for spiritual growth.

Spirit has told me that nothing in the universe is against us; that every experience is for us.

Optimism is simply the act of choosing to perceive all experiences in the light of this knowledge.

Because our understanding of 'reality' is determined almost exclusively by the way in which we choose to perceive the input of our material and mental experiences, we can and do literally and continually create our own reality.

Suppose for a moment that a stranger were to come up behind you, scream loudly, and slap your back very hard. What would your immediate reaction be? Most people would answer: "Fear, anger, and self-protection." A being who understood the energy of Optimism would probably experience momentary confusion, then await a reasonable explanation from the stranger, such as: "There was a wasp on your back, and it looked like it was getting ready to sting you. I'm sorry if I startled or hurt you, but I didn't think that there was time for me to explain it to you first."

Spirit will lovingly provide us with countless and powerful opportunities to achieve that balance through our experiences because we do create our own realities; and because we do call to us those things that we most fear (inasmuch as those are the areas of greatest imbalance). Had we been the type of person who lived in fear (a pessimist), the reply and intent of the person who struck us would almost certainly have been very different.

Spirit has told me that the obvious solution if you don't like the way something appears to be happening is to change your point of view. There are two possible ways in which to perceive any experience. One is the point of view of the student. The other is the point of view of the victim. The only real difference is that the student gets the message and moves on. The victim does not get the message and is condemned to repeat the lesson in ever evolving intensities until they, too finally understand what it is that their soul would have them learn, and move on to the next lesson.

Having established that all things work ultimately in our (karmic) favor, it is time to take a new look at events and situations that may previously have seemed to be uncomfortable or painful in your personal relationship(s). Sometimes it helps to remove yourself from the equation by imagining that someone you don't know has come to you for advice and understanding and proceeds to describe your situation exactly. What, upon reflection, would you tell them that the root issue was and what would you tell them that the lessons that you perceived as being offered were? Where is the good in the situation and how do they need to alter their perceptions in order to see things in a similar way so as to become the student rather than the victim?

The same is true of an uncomfortable situation in a general relationship. Remove yourself from the immediacy of the problem and look at it through the knowledge that there is absolutely nothing that you can experience that is not ultimately for your benefit. If the situation seems to be altogether too intense it is only because you have previously ignored all attempts by Spirit to attract your attention in the matter. Once you realize that a situation is a challenge, a lesson, and a test, almost all of the 'sting' is taken out of it and it becomes much easier to process through. Look back at the times of greatest turmoil in your past. As you processed through the hurt, confusion, and anger, look at the lessons you learned that have made you a better balanced, and stronger individual. It is all a gift. Try to see it through Optimism and the pain or discomfort is immediately lessened.

COMMENTS FROM SPIRIT:

Optimism can only survive in a reality where pessimism is a possibility. This is another of those trick words of the material duality. The very concept helps to create and maintain that duality. The ideal is to arrive and live within that point of One-ness where all things are in balance at all times. In the meantime, Dear Ones, if you must choose duality, for now, Optimism is a good place to place your consciousness. Blessings to you, Dear Ones. Remember: material plane life is only temporary. Don't despair!

CHARM

A Charm can be an object or energy that seems to bring one power or a power that one manifests that influences others to do what the bearer wishes in spite of their own beliefs, hesitance or tendencies to the contrary

Sometimes one may consciously choose to exude Charm in an effort to bring another into a personal relationship. To do so in this way is often a dishonest act. It is only when we choose to be ourselves in every moment that we will find a partner who is truly attracted to the 'real' us. The life expectancy of the relationship is directly related to the TRUE compatibility of the persons involved and if you choose to be more (or less) than you really are as the relationship is forming, the relationship is founded upon falsehood.

People will often use whatever Charm they may possess in order to manipulate others in subtle or shameless ways in the material realm. While they may seem to 'get away' with this behavior for a time -- or even for an entire lifetime -- their soul knows that this is most likely not appropriate behavior. Lessons will be required in order to bring this behavior to balance. When these karmic lessons arrive, the recipient will most likely be heard crying and moaning "Why is this happening to me? I don't deserve this. I don't understand." Remember. KARMA IS NEVER PUNISHMENT. KARMA IS ONLY YOUR SOUL SEEKING BALANCE WITHIN ITSELF! Once the conscious realization of the lesson occurs, there is no need for further lessons and the karma releases from the individual.

We are usually exempt from the influence of our own Charm and are usually aware of the facade we wear as we don it. In some cases of complete self-absorption, however, we seem to be able to fool ourselves into believing on the conscious level of our own P.R. Rest assured that Spirit will assist us in overcoming our selective blindness. Infinite Love has infinite patience, but that same Love insists that lessons be offered to help us to grow beyond the point where we currently exist.

Charm would seem to be a good thing to have, and it is, as long as it is a completely natural extension of who and what you are allowing yourself to manifest as in the moment. The problem with Charm is that it is often something that is assumed for the moment, usually for purposes of ego. Remember: Spirit has said that the definition of Evil is the misuse of Ego; placing your own desires or preferences above those of others. Display your Charm discretely and use it only for the highest good of all concerned.

COMMENTS FROM SPIRIT:

True Charm, Beloveds, is a fast peek through the tiniest of windows at the beauty of the inner self; of the Soul within; of the Creator in each of you. The beauty and Love that is your true nature above the dross of human existence and behavior, is both attractive and powerful in the lives of those around you. Manifest this inner BEingness at every opportunity and you will become the most Charming of humans. Peace be unto you.

OBSERVATION

    To Observe is the practice of experiencing a particular event or person with all possible senses and sensations WITHOUT INTERFERING IN THAT EVENT OR PERSON'S PROCESS.

    How long has it been since you have sat back and truly experienced your partner as a human as well as a heavenly being? Take some time. Quietly Observe your partner at work and at play. Marvel over the fact that this being has chosen to align themselves with you in this life experience, whether that seems 'good' or 'bad' in the moment. Find the lessons that are being offered and the ways in which your lives interact in order to provide those lessons to and for one another.

Observation of the world around you can be both educational and frightening. Remember, please: all beings are One, and that One is you, that One is me, that One is the sleaziest bum and the worst murderer. That One is Mother Theresa and that One is the Creator. Everything you see is an aspect of you; and the things that you like the least in those around you are those aspects of yourself that need the most attention and/or you fear the most.

Remember as you Observe life going on about and through you that nothing in the universe is here to harm you and that nothing ever happens TO you but only happens FOR you. It is easy to get so involved in the act of living that we forget to experience Life. When things seem to be getting to 'heavy', step back and look at the situation through the eye and understanding of Spirit. All things simply ARE at this level. There is neither good nor bad but only the experience. Each of us makes of that experience what we need it to be in order to process the lessons we are currently working on.

Observation leads one in many cases to the perceived need to perform action. There are no harsh aspects to the act of Observation as long as it is done with integrity and not from ego. Observation often seems to invite participation, and participation can often be seen as interference. Be cautious with your emotions and your ego, remember that ALL things are in Divine order at all times and in all ways and you will most likely avoid this.

COMMENTS FROM SPIRIT:

Beloveds; become the Divinities that you are. Expand until you exist as I do, with center everywhere, perimeter nowhere, existing consciously throughout all of 'space' and 'time'. Become in your consciousness the All-that-is that you are in reality, and Observe the wholeness of all from every dimension.

Blessings.

EFFICIENCY

    Efficiency deals with following the shortest path of greatest Light. It deals with cutting through the smoke screens and the illusions to find and grasp the heart of a situation.

    How many times do we 'beat around the bush' when we would like to affect a change in our relationship? Afraid of offending or angering our partner, we avoid addressing situations in a clear and readily understandable way. As a result, progress or understanding, if any, is limited or incomplete. This exacerbates problems and creates further distancing and frustration. Drawing this word invites you to sit down with your partner with a conscious, clearly stated intent to plainly, tactfully, and lovingly 'air your dirty linen' with one another in an Effort to achieve greater understanding and harmony.

Efficiency in a general relationship refers to many of the same issues, but quite often in a business or professional setting. You are invited to perform the indicated functions in a straightforward and forthright way. Spirit is here to support your Effort and your intent.

Efficiency in the personal sense implies that it is time to stop avoiding issues and face them directly. It's time to go to work!

The only harsh aspect of Efficiency would occur if you did not avail yourself of its energy. In that case, the same lessons will come around again, though perhaps not as gently.

COMMENTS FROM SPIRIT:

Efficiency is achieved by putting aside the walls and barriers associated with the human condition. It is as a direct result of these walls and barriers that the concept of Efficiency or inefficiency even exists. Live in the Light of the Creator in every moment, and you will transcend even the need for that concept.

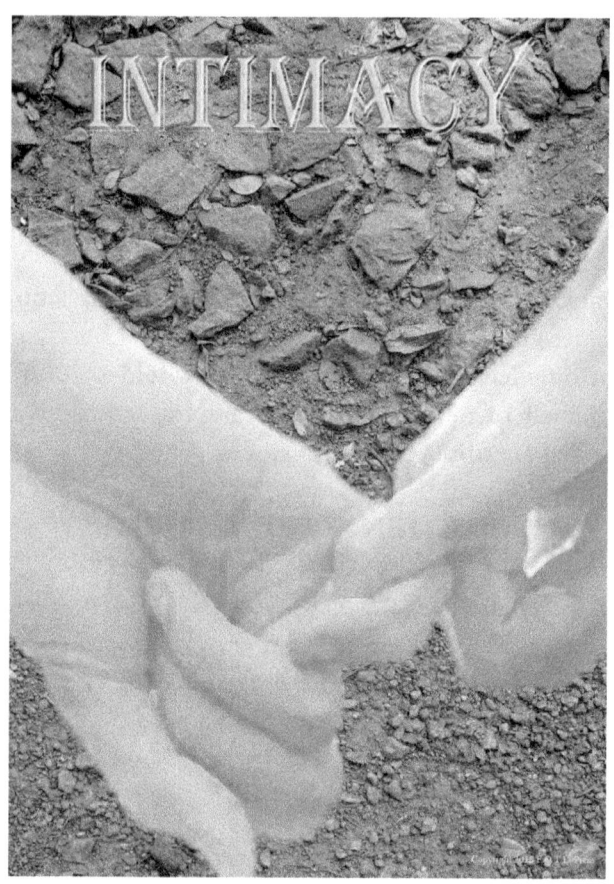

INTIMACY

Intimate means "in extremely close proximity to". Being Intimate can thus mean 'being close to' in any of the many possible forms. It can mean sharing a secret, a hope, a desire. It can be furthering the understanding one has of another. It can mean being physically close. It can mean the ultimate physical Intimate connection or it can mean something even closer; a connection in spirit.

Personal relationships contain the most Intimate connection the material realm offers. If this word has been called into your awareness this day, it is time to examine the depth and direction of that Intimacy. Spirit is suggesting that one or the other of you is holding back for some reason. While Love (and its human cousin, love) is the heart of every personal relationship worth having, communication is the blood. Without blood, the heart soon shrivels and dies. Sometimes it is extremely difficult to communicate to your partner the things that must be said, but to not communicate it dooms the partnership to death as surely as any other poison. There is an antidote. Honest and forthright communication from and with Love can often turn even the most toxic situation to one of greater depth of understanding and Intimacy.

A business or other general relationship by its very nature, in the moment it evolves Intimacy in any form, becomes a personal relationship and should be observed and treated as such.

The greatest – and the most difficult – relationship to develop and hold true Intimacy within is the relationship with self in its many forms. To allow oneself to observe oneself without bias or criticism is almost impossible, yet that is a primary requirement for true Intimacy. It is only when we simply observe and allow that ultimate closeness is possible. Every façade; every self-deception; every denial puts space between our goal and us. This day would be a good time to start the demolition of those obstacles.

There is absolutely no harsh aspect to honest and forthright Intimacy. This is Intimacy with no agenda, no ego involvement, and no manipulation or guilt. It can be an extremely frightening experience to those who are not in complete understanding of the spiritual laws of existence, as one is made to feel extremely vulnerable when one no longer maintains the 'space' of denial, fear, and deception. If, indeed, all beings are One and we are that One, what is there to fear but our own darkness?

COMMENTS FROM SPIRIT:

One to One, we issue a welcome home to those who will travel the path of ultimate Intimacy. Come once more into the heart of hearts that is your lair, your home, and your castle. Beloved Ones – welcome home!

Blessings.

SELF-IMPORTANCE

    Spirit has told me that the recognition of Self-importance rather than the expectation of Self-importance marks the boundary between Self-realization and ego. When it is recognized it can be simply set aside as the unimportant aspect that it is.

    Each 'self' IS important, though none is more important than any other as all are One with The One. Our culture urges us to feel as though we are simply tiny cogs in the wheels of a giant mechanism. Our religions teach us that we are lowly sinners and worthless helpless beings who have to go to the priests to connect with the Creator. None of this is true. We are all created of the Creator by the Creator. We are all a part of the essence of the Creator. How, then, could the

Creator which is our essence be unworthy or unimportant?

Self-importance in the higher sense is an asset within any relationship. We are urged to recognize and manifest our right to participate in the decisions and responsibilities within the relationships without usurping the rights of our partners to also participate.

The concept of Self-importance is, of course, only a matter of personal mental attitude. Perception creates reality and if you allow yourself to realize – not expect – that you are important in the unfolding of the material universe, this will manifest in your presence and your actions. Even though you have this value, remember that the universe is equally capable of existing and flowing with or without you. Spirit says that: "Everything is important but nothing matters. Everything matters and nothing is important".

For those who have not yet achieved the realization and still dwell in the expectation, remember that Spirit's definition of evil is the misuse of ego. Caution and an honest self appraisal are strongly suggested when you bring this word to yourself.

COMMENTS FROM SPIRIT:

Beloveds:

Self-importance is self deception. There is only One and you are that One as well as I. Importance requires comparison and none is possible in Unity. You are that you are. I AM that I AM. WE are that WE ARE.

Blessings.

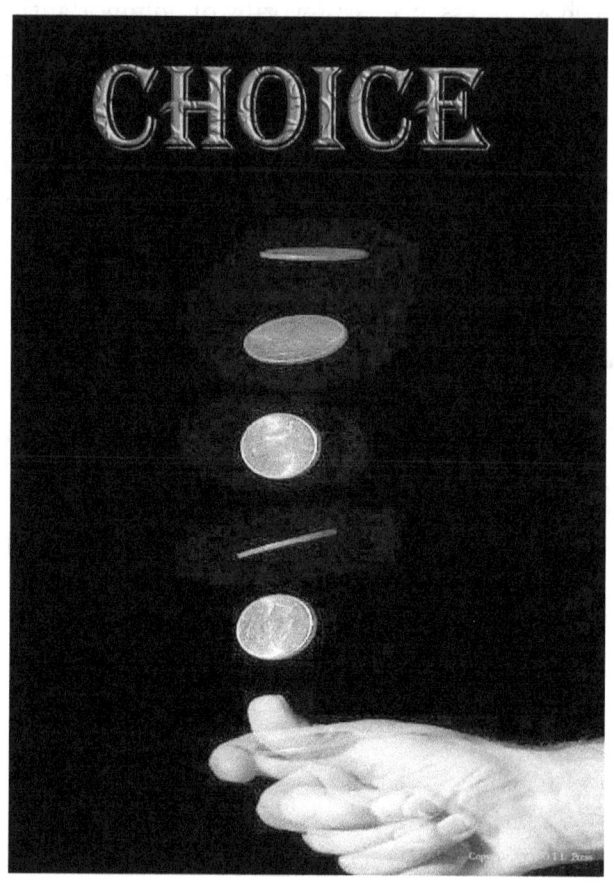

CHOICE

     Choice combined with Balance constitutes the whole purpose of human existence. Without Choice there can be no dynamic balancing. Without the need for balance, there is no purpose for Choice.

     Healthy personal relationships provide the most fertile field for growth regarding this word. Every Choice we make in a personal relationship is magnified and mirrored back to us almost instantly. If we allow ourselves to be sensitive to this input, growth is almost always assured.

     Casual relationships provide the same responses and opportunities as do personal relationships, if we will allow that to occur.

Unfortunately, in most cases this does not occur because we perceive the other(s) involved as being more separated from us than our intimate partner(s) and thus less important in their mirroring and lesson providing ability. It is of the utmost importance that we never forget that we are all One and that no one is truly separate from us. More importantly, no one is separate from Spirit and all are teachers just as all are students.

One of the most important things I have learned in this life is that every Choice we make has both costs and rewards. These costs and rewards are well known to our soul before any conscious Choice is ever made. It is of utmost importance that we be aware of that fact in every moment. While our conscious Choices determine our pathway in detail, our spiritual Choices made before birth determine the grander scheme - the very direction and hoped-for goal of our life's journey. The Choices we make determine how long, how short; how troubled, how smooth; how bright, how dark that journey seems to us. The ideal is of course to make the Choices that result in the shortest path of greatest light. Drawing this word to you today indicates that Spirit has decided to help you to accomplish just that end. What a blessing!

The mental and spiritual intent behind any Choice determines the Karmic influences it will invoke. The same Choice arrived at via two vastly different paths of reasoning will generate two vastly different Karmic responses. Always be aware of the Ultimate Commandment: to BE LOVE in every word, in every thought, in every deed, in every prayer. If this is done there will be no 'unpleasant' repercussions to your Choices.

COMMENTS FROM SPIRIT:

Beloved ones; Choice is the entire purpose of the human experience. It is the only lesson in the book of Life. Your lifelong response to this question, and your answer to this single challenge determines your placement in your next life experience. The aspects you fail to handle in a manner of which your soul approves is set aside as one of the parameters of the next existence. In this way you and you alone determine the basis and the boundaries of your next existence.

Know, Dear Ones, that there is never a 'bad' Choice and every Choice only serves to point out to your soul those areas that seem to require more experience to perfect. Blessings on you and your journey, Beloveds. Every Choice you make brings you closer to the home you have never left.

We Love you.

Blessings.

WILL

    Will can be both our best friend and our worst enemy. The only difference is whether we are in control of it or it is control of our mind and our actions. Will and mind are two very separate things. Will is the nice name for the assertive, often non-thinking part of our physical/mental self known as ego which demands that every whim be instantly gratified, regardless of the circumstances or the material and spiritual costs.
The misuse of Will (placing your wants, needs or desires above the needs or comfort of another) is) is EGO and is defined defined by Spirit as "evil" Indeed; all evil in the world seems to fit into this

pattern.

    A personal relationship is probably the single most important arena in which to practice proper management of Will. If one partner gets their way the majority of the time; if they use anger as a tool to get their way through intimidation; that is a misuse of Will. This is a technique often learned in childhood and carried into adult relationships. If you are doing this (be honest with yourself now); STOP IT! If you are in a relationship where you are the recipient of such treatment perhaps it is time to take a long hard look at your own self-image in an effort to discover why it is that you allow yourself to continually be degraded and abused. What is there in your image of self that finds a need to be punished? Only you can change the situation. There are many different paths available. It will require correct use of Will to assess and implement the correct choice for your situation. Spirit will be with you.

    Almost every non-personal relationship invites misuse of Will as human beings who are mostly unaware of their Divine nature struggle for control in small and large ways with every contact. Stand back and observe the subtle and often not-so-subtle ploys and plays; the choices of words, clothing, meeting place, posture and body language as near strangers battle for apparent superiority in the moment. Remember two things. First: BE Love in every word, in every thought, in every deed, and in every prayer. Second: No one can ever cheat or truly harm you. They can only cheat or seem to harm themselves in a way that truly matters.

    Correct use of Will is the ideal we all seek. Maintaining a state of balance between 'wants', 'needs', 'desires' and that which we KNOW to be the right action marks a mature spiritual being. In BEing Love it is important to remember that Love never possesses; it only shares. Love never takes; it only gives. If we can BE Love in every moment and in every way; if we can BE Love in every word, in every thought, in every deed, and in every prayer; then and only then will we be practicing correct and proper use of Will.

    Will is our material self's quest for power. Remember that power corrupts and that absolute power corrupts absolutely. This is the addictive power of the dark side of our spirit. By giving its practitioners a taste of power up front and with no apparent cost it appeals to the baser aspects of Will. In a spiritually weak person there is no balance to this input and the power and quest for more power takes over that person's life.

COMMENTS FROM SPIRIT:

Will, beloved Children, is often the attempt of the animal form to rule the spiritual being. Indulgence draws you away from your shortest path of greatest light, yet is totally necessary in your learning agreement with Spirit. To those of you who are challenged by Will, Blessings. To those of you who have conquered Will in this life experience, Blessings.

We Love you, each and all.

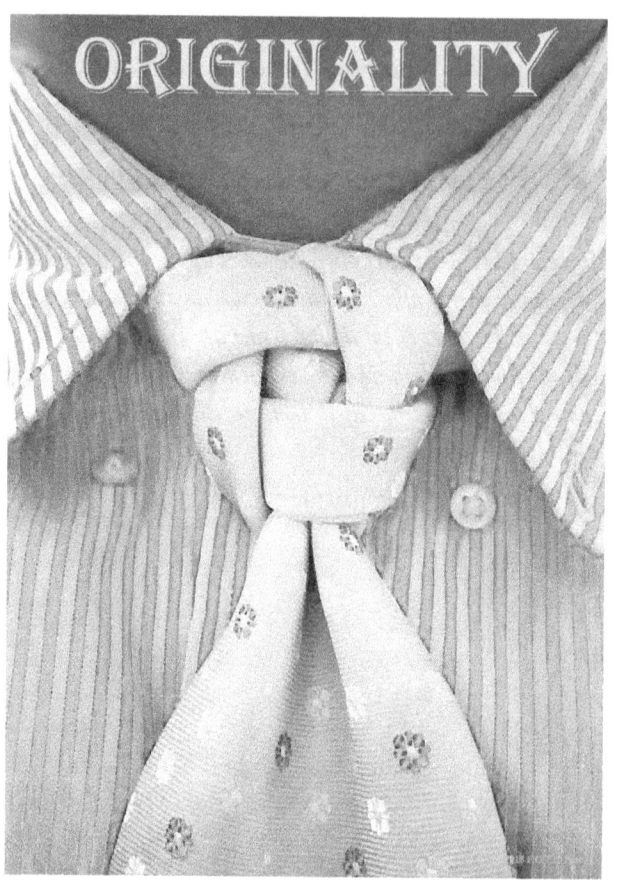

ORIGINALITY

Origin: beginning; bringing forth from non-existence.

Originality: being able and capable of bringing forth from non-existence that which has never existed before in the mind or experience of the creator.

Every close relationship is a unique entity; full of opportunities to create on a daily basis. The extent to which each partner is willing to and able to explore each unique situation to find the most elegant solution helps to determine the success or failure of the enterprise. Originality often reveals the most elegant and effective solutions. One must be willing to 'stretch the limits' in order to grow as a person and as a couple.

Originality can be one of the keys to a successful public life. It is not the person who is satisfied with letting others set their rules and limitations for them who makes a mark upon the Earth. Make your own decisions and trust yourself and Spirit enough to see them through. Always seek an elegant and Original solution to the most mundane of challenges and your personal and spiritual growth is assured. Stay 'within the lines' and you will produce the same picture as everyone else. While the 'establishment' urges us to follow the rules which keep it in power and even provides for severe punishment for some infractions, that is precisely where every step of human progress comes from. It is only when one chooses to go outside the lines of 'normalcy' that change occurs.

It is entirely up to you to guide every moment of your life. Originality does not demand change for change's sake. Rather it invites you to go beyond the perceived limitations the world would have you believe are yours. Believe instead in your innate limitlessness; as a child of the Creator, and as co-Creator.

Originality takes courage! To have the surety to go forth with what you truly feel to be 'right' regardless of the apparent costs in the material world can be quite frightening and quite difficult. Have fun! It's all a game!

COMMENTS FROM SPIRIT:

As ye are all One, and that One is All that Is, there is nothing but Originality. Ye are the Origin, the source, and the omega of all. Know ye that though we are all one, as hairs on a head are all one with the head they reside upon, Each hair is an individual unit; able to stand alone but unable to exist without the support of the greater self. Never forget that you are all. This is the source of your power and the balance of your soul.

Blessings.

SPIRITUALITY

  At our very core lies a vast sea of Spirituality, invested in our psyche as a major portion of our birthright. It is so much an integral part of who we are that it can be ignored or seemingly lost with the greatest of ease by those who are not conscious of it. It is much like a birthmark on our back. We may or may not know of its existence, but it is there nonetheless.

  Spirituality is completely different than Religion. Religion is Man's manipulation of Man in the name of God. Spirituality is each soul's intimate connection with that Creator. For more information on religion see the entry for Ceremony.

  Seen through the eyes of the conscious seeker there is no aspect of life that cannot be seen first and foremost as a Spiritual event or experience. Because of the intense nature of a personal relationship, the events and lessons of such a partnership are often more pointed and hard-hitting than outside of such a partnering. Enjoy the lessons of your partnership. They have arrived because you have requested them.

Seen through the eyes of the conscious seeker there is no aspect of life that cannot be seen first and foremost as a Spiritual event or experience. It is up to us to find the lesson and the gift of each experience whether it seems pleasant or painful in the immediate moment. If we maintain this stance of ever seeking the lesson; and more importantly of KNOWING that there IS a lesson in every event, we are well on the road to leading a truly Spiritual life.

Perception creates reality. If we choose to buy into the popular belief system that states that we are helpless 'sinners' constantly being attacked by the 'forces of evil' who are trying to get us to succumb to temptation we are the sheep they refer to us as. If we choose not to believe that we are ignorant and helpless pawns in the celestial game, then we can manifest as the Divine beings we truly are.

Some of my good Christian friends once told me that I was "so heaven-bound that I was no earthly good". Another told me that my problem was that I "loved too much". My only question is; how is either of these things possible? Would someone have said these things to Jesus of Nazareth? The only danger in Spirituality lies in the perceptions of others and their reaction to what they perceive. Would these same people berate an ascetic hermit in the Himalayas? Probably so. Be true and faithful first to your highest self and there can be no fault.

COMMENTS FROM SPIRIT:

Spirituality, Beloveds, is simply letting the gross and draining vibrations of the material realm fall away from the essence of Divinity that is your true self. Exposing the god or goddess who you truly are causes others around you to realize at some level that they are also Divine. Thus we help one another to realize our highest goals and aspirations.

We Love and Bless you all.

COMFORT

Comfort is the state or condition of feeling at ease and in balance in the moment. While Comfort can refer to several senses or areas, we will focus on the emotional and the spiritual in this text.

Comfort in a personal relationship is usually a result of a LOT of hard work between the partners and each within themselves. While Comfort CAN result from ignorance, ("ignorance is bliss"); that is a false Comfort in the context of this usage.

Coming to a place within your relationship where there is a consistently peaceful atmosphere with no nasty surprises hiding around the corner is a wonderful accomplishment. Maintaining that condition can be a lot of work but is well worth it! In a truly spiritually mature relationship, it is the norm and seems almost to maintain itself with very little conscious effort.

General relationships are a little more difficult to maintain a Comfort zone within. When that state does develop it is almost always because the general relationship has been transformed into a personal one.

Comfort with and within oneself is probably the most difficult Comfort of all to achieve and maintain. The process can be simplified by living your highest perceptions. Be the Divinity that you are and your inner Comfort is assured.

Comfort derived from and by the expense of others is not really a satisfying Comfort but only satiation and ego-based self-satisfaction. You are only fooling yourself in a situation such as this and the irreversible laws of karma dictate that in this life or another, the lesson will be brought home to you in such a way that it can not be ignored. Avoid the rush! Learn the lesson NOW!

COMMENTS FROM SPIRIT:

How can there be anything but Comfort in one who lives their Divinity?

SENSUALITY

Sensuality exists when one is immersed in or addicted to those things that are of or appear to exist in the physical realm and our perceptions regarding it. This is one of the most attractive of the traps that can ensnare us and hold our spirit in the lower vibrations. This is not to say that Sensuality is "wrong". All things and experiences are gifts of the highest Love. We only mean that as with everything, moderation is the key. A complete being experiences the highest and the lowest of human nature. It is where we choose to place our attention and our emphasis that determines what our next lessons are to be and how fast our spiritual growth occurs.

Sensuality entered into from a sacred thought pattern and pursued in a sacred way is a sacred activity just as a sexual experience generated in the same way would be. Intent is everything.

Sensuality is a state of mind and can exist within or outside of any type of relationship. In a general relationship it can be a wonderful asset or a terrible burden. The way it is perceived is always a reflection of the opinions, hopes, and fears of another member within the partnership and may or may not have anything to do with one's original intent.

Most people consider overt Sensuality to be out of place in anything but a very personal relationship. This has to do much more with that individual's own fear of their own Sensuality and sexuality and their fear of their potential reaction to those forms of expression in others. In short, most people feel threatened not because of your statements or actions, but because they fear what they feel is a demon within them that can be beyond their control. Overt sexuality and Sensuality are taboo in most of the so-called "civilized" world because they have the potential to be so disruptive in one's life (Read this as: "loss of control!" = most people's deepest fear) and because organized religions have invested so much time and effort to convince us that they are "Evil" in their continuing effort to control our lives for their benefit.

Sensuality can be one of the most honest manifestations of our deepest human self. Some, such as certain Hindu sects, feel that if one travels deeply enough into one's Sensual nature, one merges into the spiritual. To deny our Sensuality; or worse, to be unaware that it exists is to deny a major portion of our material world experience. Remember that fear, like anger, is the tool of the victim and that a tortoise goes nowhere until it sticks its neck out. Drawing this word to you today marks Spirit's attempt to have you become more aware of your Sensual nature and is an invitation to seek a more appropriate balance in this difficult and often frightening area.

Our Buddhist friends embrace "the middle path". This is an incredibly important concept, and in very few applications is it more critical than Sensuality. Whether we allow too little out of fear and denial or indulge to an excess in the pleasures of the material world we slow our journey to conscious ONE-ness by our focus on the subject to the exclusion to other lessons or by denying ourselves the experiences necessary for further growth in this area.

COMMENTS FROM SPIRIT:

Dear Ones: Do not fall into the double-sided trap of the senses. They are given to you by your request as tools for your experience and growth. They are gifts given in Love. Use them as the tools which they are; enjoy them, but do not allow them to rule you.

Blessings to all.

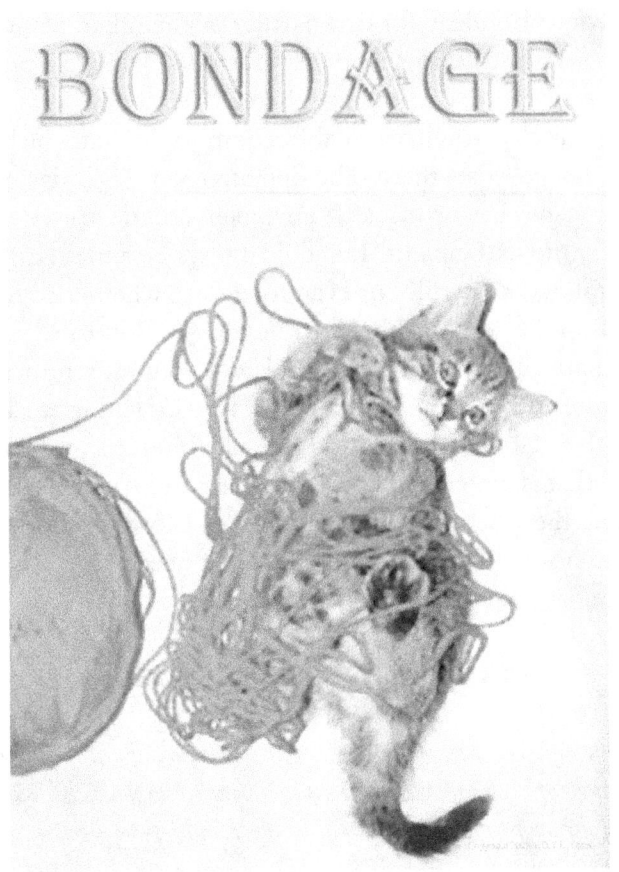

BONDAGE

Bondage is always and invariably of our own creation and exists only by our own permission. Bondage exists when we allow ourselves to be so focused on achieving a certain status or goal or when we become so focused on a certain fear that we do not allow ourselves to see our options or to see another way to perceive or deal with what seems to be happening in our lives. Whenever we feel paralyzed by fear we are held in Bondage (inability to move) by that fear. Whenever we want something above all else we are held in Bondage by our ego desires.

Unfortunately, many relationships have been allowed to

degenerate into Bondage for one partner or the other. Stand back and take a long, hard look at the relationship(s) you are a part of. Are there traces (or more) of Bondage there? If either of you is unable to honestly say that you have total freedom to do that which you choose, Bondage exists there. The operative word here is "choose". Each relationship has its (usually) unspoken and unwritten guidelines agreed to by the participants. It should always be a matter of free choice to follow those rules or even to choose whether or not to remain within the relationship. Anything less is Bondage.

We are all always in total Bondage to our current perceptions of our nature and the reality about us. Every limitation we allow, every less than Godlike perception of 'self' binds us to the material 'reality'. If that is where you choose to exist and you are satisfied and comfortable there, why then, you are home. Close this book now and find a good novel. There's nothing here you need.

Bondage is its own punishment.

COMMENTS FROM SPIRIT:

Your only Bondage, Beloveds, is your ignorance of all that you truly are. Slough off the shackles of limitations which do not exist except within your own beliefs and ye shall be truly and forever free!

BEAUTY

Beauty surrounds us in every moment. Sometimes we forget to observe it in its true form. Drawing this energy into our life helps remind us to see the Beauty in the smallest things ... and in the least likely.

There is nothing more beautiful in the human experience than a good relationship that fulfills our every human need. Being human, we sometimes think we want more (see Abundance) or otherwise forget to honor the radiance of what we have. Spirit has come to remind us of the value of what we have and what we are.

Our daily experience of life in the world brings us a rich

broth of experiences from which to draw our lessons and growth. It is important to remember that this process is a thing of Beauty in its entirety. From the stranger who comes over to complement your appearance to the jerk who cut you off on the freeway, all are One with the Creator, and all is done in Divine Love and Beauty for your soul's benefit

So many of us spend many hours and dollars to present to the world an appearance that we think of as pleasing or beautiful; what a shame that we do not spend as much on our own self-image. I have yet to meet even one person who was truly happy with every aspect of their inner self. This is your opportunity to remove one more layer of inner ugly. When you can truly love every aspect of your inner self you will have achieved real Beauty.

Sometimes in the quest for Beauty you must experience the most repulsive aspects of the world. Remember that these, too, serve you.

COMMENTS FROM SPIRIT:

Beauty is not in the eye but in the heart of the beholder. How can one who is at peace with self and who is of the flow of the Universe see any portion of that flow as more or less beautiful than any other portion? The flow is the flow -- it simply is. All things and situations are created of the Creator by the Creator through Divine Love. Thus all things are part of the flesh of the Creator and reflect that Love. This, then, is true Beauty.

Blessings.

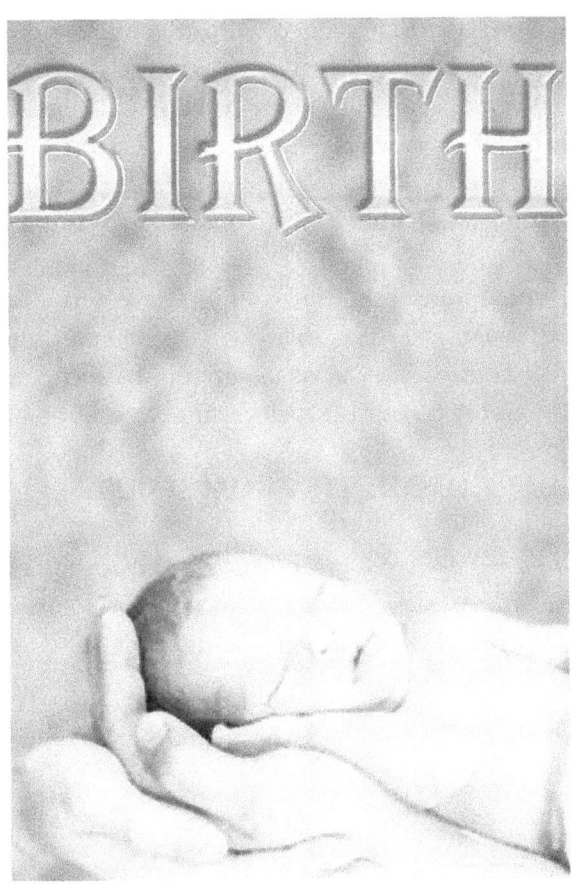

BIRTH

Drawing the word Birth marks powerful new beginnings. Birth is coming into the light from the darkness; into full consciousness from partial awareness. It says that you are merging into the world as a being who has completed one area of learning and is now ready to begin growing even more.

The energy of Birth in a relationship opens many doors. Drawing this word can mean the initialization of a relationship, a further opening of an existing relationship, a change in direction or whole new areas of understanding within the relationships you currently are a part of.

This word is closely aligned with Adventure and Growth.

On the personal level Birth is an extremely exciting prospect. This usually indicates growth to a new level of understanding or a further awakening of awareness of self or the Universe to a degree previously unsuspected. You will frequently find yourself operating and understanding at a higher level after bringing this energy into your life.

One would not suspect this word to have a harsh aspect but remember in the physical realm that Birth is often accompanied by a great deal of discomfort and a certain amount of recuperation time. Also, keep in mind that your life is never the same after a Birth.

COMMENTS FROM SPIRIT:

Awakening is another word for Birth. Expanding your consciousness to previously unknown levels is the excitement and the reward. Child of the Creator! Open your eyes! Dawn is near!

BROTHERHOOD

This energy knows no gender. It is the mind of the human species that gives it that energy. Brotherhood is identical in meaning to NAMASTE. Each means "the Creator in me sees, recognizes, and Loves the Creator in you." Brotherhood means putting the emphasis on others first -- not self – while recognizing that they are not truly 'others' but 'self' in another body.

Brotherhood is not to be confused with romantic love (small 'l' for human love), but rather Divine Love (large 'L'). Spirit defines Divine Love as: "Love not for or of; but simply Love." Divine Love is the love you would have for the concept of a wonderful spring meadow full of lambs and butterflies. It is unfocused and all encompassing. This word coming to you today invites you to explore this aspect in all of your relationships.

It is simple to see that our day-to-day existence and the experiences of those we interact with could be greatly improved by focusing on the energy of Brotherhood. Try consciously to demonstrate an extra helping of this force at least once a day, and bring more Love into the world.

Once more we are focused on learning to accept and Love ourselves for the Divine being we truly are. Perhaps the most difficult person to feel Brotherhood for is our self. It can be quite difficult to offer ourselves the Brotherhood that we freely give to others when we are intimately reminded of our perceived faults and failings on a daily basis. Receiving this word today is an invitation to remember and manifest your Divine nature and your Brotherhood with All that IS!

If we continue to ignore the energy of Brotherhood Spirit may place us in a position requiring Brotherhood in order to get out of a tight spot. This enables us to more readily see the importance of knowing and living the Oneness of all beings.

COMMENTS FROM SPIRIT:

Brotherhood of the highest order was demonstrated by Jesus of Nazareth, Siddhartha Guatama, and many other teachers. It is also demonstrated in every person's life as they stop to help another for no other purpose than to be of assistance. Nourish and nurture this place in your being for these actions reflect the Creator into the world for all to experience. No greater Love is there than to Love and support one another from the Loving energy of Brotherhood.

Blessings.

CLARITY

What a gift this is; to be able to cut through all of the symptoms; the smoke and mirrors, in order to find and remove the ultimate cause. So many times we wear ourselves out from discord within; not understanding why we can't seem to make any progress. Help is here. One of the greatest gifts Spirit can bring is Clarity. Trust it and use it wisely, for it is a rare gift.

Because of the central role personal relationships play in our lives, this is a particularly valuable gift in that arena. Even in the best relationship there is imbalance in some areas. Clarity will assist you in seeing past the manifestation to the root cause. It is usually a simple matter to then fine-tune that fundamental difficulty into something less abrasive and more tolerable.

As with personal relationships, there are many areas of interaction that are out of balance daily in our casual relationships. Many times we blissfully go on through our life; accepting these circumstances as 'the way things are'. Clarity will assist you in becoming more aware of which of those areas are not comfortable to you; why they are there and what changes you can make to improve them.

Robert Burns understood the meaning of Clarity in our personal existence several hundred years ago when he wrote: "Oh the gift that God would gi' us, to see ourselves as others see us.".
Many of us have a persona that we put on like a mask or a suit of armor when we go into public. Most of us are totally unaware of it. We wear this disguise in order to appear to the world to be more than we think we are and to hide our self-perceived flaws. What a gift it would be, then, to acquire a flash of insight that would allow us to see ourselves differently -- in a more positive light and more in keeping with our Divine origin and source. This is the gift that Clarity brings; an understanding of why we are as we are and how to change our lives to more closely reflect that if we wish.

Spirit has told me "In the Light all things are made visible." Be prepared to see something you may not like when Clarity comes to you. Disliking it is the pivot upon which your changing life turns as you then determine a new and more light-filled path. What a gift!

COMMENTS FROM SPIRIT:

Each of us functions a lens, focusing the Eternal Light through our being. A smudged or dirty lens transmits little Light. Clarity is essential to one who would be thought a Light-worker.

Blessings.

COMMUNICATION

Communication lies at the heart of all human endeavors. Unless we are able to accurately express our wants, needs, feelings, fears, and thoughts to others, we might as well be locked in a padded cell. Interactive relationships are extremely important to our development as human beings and depend heavily on accurate Communication.

Expect to hear things in conversations with your partner that has always been there, but that you were not aware of before. These nuances are often at least as important as the face value of the words themselves. Love is the heart of any personal relationship, but deep, continuing and honest Communication is the lifeblood. Without it, you are living in a shell that could collapse from the slightest shock. Without Communication, the heart will soon wither and die.

Drawing Communication brings into your awareness the necessity and the ability to send and receive messages of all sorts in a more accurate and efficient manner.

The single most important Communication we can have is with our selves. This can be at the conscious, sub-conscious, super-conscious (soul), or Divine level. Receiving Communication in response to a question about self invites closer scrutiny of information from other levels. Communication is a two-way street. Listen with your heart.

We don't have to like what we hear, but there is a good reason for us to look into why we have chosen to hear it – or not. In even the greatest lie is a grain of truth. Seek out the truth of what you have heard and use it to grow from within.

COMMENTS FROM SPIRIT:

Communication at all levels is only a matter of completely opening yourself to the universe. All information is available to each soul.

At the highest level we are all One and One with All that Is. As we approach this level of conscious existence, Communication becomes effortless, instantaneous and complete.

Blessings.

DELIGHT

Delight is Joy with a playful twist and a sparkle.

This is a time to play -- to enjoy your partner and your partnership in every way. Let go of all heaviness of spirit or depression. This is a time of Light and of lightness!

Spirit has given you rose-colored glasses on this occasion. You are going to be able to see the humor in situations where that aspect would usually be hidden. You will be the spark of Light in the lives of those around you and a blessing to the world while this energy is in your corner. May it ever be so.

Delight brings a lightness of heart and spirit to you. Enjoy life to the fullest. Become even more child-like for the time being. "You must become as a child to enter the kingdom of Heaven". You've been handed the key today.

The only harsh aspect might be that you would offend someone who was not prepared to experience such playfulness this day. They probably needed it, though.

COMMENTS FROM SPIRIT:

Delight strips away the concrete of morbid sameness that we allow ourselves and others to encase us in. Delight invites absolute freedom; loss of restrictions and total joy. It is one of the greatest blessings we can allow ourselves. Enjoy! Live in the glory of your own being!

EXPECTATION

    Drawing this word indicates you are aware at some level that something is about to change in your life. You may even think you know what that something is and you may even go so far as to think that you have figured out how it is going to happen. (You will almost always be wrong -- Spirit loves to let us play guessing games but rarely lets us figure it out in advance.) Your feelings about this situation may range from hopefully excited to fearful. Rest assured that like it or not, understand it or not, all things that are about to occur are exactly what our soul has requested in an effort to encourage our understanding and growth.

Expectation in a personal relationship can have meanings in a couple of areas. The most mundane, though quite exciting meaning deals with the addition to the relationship by birth. Other than that, it indicates looking into the future to see the prospect of a marked change of some nature to some core area of the relationship.

Drawing this word in response to a question regarding general relationships brings the energy of conscious change into the transactional matrix. It offers awareness of the potential consequences of forthcoming patterns within ongoing transactions.

Awareness of approaching change can be very exciting or very worrisome, depending on your frame of mind. Worry is another form of fear. Fear is a lack of Love. Love yourself, the Creator, and this process enough to enter into this period without fear. It is all in order. Remember that everything is happening FOR you – not TO you!

The harsh aspect of Expectation occurs when we allow our focus to be on the future instead of in the present. Be here now. The future takes care of itself and is always in Divine order.

COMMENTS FROM SPIRIT:

Expectation occurs when we allow our focus to fall away from the moment; when we reach into the future with our fears or hopes. The future is in the moment. There is no such thing as time except to your perception and no need to hope or fear; as all things simply are.

Blessings.

FREEDOM

There is a line from a song that says "Freedom's just another word for nothing left to lose." Surprisingly, this is quite accurate; although probably not in the way the songwriter intended. We create entanglements throughout the length and breadth of our lives. Relationships, material goods, financial and other self-imposed commitments form the walls and limitations of our existence. Some we bear gladly -- even proudly. Others chafe us with every movement. True Freedom is marked by the mental and philosophical position that allows us to move in an unattached yet honorable manner through these entanglements.

Freedom in a personal relationship is a rare, beautiful and sometimes dangerous thing. When two complete, whole and healed people choose to come together in a healthy relationship each has total Freedom of thought and action and the personal responsibility to act with and from Love at all times. If you are not yet in this place in your relationship, this word invites you to take a step or two in that direction. Freedom within the format of a personal relationship can have two meanings. The first, which is really not a long-term possibility nor is it even desirable for most of us, is Freedom from a personal relationship. Because of the intense teaching and growing nature inherent in most relationships, they represent an extremely important tool in our material world learning experiences. The second and more pertinent meaning is to find Freedom within that relationship. Freedom within a relationship comes when each partner knows themselves to be whole and complete and the partnership occurs as a result of these whole and complete individuals choosing to come together to share life. There is no ownership and no 'boss of the family'. Each partner is Free to do those things they feel to be important and correct within the framework of that relationship. Love does not possess; it only shares. Love does not take; it only gives. If you so choose and are able to live together in this manner you will discover the true meaning of Freedom within a personal relationship.

There is only one law in any relationship. That law is to be Love in all matters and in every manner. Few of us operate at this level at all times. The word 'Freedom' invites us to slip the bonds of our own limitations and perceived faults. The only way to truly be Free is to Free yourself!

If you could see inside your own energy pattern, you would probably see something akin to Marley's ghost from "A Christmas Carol." As with Marley, the chains we wear are the ones we have forged link by link in life. We also have the power to release ourselves from these bonds; link by link or all at once. The choice is ours. Take a moment, ground and center yourself, and go within in meditation. Visualize those bonds and chains you wear; ask them what they represent and see the ones you are ready to release. The greatest Freedom we can have is the Freedom to be our highest selves without fear of censure or reprisal. Only we can give ourselves this gift; for the censure and reprisal we most often face comes from the darkness and fear within. Bringing this word into your reading at this moment invites you to judge yourself less harshly and Love yourself more. Do not fear the changes that appear in your life stream (remember that fear is only the absence of Love), but accept them as growth opportunities in every detail.

Your perceived lack of bonds does not mean that you are Free from the need to act responsibly and with Love at all times . Freedom, as with any aspect of Free will, can be and often is abused as a result of ego stepping into the picture. In the lexicon of American jurisprudence -- "your Freedom to swing your fist ends at the point of my nose". Be certain that in your exercise of Freedom you do not create a disharmony for yourself or others around you. The Karma Kops will be glad to remind you if you have trouble remembering this.

COMMENTS FROM SPIRIT:

The essence of Freedom is Divine Love -- that Love with which the Creator has created you; that energy with which you are surrounded daily. Freedom is found within. It is yours whether or not you are aware of it or choose to claim it as your birthright. It is the source and the result of complete balance regarding a particular facet of self. Try to achieve Freedom in as many areas as possible. The more you gain, the easier each new conquest becomes. Conquer yourself and the universe is yours. The only times that you experience less than total Freedom is when you choose to limit yourself in that form known as fear.

Love yourselves and realize that all of you are One, and you shall experience the total Freedom of total Love.

Blessings.

BUILDING

Building is the ongoing act of becoming or making something larger. Building awareness or assets or knowledge is a common use for this concept. Building spiritual growth is not. In the spiritual realm, there is no such thing as growing more or Building. There is only limiting less as we are already One with All that Is. There can be nothing beyond that. The concept 'Building' assumes that there is a need to add to that which we already are in order to manifest as greater than we have manifested in the past. The Spiritual reality is that we are already greater than we could possibly imagine and it is only the limitations that we have been taught to accept which keeps us from realizing that in action and deep awareness.

Building in the material realm involves almost an infinite array of aspects; from the Building of trust and relationship to the Building of individual skills and talents. While all of these aspects are only symptoms, they can be reflections of an inner, spiritual lessening of limitation.

On the other hand, casual relationships, being material realm manifestations, are ALL about Building. Building trust, love, comfort, rapport, and all of the other aspects of material existence require constant effort and focus on adding to what currently exists. Calling this word to yourself today suggests that perhaps not enough focus has been placed on material realm Building of late, and Spirit has arrived to assist you in regaining that focus. The more open and responsive you are to the subtle signals from Spirit, the less likely you are to experience the harsher aspects. The choice is as always yours and yours alone.

Building self consists of only one thing: increasing awareness of your greater self.

Spirit has taught me that there is no such thing as (spiritually) growing more; there is only limiting less.

Spirit continues "And if you continue each day to limit less eventually you will become LIMITLESS!"

According to Spirit there are five aspects to growing more (Building your spiritual awareness).

These are: trust, believe, allow, appropriate and Love.

Each one of these Builds upon the previous.

The first two, trust and believe, are almost one. Spirit requests that we trust ourselves and believe (in) Spirit.

Once that is accomplished, the next step is to allow Spirit to have its way in our life without interference from our egos. (Spirit told one client of mine to: "Please let go of the reins - you're making it very hard to steer."). Most of us spend the majority of our lives trying to achieve certain material-realm goals that we have set for ourselves or accepted from others. Few if any succeed in achieving those goals. Our entire life is taken up with 'trying'.

Trying is an aggressive, acquisitive and manipulative thing.

"Allowing" is the preparation of a soft, deep feathered nest in preparation for something of value to be placed into it by an apparently separate and outside agency.

Which of these two methods reminds you more of your concepts regarding Spirit and which more closely resemble your perceptions of mankind's techniques?

Once we have arrived at the spiritual place of trusting and believing enough that we have begun to ' allow', the next step is to understand and KNOW that ALL things are totally appropriate within the eye, the mind, the heart of the Creator and that all things ARE in Divine order in all ways and at all times whether we understand them or like them in the moment, or not.

The fifth parameter; Love, is the most important of all. Love is literally the alpha and the omega of this process. Love is required in order to begin the process, to walk through every step and phase of spiritual growth and stands alone at the end of the process. Love; as it is used here refers to Divine Love as opposed to human love. Divine Love is Love not 'for' or 'of' but simply Love. It is the Love one would have for the CONCEPT of a new baby or a springtime field bursting with new flowers.

After sharing this teaching of the five elements for about seven years I was in Seattle for an Expo when a young man came to me for advice. Spirit had me share with him this teaching and then had me offer these five concepts as a mantra - a single sentence. When offered in this way, the mantra is: "Trust, Believe; Allow appropriate Love!'

The only harsh reality associated with Building occurs when we seek that growth from outside ourselves rather than from our greater selves within. To do so only reinforces the material realm's set of limitations.

COMMENTS FROM SPIRIT:

Dearest Ones:
The Building is complete and has been for eternity. Becoming is still progressing. Become that which I have Built and your task is complete.

Blessings,

INCOMPETENCE

Contrary to one's first impression, this word is not to be used as an insult but as a promise. Incompetence is simply a way of stating that one is not (yet) skilled (competent) in a given area. It is a promise of room to grow and of incentive to do so. Whatever the question or the issue which brought this word to you this day, drawing it is a promise from Spirit that lessons and opportunities shall be made manifest in your life which will afford you the opportunity to increase your competence and effectiveness! What a gift!

Incompetence reveals itself in a relationship by its awkward nature. If you and your partner are constantly at odds with one another it is a direct result of Incompetence of one or both of you regarding the nuances of a successful relationship.

One of the more difficult things to admit to ourselves is our own areas of Incompetence. It is far easier and much more comfortable to see ourselves through non-critical eyes; to see ourselves as comfortable and competent in every field and area. If Spirit has brought this word to your awareness today be prepared to have your eyes opened to areas of potential growth. The discomfort associated with this new awakening will be inversely proportional to how open you are to receiving the lesson.

Being less than competent is an Inconvenience. Failing to attempt to increase your competence is a disservice to your self and to those around you. The greatest failure of all is the failure to try. Spirit, as always, is here to help, with the greatest of Love.

COMMENTS FROM SPIRIT:

That which you refer to as Incompetence is simply a lack of awareness of your truly limitless nature. It is a temporary human condition and is not nearly as important as you make it seem. Immerse yourself in the wonder of total One-ness and you shall be competent in every important way.

Blessings.

This concludes Volume One.
Watch for Volume Two!

You are cordially invited to visit Mani's website at:

www.ManiPureheart.com

If you do not meditate, or if you have difficulty achieving a good meditative state, I offer – for free – 7 meditations. I VERY strongly recommend practicing the "Grounding and Centering" meditation until you can achieve that state without having to listen to my voice. At that point, you are ready to try some of the others at:

https://tinyurl.com/7Meditations

...and if you want to learn more about me and my work, please visit:

https://tiny.one/ManiOnYouTube

You can also visit our group on Facebook:
T.I.N.G.L.E:
The International New-thought Group - Light Enclave at:

https://tinyurl.com/TINGLE-group

ALSO AVAILABLE IS A DECK OF 216 ORACLE CARDS THAT ACCOMPANY AND ARE SUPPORTED BY THIS BOOK.

That is the equivalent of 2 2/3 Tarot Decks!
The image below is an example card from the deck. The circular cards are 3 ¼ inches in diameter.

They can be ordered from **manipureheart.com** for $47.50, with free shipping in the continental U.S

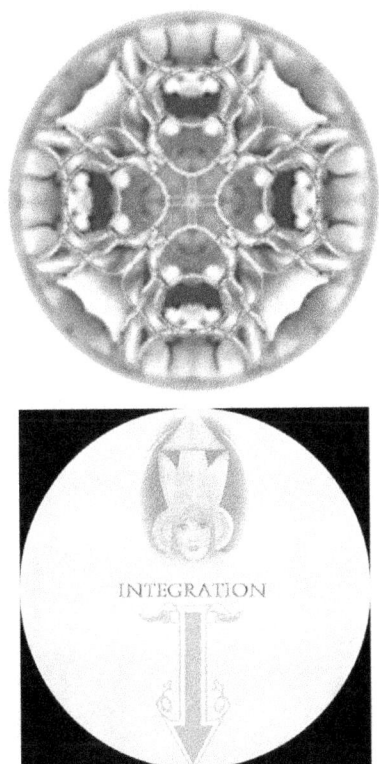

www.ingramcontent.com/pod-product-compliance
Lightning Source LLC
Chambersburg PA
CBHW071430300426
44114CB00013B/1379